SUBMARINE

VERSUS

SUBMARINE

SUBMARINE

VERSUS

SUBMARINE

THE TACTICS AND TECHNOLOGY OF UNDERWATER CONFRONTATION

RICHARD COMPTON-HALL

A David & Charles Military Book

Submarine versus Submarine was conceived and produced by Grub Street, London.

© Grub Street, 1988
Text © Richard Compton-Hall, 1988

Designed by Jerry Goldie
Colour artwork by Terry Hadler and Steven Seymour
Line artwork by Tony Garrett

British Library Cataloguing in Publication Data

Compton-Hall, Richard
  Submarine versus submarine.
  1. Naval operations by submarines
  I. Title
  359.3'257

  ISBN 0-7153-9178-X

First Published 1988 and printed in Great Britain by Eagle Press PLC, Glasgow for David & Charles Publishers plc Brunel House Newton Abbot Devon

Typeset by Chapterhouse, The Cloisters, Formby, England

DEDICATION

To Eve, as always.

ACKNOWLEDGEMENTS

Numerous firms (notably CAP Scientific, Marconi, Maritalia, Ferranti and RACAL) and submarine specialists in several countries have helped me to compile the material and provide the photographs (most from the RN Submarine Museum Collection) needed for this book. Too many people have been involved, at one time or another, to mention them individually — and some of the more controversial passages anyway arose from discussions which were non-attributable by request — but I am very grateful to everybody concerned.

My gratitude also goes to:

My wife, Eve, for patient, expert and continual assistance.
David Hill for his accurate line drawings, technical comments and very sensible advice.
Terry Hadler for his superb scenarios.
Tony Garrat and Stephen Seymour for additional artwork.
David Foxwell, Managing Editor of the excellent international journal *Naval Forces*, for photographs and for permission to reproduce some paragraphs which I had previously written for him.
The invaluable *Jane's Fighting Ships* (and its former editor Captain John E Moore); *Jane's Weapon Systems*; *Jane's Defence Weekly*; *US Naval Institute Proceedings*; *Military Technology*; and the outstandingly good *Submarine Review* published by the Naval Submarine League (which offers membership abroad as well as in the USA from Box 1146, Annandale, Virginia 22003) — all for up to date and reliable information.
Members of the Naval Research Institute PLA, Beijing; the Submarine Academy Qingdao; and the Chinese submarine officers to whom I was privileged to lecture recently — all for a warm welcome and stimulating discussions.
And, finally, John Davies and Jerry Goldie of Grub Street for thoroughly professional packaging and much help.

CONTENTS

PART ONE
UNDERSTANDING THE TECHNOLOGY

1.1	THE SOVIET THREAT	10
1.2	SUBMARINE CONSTRUCTION	13
1.3	PROPULSION, SPEED AND ENDURANCE	23
1.4	SOUND, SONAR AND NON-ACOUSTIC INDICATORS	32
1.5	SECONDARY SENSORS	41
1.6	NAVIGATION AND COMMUNICATIONS	45
1.7	SUBMARINE ANTI-SUBMARINE WEAPON SYSTEMS	51
1.8	SUBMARINE-LAUNCHED MISSILES	65
1.9	UNDER THE ARCTIC ICE	79
1.10	RE-EMERGENCE OF THE MIDGETS	86
1.11	SELF-DEFENSE	102
1.12	POWERFUL FORCES, PRACTICAL PROBLEMS	107

PART TWO
ACTION AND FACTION

2.1	SOVIET SSK TACTICS	116
2.2	SOVIET SSN TACTICS	125
2.3	BLACKMAIL	133
2.4	SUBMARINE PIRATES	138
2.5	SPIES AND TRACKERS	145
2.6	MIDGET MARAUDERS	151
2.7	SKIRMISHING IN THE PACIFIC	165
2.8	ARCTIC ASSAULT	173
2.9	RUSSIAN CHESS	181
2.10	THE SURVIVORS	188
	INDEX	190

INTRODUCTION

Open Note to:

Admiral of the Fleet VN Chernavin, Commander-in-Chief of the Soviet Navy, Deputy Minister of Defense, and Submariner.
General of the Army PI Ivashutin, Head of the Chief Intelligence Directorate (GRU) of the Soviet General Staff.

This book is written through a submariner's eyes and principally from your standpoint. Please tell us if our interpretation differs from yours: we would be interested to know.

It is sometime — today, tomorrow, any time — in, say, the northern ice-bound confines of the Barents Sea. Two monstrous shapes are stealthily twisting and turning, probing and questing uncertainly far below the surface as if following some faint elusive scent. Obviously, each is trying to find out all it can about the other. Suddenly, they come together in the blackness. One has made a momentary mistake: the deep-sea silence is harshly broken by the sound of metal being torn. Part of what appears to be a dorsal fin hangs bent; a thin trickle of hydraulic fluid — life-blood apparently — streams astern and a long, stringy appendage sinks lazily to the bottom while the monsters part to attend to their injuries.

A minor underseas drama has just been enacted. It will not be reported in the Press: the world will know nothing of a brief encounter in one small corner of that unlit theater which is the vast inner space of seas and oceans, where the players are submarines and between two and three hundred are fully armed and constantly on stage unseen by any audience. Another seventeen hundred await their cue. Even more lie strewn across the seabed, entombing the remains of some 60 000 men.

Undersea maneuvers, with potential enemies in close proximity, are actually happening; it is very reasonable to assume that, if, God help us all, World War III ever happens, it will happen here in inner space. This inner space has always been a world apart, dark and intensely hostile. At one thousand feet below the surface, quite a modest depth nowadays, the sea exerts a force of more than 140 tons on a conning tower hatch. The steel sharks which have systematically sought and killed their surface prey during bitter years of warfare have themselves been destroyed in huge numbers: the sea is relentless when their skins are ruptured. From the earliest days two centuries ago, 302 have been lost by accident — while during the World Wars for example, 1442 submarines failed to return from patrol and six were sunk in minor conflicts.

The German balance sheet alone for the second underwater war from 1939–1945, indicates the horrendous costs. About 2800 Allied merchant ships amounting to 14 573 000 tons of shipping — 94% of it in the Atlantic — went to the bottom; but 784 U-boats and 33 000 German submariners were lost, from all causes, in exchange.

Few, if any, submariners today are conscious of these daunting statistics: still less do they care about them. A peculiar greyish sense of comedy masks past tragedies and carries them through events which, in British terms, are 'fraught with interest': 'What', an electrician was heard to enquire when the compass failed, deep beneath the Arctic ice-pack, and started a fire, 'what comes after "Hallowed be Thy Name?"'.' Submariners, albeit highly skilled in their peculiar trade, are ordinary people but not all their reactions in a given situation are easily predictable: and the same has to be admitted about their future operations.

Merchant vessels, as well as important naval units, are still a prime target for the

A Soviet 'Tango' SSK head on

underwater marauders; but today the sharks, enormously more powerful than their predecessors, are stalking their own kind. A future undersea battle will be three-dimensional. Will it be as costly? Will shark kill shark on a grand scale? These questions are important: the answers could affect the future of mankind.

There has been precious little practical experience to base our study on. To date there has been only one case of a submarine sinking another when both boats were submerged and the story is not really meaningful in the present context. However, it is worth relating.

On 9 February, 1945 HMS *Venturer*, patrolling off Norway, heard very faint hydrophone effect on her primitive ASDIC (Sonar) set. The noise steadily increased and at 1050 the Officer-of-the-Watch briefly sighted a periscope on the hydrophone bearing. Course was immediately altered northwards to intercept and at 1115 the periscope was again sighted. Although the machinery of the U-boat was very noisy there was no sign of a 'schnorchel', and *Venturer*'s Captain, Lieutenant Launders, deduced that the U-boat was making port submerged on electric motors and probably zig-zagging. Being unsure of the enemy's course and speed, Launders tracked his prey and for the next hour plotted it by Asdic bearings — very inaccurate by today's standards — assisted by a further generous view of the periscope at 1122.

At 1212 Launders, satisfied that the plot was reasonably correct, brought his boat round to a firing course. Two minutes later *U-864* paid the penalty of what was described as 'most shameful periscope drill' and sank with all hands. *Venturer*'s torpedoes were not, of course, 'smart' homing weapons: they were ordinary straight-running 45-knot Mark VIII torpedoes which happily ran straight in a 'hosepipe' salvo set to the correct depth.

Although fratricide was extensively practised in both World Wars the victims were, except for this one occasion, invariably on the surface. Despite continual and increasingly advanced trials and exercises, the question of what will actually happen today or tomorrow when submarine meets submarine, each armed with specifically designed anti-submarine weapons, is open to speculation. History is clear about one thing: nothing in war ever follows the pattern predicted in peace. Because of this, and without the benefit of actual historical data, the author has kept an open mind and examined the possibilities objectively — however much some of them differ from doctrine — against a background of fairly intimate knowledge of the subject, educated guesswork and some informed imagination. In that way there is perhaps some chance that we shall be ready to accept the sort of surprises which war is bound to spring, while not being too inhibited by partisan peacetime pronouncements.

Part I of this book explains the mechanics which underlie submarine anti-submarine warfare. Part II is set a few years ahead — say the mid 1990s — and envisages, as action and faction, what might happen, possibly will, when various underwater opponents come up against each other in war.

Author's Note

Part II stands by itself and can be read first, if preferred, returning to Part I afterwards for the supporting facts.

Measurements are given initially in metric or imperial figures according to the practice of the country concerned. One meter equals 3.2808 feet and one foot equals 0.3048 meters. One (international) nautical mile (the measurement used at sea and for missile ranges) equals, for practical purposes, 2000 yards — or more accurately, about 6076 feet or 1852 meters. Speeds are expressed in knots: one knot is one nautical mile per hour.

PART I

UNDERSTANDING THE TECHNOLOGY

1.1

THE SOVIET THREAT

The Soviet Union has a much larger underwater fleet than any other nation or alliance; so it seems sensible to focus an examination of future underwater warfare on Soviet capabilities and probable intentions — and both from a submariner's viewpoint. Assuming, pessimistically, that Strategic Arms Limitation agreements do not appreciably diminish the missile force, some 75 ballistic-missile submarines (about 950 missiles), 67 cruise-missile submarines, the best part of 200 attack submarines, 14 special-purpose submarines (eg, communications and research) and three score boats in reserve constitute a demonstrable and major threat.[1] In the principal groups, nuclear plants power practically all of the first (ie, SSBNs), three-quarters of the second (ie, SSGNs) and about 35% of the third (ie, SSNs). Most of the attack submarines are still diesel-electric (ie, 65% are SSKs) but the newer boats have a long submerged endurance and are capable of high burst speed.

There are lesser potential threats from other navies but the Russian menace must be foremost. If that can be faced, we in the West should be able to cope with smaller submarine forces, although not necessarily by the same methods.

A primary aim of the Soviet Navy at the outbreak of war must be the protection of nuclear ballistic-missile submarines (SSBNs) on passage or on station, the most powerful SSBNs patrolling relatively close to home. This task, equally applicable to the Northern and Pacific Fleets, would be shared amongst all branches, including the Naval Air Force, but some of the nuclear and diesel-electric attack submarines (SSNs and SSKs) would endeavor to hunt down and destroy enemy (pro-Western and/or Chinese) submarines, seeking out SSBNs as priority targets. This is a totally new commitment.

Meanwhile, a proportion of the torpedo-attack boats (SSNs and SSKs) together with nuclear and diesel cruise-missile submarines (SSGNs and SSGs) will be vectored against naval Task Groups threatening the *Rodina* (Motherland) while a substantial number will be deployed, in traditional U-boat fashion, across the crucial trans-Atlantic supply lines. Other SSGNs and some SSNs equipped with cruise missiles will direct their weapons at shore targets. Elsewhere, submarine mine-laying, reconnaissance, the landing of agents and raiders will have their place.

Anti-submarine (ASW) submarines on both sides will have a very important part to play in countering all kinds of aggressive submarine activity in a conflict. We are principally concerned with these submarine-versus-submarine engagements — shark against shark — because they are new, they are likely to be crucial, and they are certainly intriguing; but there are many other ASW players involved — on the seabed, on the surface, in the air and outside the atmosphere — and these have to be taken into account. Soviet submarines depend heavily upon co-operation with other units as well as amongst themselves. Submarines cannot be regarded in isolation even if they hold the key to most of what happens at sea and much that may happen on land. It is well known, for instance, that Britain came perilously close to defeat at a critical stage in World War II because of German U-boat anti-shipping onslaughts; but submarines can and did also exercise great influence on theater land battles.

The USSR very obviously appreciates, to the full, the value of submarines, and has found the means to speed the development of

new boats and weapon systems. Where in the West it usually takes a decade or more to produce a new weapon system, whether or not embodied in a new hull, and longer to put it to work throughout the fleet (where it has to last for many years to be economically viable) the Russians have taken short cuts — by fair means or foul according to your standpoint.

KGB and GRU espionage, augmented by more or less innocent business deals, greatly assist Soviet progress in certain areas — notably in the fields of underwater sound, electronics, computers, metallurgy and advanced construction methods. If the fruits of research are acquired from democracies they provide a springboard, at little cost or effort, from which to leapfrog. Actual technological transfers make things even quicker; and these include packages like fiber optics or micro-processors which might seem purely commercial and have no obvious connection with military matters.

A submarine's normal life is at least 20 years so, allowing time for development, a

A submarine's value

The German Lieutenant General Bayerlein, Chief of Staff of the Afrika Korps, admitted that the Axis defeat in North Africa in May 1943 was due in no small way to the onslaught by a handful of British and Allied submarines, operating from Malta under siege, on the seaborne supply lines across the narrow Mediterranean Sea.

From still further back there remains an echo of Mahon's ringing words about the Royal Navy in the Napoleonic Wars: 'The world has never seen a more impressive demonstration of the influence of sea power upon its history. Those far distant, storm beaten ships, upon which the Grand Army never looked, stood between it and the Dominion of the world'. Submarines, upon which no army ever looks, could be reckoned just as influential today and tomorrow.

Above: The wartime 10th S/m Flotilla (British, French, Greek and Polish boats) often had to dive in harbor because of air attacks on Malta. Crews had little rest.

planning team today has to look far beyond the immediate horizon and well into the 21st century. There is no choice but to be futuristic — and Russian scientific journals show that Soviet planners are unquestionably that. While the West prefers evolution the Soviet Navy is not afraid of revolution despite the risks which go with it, and the serious disasters which are never reported to the

Russian 'Yankees'

When the first Soviet 'Yankee'-class SSBN was commissioned in 1967 it bore a marked external resemblance to the early American SSBNs — which is not surprising because take-apart models of the first USN 'Boomer', *George Washington*, were on sale in toyshops by December 1960 a year after commissioning; and model makers, supplied with adequate drawings, were equally quick of the mark with *Ethan Allen* when she went to sea in 1961.

Right: USS *Woodrow Wilson* (SSBN 624), seventeenth FBM submarine. The broad family resemblance between the first generations of US SSBN and early Soviet PLARBs is obvious.

Below: A Soviet 'Yankee' PLARB, evidently clearing main ballast tanks with low pressure air after surfacing.

Soviet people. They know nothing about the 200 or more bad accidents, some of them with nuclear connections, which have occurred since 1975; and they are not aware of the unfortunate irradiated sailors who have suffered from inadequate reactor shielding. Neither have they been informed of the astronomical costs which constantly rock the shaky economy. Secrecy enables the Soviet Navy to take giant strides which are simply not feasible in a democratic society.

Inevitably, a totalitarian state enjoys significant advantages in the field of weaponry.[2] This fact of life has to be remembered when going on to review the Soviet submarine force in detail and compare it, sometimes enviously, with other undersea arms around the world. Russian submariners are convinced that they have the finest fleet in the world. They could be right — at least in terms of hardware.

END NOTES

1. Predicted figures for 1990. The total number for the mid 1990s will be rather less but individual capabilities of new SSGNs, SSNs and SSKs will probably more than compensate for any diminution of the force.
2. Rear Admiral A T Mahan USN recognised the dilemma a century ago: 'Free governments have sometimes fallen short while, on the other hand, despotic power, wielded with judgement and consistency, has created at times a great sea commerce and a brilliant navy with greater directness than can be reached by the slower purposes of a free people'. (*Influence of Sea Power on History*, Chapter 1, Part VI, page 58 of 1889 edition).

1.2

SUBMARINE CONSTRUCTION

I t is 1956. The old tyrant Stalin has been dead for three years. Krushchev is in power and he has just appointed the innovative 46-year-old Admiral Sergei Georgiyevich Gorshkov — a proven commander in battle — as Commander-in-Chief of the Soviet Navy: he is a good deal younger than his Western contemporaries and a born survivor.

The Korean War, prompted and inspired by Stalin, was terminated unsatisfactorily soon after his death and Allied warships have now vacated the North West Pacific. While they were there a great deal was learned about their capabilities. Elsewhere, the KGB together with the rival GRU Military Intelligence Directorate (a much less efficient organisation in those days) has been busy: activities have been concentrated in the United States and Great Britain where naval expertise is reckoned to be the best. Practically every significant aspect of America's nuclear submarine construction programme has been assimilated in Moscow and passed to the shipyards at Severodvinsk on the White Sea and Gorky on the River Volga. Severodvinsk will have seven times the potential capacity of all the American yards together in a few years. Other yards in the Baltic at Leningrad and Sudomekh, and at Komsomolsk on the River Amur in the East, are being expanded to help build a new generation of submarines.

Some particularly valuable information about new sonar equipment has been derived from the Admiralty Underwater Weapons Establishment at Portland, England, where two of the staff — Ethel Gee and Master-at-Arms (Senior naval policeman and disciplinarian!) Ron Houghton — have been suborned with remarkable ease; but extraordinarily few reports have come in about homing torpedoes. There are indications that the Royal Navy has developed a weapon of this type for use by submarines against others and the Portland traitors (despised in the

USSR as much as they were in England when discovered) have supplied statistics. There are also reports of similar torpedoes under way in the United States. But the Soviet Naval Staff cannot understand the apparent in-effectiveness of these so-called intelligent or 'smart' fish. (And well they might be puzzled because they were not very much better than the wartime German 'Gnat' used against ASW vessels.) Indeed, progress towards modernising submarine weapon systems in the West appears to be very slow. Attention there is concentrated on hulls and propulsion although sonar sensors are way ahead of any equipment in the Soviet fleet.

Presumably, the West's two largest navies will apply more effort to weapon systems when they are happy with the new range of boats to carry them. It seems a crazy way to proceed. Gorshkov and his team believe it is more logical to designate future targets, design weapons to sink them and only then decide on the best types of submarines to carry them. In their opinion, the Westerners are going about their business back to front.

Gorshkov is far-sighted and politically astute — he would not otherwise have survived the turmoil of internal changes after Stalin's death. He is not a submariner but he is indoctrinated with the traditional Russian belief that the first duty of an underwater force is to defend the *Rodina*. The threat from the West, most notably the American Strike Fleet with its nuclear-armed aircraft, is alarming. The Motherland must never let itself become vulnerable to attack and invasion again. But, with the Strike Fleet

Top to bottom: Kuznetsov, Gorshkov and Chernavin, successive Cs-in-C of the Soviet Navy. The post equals the US Chief of Naval Operations and Secretary of the Navy combined: the holder is also a Deputy Minister of Defense.

Wartime Russian Submariners

Wartime Russian submariners tended to trust guns more than torpedoes for the excellent reason that most of them had only the sketchiest idea of how to calculate torpedo deflection angle; and the inexperienced Staff Officers were not competent to train them. Time and again hits were reported when there was not a shred of justification for the claims. For example, *K-21* (Captain Lt N A Lunin) confidently boasted that he had torpedoed and hit the German battleship *Tirpitz* and an accompanying destroyer during the disastrous passage of the British Convoy PQ 17 to Murmansk. The Germans did not even notice an attack had taken place; but no amount of evidence has since convinced the Soviet historians that the attempt was abortive. Lunin was made a Hero of the Soviet Union.

Engineer officers remained for long years in their boats (they still do) and knew their business better than the bosses. One, Karatayev, saved the day for *M-172* whose captain, Lysenko, had been a sound (meaning politically sound) peacetime commanding officer who handled his submarine 'without any glaring errors' but found the strain of war too much for him. One day, returning from patrol, Lysenko mistook a friendly aircraft for an enemy and hastily dived in shallow water close to the coast, whereupon the boat hit a submerged rock and stuck there. According to his Division Commander he immediately panicked and screamed 'It's a magnet! The Germans have

Above: M-172 (Capt Lt Fisanovich), one of more than 200 205/256-ton 'baby' boats commissioned between 1934 and 1944.

Below: A Party meeting in the large *K-21* (Lunin), probably held to discuss the supposedly successful attack on *Tirpitz* 5 July, 1942.

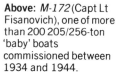

Above: Shch-class 590/705-ton 'Pike': 31 of this type were lost.

special magnets to attract our submarines. We are trapped!' However, the Engineer Officer with 'skill and presence of mind', sorted the situation out and made sure that the submarine surfaced and reached base safely.

Shch-421 (Captain Third Rank F A Vadyaev) struck a mine whilst surfacing. All propulsion was put out of action; but Vadyaev, prompted by Flotilla Commander Kolyshkin, who was on board, raised both periscopes and hoisted diesel-engine covers between them as a sail in the hope that wind and tide would carry the heavily damaged boat out to sea and away from the

enemy-occupied Norwegian coastline. The improvised rig worked well enough for some three hours but then the wind changed leaving *Shch-421* still in sight from shore. Reluctantly, the boat was made ready for scuttling and, in accordance with Russian naval tradition, she was cleaned throughout and the brightwork polished as if for an Admiral's Inspection. When all this was done an Open Party Meeting was held. Those sailors who were not already Party Members were accepted into the All-Union Communist Party of Bolsheviks. Soon after this prudent precaution had been taken a rescue boat *K-22* (whose

navigation had been erratic) at last succeeded in finding *Shch-421*. After several fruitless attempts to take the stricken submarine in tow, and with enemy reconnaissance aircraft gathering ominously overhead, the crew were taken off and the boat was scuttled. The Flotilla Commander and the Captain left last, in that order.

Vadyaev went on to command *Shch-422* replacing the former Captain Malyshev who had been court-martialled for cowardice despite acknowledged displays of courage earlier. The evidence given at the court-martial throws a particularly sinister light on the role of political

officers. Malyshev was said to have returned from patrol on several occasions with unexpended torpedoes. Senior Political Instructor Dubik reported that there had been ample opportunity to fire them and that the Commanding Officer 'bore the stamp of excessive inexplicable caution'. When a new Commissar, Senior Political Instructor Tabenkin, relieved Dubik and went on patrol he soon signalled the base (in his private code) asking for recall in view of the Captain's palpable cowardice. It transpired that the boat's gyro had

Above: Wartime signalmen needed good balance, especially when cradling a flashing lamp, but this one semaphoring on a Soviet 'D' was almost a trapeze artist.

become unserviceable and that the Captain, formerly the Division's Navigating Officer, personally tried to repair it. His efforts succeeded in putting the gyro completely out of action. Presumably after some preliminary softening-up on shore, Malyshev admitted to having caused the damage deliberately 'because he was afraid to carry on with his patrol'. It was laconically noted, a while later, that Malyshev was killed when the building in which he was being held was hit during an enemy air raid. This small fragment of Soviet submarine history makes abundantly clear the reasons for commanding officers firing torpedoes extravagantly at small (but purportedly large) targets and announcing wild successes when they returned to base.

However, the Baltic submariners were evidently more capable than their Northern Fleet comrades. There was one, Captain Third Rank A E Marensko in *S-13* who could, in comparative terms anyway, be called an ace. On 30 January, 1945 he torpedoed and sank the 25 000-ton liner

Wilhelm Gustlof off the Bay of Danzig: he hit with three torpedoes — quite possibly a Soviet fire-control record. The liner was urgently ferrying 6000 fugitives, including U-boat men, from Pilau and it had no escort: nor was the ship zig-zagging so it was not a difficult target. On 10 February, Marensko torpedoed another large liner in similar circumstances, the *General Stuben*, which was escorted but thinly. Between January and May 1945, Baltic Soviet submarines torpedoed 13 transports altogether, totalling 63 000 tons, and three other ships totalling 4000 tons. Four warships were sunk by submarine-laid mines (submarine minelaying was effective in several areas) and the Russian boats were an admitted menace to German supply vessels and troop-transports.

There was sometimes direct co-operation between submarines and reconnaissance aircraft: sub-air tactics worked quite well — perhaps better than contemporary American SUBAIR procedures in the Pacific. A handful of Soviet submarines were reasonably efficient but they formed only a very small proportion of the force and they were operating in waters where anti-submarine warfare (ASW) was notoriously difficult.

hovering in the Atlantic, that seems a real possibility. Moreover, a glance at the great globe in the Commander-in-Chief's office shows that the USSR is almost entirely surrounded by enemies.

Submarines are the answer to prevent the Strike Fleet surging up the Norwegian Sea or, equally, the giant American Pacific Fleet attacking from the East. The boats will have to be much more powerful than in the past because enemy anti-submarine warfare (ASW) methods are good; intelligence is sure of that.

The performance of Soviet submarines against Germany throughout the Great Patriotic War was abysmal but Gorshkov has no more than a sneaking suspicion about how bad it actually was: he knows full well that Stalin's pre-war purge cut a broad and damaging swathe through the officer ranks but as a late-comer to the Party (he was eventually nudged into joining when a Vice Admiral) he does not concede, even to himself, that this was because good submarine captains are individualists — and individualists are bad Communists. To objective Western historians, rigid political control was a prime cause of Soviet failure from 1941–1945 but Gorshkov has no intention whatever of relinquishing *absolute* control. It will continue to be enforced in every ship and submarine by the omnipresent *Zampolit* (political officer) and anonymous planted *stukachy* (informers) from the Main Political Administration wing in Moscow. Therefore, neither the Commander-in-Chief nor his submarine Fleet Brigade and Division commanders — albeit keen students of history like all Soviet Staff officers — have accepted the most significant single lesson learned from wartime experience in other navies: a successful submarine captain must be given free rein to be his own master.

History tells why submarine performance was so poor but the reasons are hidden from the new Soviet submariners. The more perceptive officers might garner some hints from memoirs like *With the Red Fleet*[1] and *Submarines in Arctic Waters*[2] by senior wartime officers who artlessly recount stories of commanding officers caught out for admitting their failings. But it is contrived to appear that these were the exceptions who proved the rule and that the fleet as a whole was heroic and magnificent.

The appallingly long list of failures is concealed by almost wholly falsified claims of success. Nobody, not even Gorshkov, knows

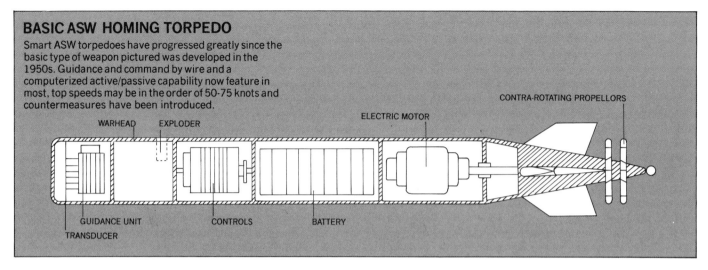

BASIC ASW HOMING TORPEDO

Smart ASW torpedoes have progressed greatly since the basic type of weapon pictured was developed in the 1950s. Guidance and command by wire and a computerized active/passive capability now feature in most, top speeds may be in the order of 50-75 knots and countermeasures have been introduced.

WARHEAD   EXPLODER   ELECTRIC MOTOR   CONTRA-ROTATING PROPELLORS

GUIDANCE UNIT   CONTROLS   BATTERY

TRANSDUCER

the truth: Soviet submarines contributed virtually nothing of value to the campaign at sea. There were a few sinkings but the targets, save in a couple of instances, were easy meat and of little consequence.

Unburdened by pointers from the past, Gorshkov sets out to build a modern submarine fleet without overmuch regard for the personnel factors which, unknown to him, had largely been responsible for such disappointing results in general during the war. He has a lot on his plate.

In 1948 Stalin had ordered 1200 conventional boats to be built in three successive five-year plans between 1950 and 1965. In the event only 388 were to be constructed during that period because quality had to take precedence over quantity — but the number was still impressive.

By 1958, a couple of years in to his task, Gorshkov has two SSNs[3] at sea. They are named the *Leninsky Komsomolets* and *Seljabinsky Komsomolets* after prominent Young Communist League organisations. One is commanded by Captain Vladimir Nikolayevich Chernavin, a brilliant young Party member, who will one day, 30 years hence, relieve Gorshkov as head of the navy.

The design for what Westerners will designate the 'November' class was personally approved by Stalin at the recommendation of Kuznetsov, the former C-in-C who fell out with the KGB at one stage: accused of complicity with the West, he was temporarily demoted to Rear Admiral. Sergei Georgiyevich is not going to make that mistake.

Thirteen more 'Novembers' are to be brought forward with great urgency at Severodvinsk to gain experience for future types and strengthen defenses not only against the

American carriers but also to combat a new menace from the United States where five SSBNs have been laid down and are nearing completion. Many more will undoubtedly follow.

The 'Novembers' and their successors must be submarine-hunters as well as carrier-killers: sonar secrets stolen from England are hugely beneficial and the 'forehead' equipment fitted around the bow is basically a Portland product. Unfortunately the SSNs are very noisy and they can't hear themselves think. Something will have to be done about that.

The policy is for the machinery to be duplicated in SSNs — two steam turbines generating 30 000 shp for two propellers. Redundancy is advisable because there can be no risk of engine failure under the ice or, worse, in enemy waters: there is not much faith in reactor reliability. Twin plants need space so a 'November' is 361 ft long with an unhandy length to beam (L/B) ratio of 12:1. It will be difficult, even dangerous, to control at speed. Such a big awkwardly shaped boat needs two reactors anyway to attain the 30-knot Staff Target. Chicken and egg!

By contrast the contemporary USS *Skipjack* is 252 ft long with an ideal tear-drop hull for an L/B ratio of 8:1. She is extremely maneuvrable and can easily exceed 30 knots. Thanks to Admiral Rickover's insistence on excellence as the norm she has only one reactor, one turbine delivering 15 000 shp and a single screw.

Gorshkov is a realist: he knows that excellence is not a feature of Soviet workmanship. And if he is prudent he will not spend too long inspecting reactor spaces: the shielding is apt to be less than adequate. So far as physical safety is concerned boats are to be built with double hulls comprising a thin outer hull displaced from the main pressure hull to minimise the effects of a torpedo hit: they will also have an exceptionally high reserve of buoyancy thereby in the order of 30–40% of total displacement.

The drawing boards multiply; covered building slips spring up; canals and waterways are dredged and widened; universities and colleges turn out specialised scientists and technicians in their thousands; whole armies of workmen are drafted to the yards from 15 republics all over the Union.

Western intelligence is decidedly sniffy about 'Novembers' but much better boats are on their way. Meanwhile the diesel-electric fleet is a force to be reckoned with — 240 basic but serviceable 'Whiskeys', 20 'Romeos' and 26 'Zulus'. The little coastal defense 'Quebecs', powered by High Test Peroxide (HTP), are submersible disaster areas but the long-range 'Foxtrots' now starting to commission are first-class.

Gorshkov's inheritance reflects Stalin's decree modified in mid-stream. He now has to formulate further five-year plans for the Defense Council consisting of the General Secretary, his Deputy and three members representing the eternal triangle — the Party, the KGB and the Red Army (meaning all the armed forces). How is he to persuade this all-powerful cut-throat inner cabinet of the navy's needs?

The threat from America and the NATO Alliance is obvious. There can be no argument about that. But there has been a profound change in the balance of power since Stalin's death because, thanks to Klaus Fuchs and other spies, the Soviet Navy has had nuclear weapons, including hydrogen bombs for the aviation arm, since 1954. The United States no longer has a monopoly.

The overriding strategic objectives for the navy are now threefold: to target the American mainland with nuclear ballistic missiles; to prevent the American Strike Fleet from launching aircraft against the Mother Country; and to hunt down enemy SSBNs.

It is difficult to pry into a Russian mind and Gorshkov's writings[4] are not altogether revealing but it is probably at about this time that the wily admiral shifts his stance in the face of protests about costs from the Defense Council and Politburo. Submarines have traditionally been assigned an almost wholly defensive role although this logically includes the interception of transatlantic shipping.

But it is fair to conjecture, bearing in mind the extensive 'out of area' submarine operations which soon commence, that he puts a fresh case for numbers and quality forward.

The Soviet Naval Staff appreciates that it has always been vastly more expensive to mount anti-submarine defenses against a submarine (U-boat) campaign than to build and man the submarines in the first place. As a tiny example of this they read that German midget submersibles, despatched in desperation to try and help stem the Allied invasion flood in 1944, were inadequately prepared, poorly equipped and for the most part ineffectual: yet 500 escorts and 1000 aircraft were diverted from more important offensive tasks to guard against them.

Gorshkov may well have argued, therefore, that if the West could be obliged, by an ubiquitous underwater presence, to pour its money into ASW defenses, spread over diverse ocean areas, its capability for conducting a concentrated offensive against the *Rodina*, or the expanding Soviet Empire, would be much reduced. This line of thought would have aligned splendidly with the projection of power and influence by Soviet maritime forces.

Moreover, underwater pressure would not necessarily have to be real or constant: it need only be supposed. There is ample scope for bluff. The admiral doubtless points out that a Soviet *Principle of War* is Surprise and Deception — which submarines suit admirably.

Of course, some of the submarines sent out of area will be SSBNs while others, SSNs, will seek the opposition's 'Boomers'. This will complicate their problem of concealment and possibly force the enemy to employ some of his SSNs as sweepers to clear initial transit routes — lessening his striking power against the Soviet ballistic boats. A case of chicken and egg again! Submarine-versus-submarine warfare is becoming more and more significant.

While the Americans — and before long the British, French and Chinese — are forging ahead with their SSBN programs the Soviet Union is well acquainted with ballistic missiles. Although the master-mind, Von Braun, is in the USA, most of the German rocket experts were hauled to Russia where they have been strenuously engaged on cruise and ballistic-missile projects: the working conditions in the laboratories and factories are rather better than in the forced labor camps which were offered as an alternative.

The first Submarine Ballistic Missile

By 1944 the V-2 could be launched from capsules towed by U-boats; but there were practical difficulties and subsequent Russian trials with Golem missiles were not encouraging. Tube launch was clearly the way ahead for submarine launched ballistic missiles (SLBMs).

The world's first SLBM launch took place, from a modified 'Zulu V' diesel boat, in 1955 — five years before the USS *George Washington* despatched a Polaris missile down the test range. A number of 'Whiskey' boats were fitted with 450-mile SS-N-3C (Shaddock) cruise missiles at about the same time. The picture above shows a very early Soviet SLBM test firing.

The starting points were Hitler's secret weapons — the V-1 pilotless flying bomb and the V-2 (A4) ballistic missile. Both were used against London with considerable effect: now similar 'birds' can be equipped with infinitely more destructive megaton warheads.

The C-in-C is advised that, in view of control problems against ships, the 'Whiskey' Shaddocks can only be used for shore bombardment. Targetting difficulties will have to be resolved speedily; but the Strike Fleet may have to be dealt with immediately — and current anti-ship torpedoes are not good enough either. Worse, ASW torpedoes are primitive. A concerted effort is made to acquire information from the West in all areas: France is showing exceptional promise in the missile field but nobody yet has an effective submarine ASW weapon.

Problems, problems. But the Defense Council is firmly on the navy's side with a bias towards submarine warfare and a conviction shared with the Royal Navy's Admiral Sir John Eccles — a non-submariner incidentally — that 'the only answer to a nuclear submarine is another one'.[5]

The Soviet land forces are certainly not prepared for war — a fact not conceded by the Red Army in Council but the KGB is sure of it; the Party doubts if another invasion

Post-war Soviet submarines. Clockwise from top, a 'November' SSN, the sole 'Hotel III' SSBN converted to carry six SS-N-8 missiles for trials (original 'Hotels' were completed 1958-1960 with three tubes); a 'Romeo' SSK (widely exported); and a 'Whiskey twin-cylinder' SSG ahead of a 'Tango' SSK.

could be repelled; and the General Secretary wants to fend off a major conflict at all costs as the State is far too weak.

Defense in depth (literally) is the solution. No expense is to be spared despite the poor state of the economy. Gorshkov's Staff Appreciation is accepted virtually 'as is'. A revolutionary range of weapon systems, with SSBNs, SSGNs, SSNs and SSKs tailored to carry them, is on its way.

The Admiralty, London
An agreement with the United States is concluded in 1958 for the purchase of a complete set of propulsion machinery of the type fitted in USS *Skipjack* (SSN 585) to speed production of the Royal Navy's HMS *Dreadnought* (SSN-01) which will be laid down at Vickers next year. A personal approach to Admiral Hyman G Rickover USN by the First Sea Lord, Lord Louis Mountbatten succeeds where others have failed: it is, perhaps, a help to be an Earl. Nuclear training facilities in the States are secured for the first crew and CNO Admiral Arleigh Burke agrees to the appointment of an additional officer to the British Staff in Washington for liaison with the Polaris project team.

The Type 2001 active/passive sonar planned for *Dreadnought* is outstandingly good (as the Soviets have noted) but her weapons will be way astern of station. As a submarine hunter-killer she will be able to hunt but her ability to kill will, predictably, be marginal at best.

New London, Connecticut, USA
By 1958 the Submarine Development Group at New London is concerned, almost exclusively, with pitting submarines against submarines. It has a small diesel-electric squadron of its own — nuclear boats will join later — and all kinds of weapons and sensors are tested. The Mk 37 ASW torpedo looks promising although there are plenty of teething troubles. Low frequency passive sonar is detecting snorkel and nuclear submarines at exceptional ranges — but unfortunately they are American boats: drastic noise-reduction measures are indicated. Passive ranging by PUFFS is rather disappointing and so is SUBAIR co-operation whereby an aircraft is vectored out along a directing submarine's line of bearing.

It is a matter for concern in Moscow that the GRU is failing to gain access to the invaluable results generated by the tiny non-partisan DEVGRU staff.

Leningrad RSFSR
The largest submarine training establishment is at Leningrad. By 1967, ten years into Gorshkov's program, it has to cater for a lion's share of the 65 000 submariners, with half as many again in reserve as 'spare crews', who are required to man the underwater fleet of 407 boats. The total throughput of the giant training machine amounts to 30 000 every year. Western training officers do not envy their Russian opposite numbers: quite apart from the sheer volume of training involved they have to cope with numerous different nationalities from within the Empire and a fair amount of Soviet sympathisers from overseas.

USS *Skipjack* (SSN 585), commissioned 15 April, 1959, on an early visit to Portland, England where her excellent performance and ideal tear-drop shape, contrasting with the unhandy Soviet 'November'(opposite page), were fully recognised. HMS *Dreadnought*, looking very similar to *Skipjack*, was laid down two days after the latter commissioned.

Early Mass production

Russia had long experience of mass production from 1926 when the first naval building program was tabled with a high proportion of submarines: by June 1954[1], when Germany launched Operation Barbarossa, the Soviet Navy had 280 boats — the largest national fleet in the world.

Moscow RSFSR

His task complete — although vigorous submarine developments will be continuing — Gorshkov retires in December 1985 at the age of seventy-five. He has twice been made a Hero of the Soviet Union and he wears six Lenin medals. He is relieved by the 57-year-old Admiral Chernavin who has been, amongst other things, Commander of the Submarine Force, Northern Fleet, and C-in-C Northern Fleet.

The Defense Council is glad to say goodbye to Sergei Georgiyevich because the stubborn old sea dog insisted on independence for the Navy, including control of the SSBNs. Chernavin is a team player — a better Communist in fact.

General of the Army Maksimov, C-in-C Strategic Rocket Forces (RSVN), can now integrate all Soviet strategic nuclear weapons under a unified command. Chernavin goes along with that, which is one good reason for his being given the post.

Chernavin's inheritance is rich and getting richer still. Besides 50 or 60 SSBN (PLARB)[6] types which belong to Maksimov (the number depending on SALT agreements and on how many missiles/warheads are carried) he can reckon to have, by the 1990s, a large and predominantly modern attack fleet comprising SSGNs (PLARKs)[7], diesel SSGs (PLRKs)[8], SSNs (PLAs)[3], and diesel SSKs (PLs)[9].

The numerical total will be less than when he took over from Gorshkov but most of the boats will be very well armed, fast and tough. He absolutely refuses to ease back on the qualities which personal experience, dating back to his 'November' command days, has taught him are essential:

1. A mix of powerful weapons for flexibility. A boat may be attacking other submarines one day and surface forces the next; or it may be diverted to bombard shore targets. The penalty is size — an adequate mix cannot be accommodated (yet) in an attack submarine of less than eight or nine thousand tons.
2. Speed to break out, break in and break away.
3. Silence.
4. Deep diving depth.
5. Range to operate world-wide.
6. Surviveability.

He is well on the way to getting all these qualities over a wide range and in good measure as successive chapters will show.

Gorshkov's framed admonition, *Better is the Enemy of Good Enough*, still hangs in the office but it hardly accords with practice.

It is not really rational to separate Chernavin's requirements into categories: he, more than anyone, recognises that a submarine must be a fully integrated weapon system in itself and that nothing is unrelated to the whole. However, for the sake of simplicity it is a lot easier for us to start with hull construction, then go on to propulsion, sensors and fringe benefits before considering weapons and returning full circle to the total system which supports them.

Hull construction

Hulls used invariably to be circular in cross section and domed or tapered at the ends: most of them still are but some Swedish designs now substitute a thick flat plate (faired by the bow casing) for the forward dome. This makes construction, tube and sonar fittings easier and it might be attractive for the forthcoming new Soviet SSK.

For deep-diving boats the inadjustable domed and circular rule must continue to apply. But it can be less awkward in some cases to put certain weapons — cruise missiles and mines — outside the pressure hull (which is the submarine proper) and inside a light outer hull surrounding it. Double-hull construction is favored by Soviet submariners partly for this reason; partly for large ballast tanks and buoyancy; and perhaps even more for the protection it affords against ASW weapons.

If a torpedo detonates against the outer hull, well displaced from the inner hull, the effect is very much reduced. Chernavin is perfectly aware that new ASW torpedoes are threatening to penetrate the barrier, but his submariners (who have no strict 'need to know') may not be aware that immensely strong (and, incidentally, toxic) titanium, now widely used, transmits more shock than the steel it replaced. The pressure hulls themselves are highly compartmented for damage control, which is just as well in light of the fires and floodings which have been so common. There are also many more separate main ballast tanks than in Western boats — the simple 'Romeo' SSKs, for example, have 14 and Kingston valves are fitted on six of the flood holes.

An outer hull can, in addition, accommodate some sonar equipment and air bottles; and meanwhile it greatly helps to prevent noise being transmitted to the sea — especially if the space between the hulls is packed with honeycomb material which would have the added advantage of attenuating shock. (See also Chapter 1.11).

The NATO and French navies have not opted for double-hulled nuclear boats; and their ballast tanks are usually situated in an external continuation of the smooth cylindrical pressure hull forward and aft. The Soviet designers understand that this is because a lesser wetted area means less drag. But they doubtless ask why that is considered so important when they themselves have known how to make submarines slippery for ages. Turbulence can be dampened by well shaped hulls and by synthetic hull coatings. Drag can be lessened by ejecting drag-reducing substances (polymers) around the hull or applying them directly as a paint; or by covering the hull surface with gases; or by aviation flow techniques. A great deal can be learned by studying fish and sea-mammals — as Soviet scientists have done. Methods like these compensate for size and the upshot is more speed for less power.

There is potential weakness wherever the pressure hull is breached by hatches, weapon tubes, periscopes, masts, propulsion shafts and hull valves. It is therefore likely that the latest Soviet boats have only the minimum number of hull penetrations — certainly that is the intention for the American and British boats which will appear in the 1990s. Nuclear boats have a particular problem: most of the hull penetrations and systems in a diesel-electric boat can be secured when going deep but a number of vital systems in a nuclear submarine must continue to operate.

There are several ways in which some of the traditional holes in the main hull can be avoided. If periscopes and masts (possibly telescopic) are electronically rather than physically connected to the users they can be contained within the external sail or fin — and there is no need for that to be amidships. Or they can be let into a small strong cylinder, on top of the principal hull, housing the attack center. This was the case in many previous Soviet, American, German and French boats and it is probably how several Russian types are built today. In fact, the monstrous 25 000-ton 'Typhoon' SSBN consists of four separate cylinders — two pressure hulls side by side, the command post above and yet another cylinder for the torpedo tubes forward.

Wartime Monsters

The Japanese 'I-400' class (6560-tons submerged) heavily armed aircraft-carrying submarines completed between 1944 and 1945 went some way towards a twin hull by forming much of the pressure hull into two intersecting circles laid side by side, spectacle fashion, with a common longitudinal bulkhead running between them, while the two torpedo rooms forward were one above the other in a vertical figure-of-eight. This arrangement was primarily to achieve stability for surface operations while launching aircraft and to accommodate eight torpedo tubes with twenty reloads. Diving depth was no more than 325 ft (100m): the boats, huge for their time, were rivetted rather than welded and Allied experts after the war reported a 'definite impression of careless construction' — but the germ of a good idea was there.

Recognising the active sonar detectability of such bulky submarines, external surfaces were coated with an absorbent anti-sound reflecting substance comprising a resilient foundation of synthetic rubber and sand with a thin cement or plastic covering — the forerunner of the coatings extensively employed today, especially on the large new Soviet boats. The effectiveness of the Japanese covering was never demonstrated in wartime.

Above: The *I-400*, *I-401* and *I-14* aircraft carriers alongside the tender USS *Proteus*, soon after surrender with the hangar door of *I-400* open.

Many modern Soviet boats are covered with non-reflective anechoic tiles (NATO codename Cluster Guard) sometimes combined with an under-mattress of rubbery material for absorbing emitted sound. It is not easy to apply drag reduction methods as well: usually, a boat can either be protected acoustically or it can be slippery, but it is conceivable that the two techniques can be combined. In any case external surfaces can easily be made less reflective (and less prone to drag) by rounding them and avoiding angles: Russian designers must wonder why the Westerners insist on slab-like sails and angular superstructures.

Depth

Diving depth (and resistance to explosions) depends upon the material used for the pressure hull, its thickness, overcoming weaknesses caused by hull penetration — and the efficiency of the builders. An American or British submariner is confident in a boat built by, say, Electric Boat or Vickers (although the USS *Thresher* disaster in 1963 raised some doubts) but he might be a little hesitant to plunge to the depths in a submarine from a Russian yard where standards are not too exacting.

Welding sections together is easier now that the Russian building slips are covered and weather-proof; but it is still an exceedingly skilled business when the metal is two or more inches thick and not ordinary steel at that.

There are normally (but not universally) two depth figures quoted — safe (or test) and collapse. There is a considerable margin between them: the predicted collapse depth has usually exceeded the maximum safe operating depth by a factor of 1.7 or 2. German U-boats were often taken to the utmost limit during the war and plenty of unmanned trials have demonstrated that the constructors' calculations were correct. For example, a British A-boat, vintage 1945, had a safe depth of 500 ft and collapsed at rather more than 850 ft — which was to be expected from the 1.7 safety factor.

Assuming, charitably, a degree of integrity amongst Russian builders, an 'Alfa' SSN can go down to about 1000 m (approx 3000 ft) which is twice the safe depth for the US Navy's 'Los Angeles' class. But the latter is nearly twice the size of the little 'Alfa' and, to be fair, the 'Alfa' normally operates no deeper than 600 m — presumably to limit

'ageing' of the hull caused by frequent excursions to the maximum. It would be surprising if the larger 'Sierra', 'Mike' and 'Akula' SSNs are intended for operations at much more than 450 m because deep sound channels can now be exploited without the vehicle itself descending to them (see Chapter 4). Nor need the safety margin be as wide as it used to be: an additional 200 m, representing a factor of 1.4, should be enough for recovering from an unintentionally large pitch angle at speed.

However, there is at least one area where construction might be suspect. All machinery and electronic equipment must be shock-mounted and moving parts must be sound-insulated. It is a tedious business to install flexible supports properly, tempting to neglect them at sea and hard to check that they are doing their job.

Maneuverability was certainly a desirable attribute when Chernavin took over but recently it has become crucial for close-range submarine-versus-submarine engagements. Fortunately for the Russian submariners their newer types can turn on a kopek, and pitch angles of 20 or 30° ought to be safe if somewhat exhilarating.

The diversity of effort — two new diesel and seven different nuclear classes in eight years since 1980 — arises from experimentation and diversity of targets. But practically all submarines can assume an anti-submarine role.

To all appearances Soviet submarine construction is better than good enough, more advanced than anywhere else and the yards are theoretically capable of turning out 20 nuclear submarines a year. But how the boats will perform in action is another matter: underwater warfare is not always what it seems from the surface. We shall be observing it from below.

END NOTES

1. By Admiral A G Golovko, published in English by Putnam in 1965.
2. By Rear Admiral I Kolyshkin, first published in English by Progress Publishers Moscow in 1966.
3. Soviet equivalent to SSN is PLA — *Podvodnaya Lodka Atomnaya* (atomic underwater boat).
4. Eg 'The Sea Power of the State' published in English by Pergamon Press in 1979.
5. Admiral Eccles, C-in-C Home Fleet, while flying his flag in the submarine depot ship HMS *Maidstone*, 1957.
6. PLARB: *Podvodnaya Lodka Atomnaya Raketnaya Ballisticheskaya.*
7. PLARK: *Podvodnaya Lodka Atomnaya Raketnaya Krylataya.*
8. PLRK: *Podvodnaya Lodka Raketnaya Krylataya.*
9. PL: *Podvodnaya Lodka.*

U-boat welding problems

It was rumored during the last war — and it does not seem to have been a propaganda invention — that some German U-boat welders were publicly executed with an axe for speeding up their task by laying spent welding rods at the bottom of a 'V' join and welding over the top. It has, regrettably, proved impossible to verify this story but it has a ring of truth about it: submariners concur with the sentiments anyway!

1.3

PROPULSION, SPEED AND ENDURANCE

The traditional propulsion for submarines, when highly dangerous gasoline engines were thankfully abandoned before the First World War, has long been diesel-electric. It has the obvious disadvantage of obliging a boat to snorkel intermittently in order to transmit at a respectable speed and/or to recharge the main storage batteries. Consequently a diesel submarine (SSK) is sometimes disparagingly referred to as a submersible because it is dependent upon the atmosphere while a true (nuclear) submarine is not.

At first sight, with all the massive ASW systems arrayed against it, a boat which is dependent upon conventional diesels is poorly placed because snorkelling is noisy (although much less so than formerly) and it has to expose masts above the surface where it is liable to visual or radar detection. Moreover, its sonar is severely hampered by self-noise during snorkelling periods. Nevertheless, in practise there are many circumstances in which an SSK can still patrol and attack very effectively with a reasonable degree of security. In fact, there are confined and shallow water areas where a small submarine with diesel-electric propulsion is much better off than a large submarine with nuclear power.

It is a great mistake to denigrate SSKs: they will continue to be a menace for the foreseeable future and the Soviet Navy knows it. However, it is equally a mistake to treat them as second-class nuclear attack submarines (SSNs): they have limitations and they are at risk in heavily patrolled ocean areas. Although Soviet SSKs may be obliged to take that risk they are best deployed, if not for ASW defense close to home, in coastal waters: here they can make good use of what might be called natural cover while attacking inshore traffic and incoming convoys, laying mines, discharging combat swimmers and Swimmer Delivery Vehicles, surveying coastlines or gathering intelligence. ASW against diesel boats is like hunting foxes: they can be seen and shot running across a field but they are a lot more difficult to catch nipping in and out of the hedgerows.

Even in the open ocean NATO fleet exercises demonstrate, time and again, that a proportion of SSKs will get through the screen. Numbers are the key to success and the Soviet Navy has plenty. Russian approaches are co-ordinated and ASW defenses could be swamped by a massed attack.

Meanwhile a modern SSK is virtually silent on main motors and can be a good ASW vehicle when away from the surface turmoil.

Soviet diesel-electric performance

An elderly unsophisticated Soviet 'Foxtrot' SSK, with three shafts, can make 15.5 knots submerged for one hour, run for 100 nautical miles at eight knots or about 220 nautical miles at three knots: endurance is nearly doubled for the boats equipped with silver-zinc rather than standard lead-acid batteries. Snorkel speed, with a small battery charge, is around 10 knots.

The quite big 'Tangos', 1500 tons heavier than a 'Foxtrot' at 3900 tons submerged, have a higher capacity battery and significantly greater dived endurance to fit them for anti-submarine work. They carry torpedoes and ASW missiles. They are also being given anti-aircraft (SAM) missiles so they may feel more able to come out of the hedgerows in war.

The 'Kilos', at sea since 1982 and still building, are a little smaller at 3000 tons submerged and are ideally shaped with a 'tear-drop' hull. Unlike the 'Tangos', which have three shafts, thay have a single six-bladed propellor. The top speed submerged is 25 knots and it can probably be maintained for a couple of hours — quite enough to tear into a convoy and out again. They, too, probably have a SAM system and they carry 12 ASW torpedoes.

Nothing is yet known about the new Soviet SSK which will soon appear but some clues can be gathered from projected non-nuclear propulsion systems.

Non-nuclear air independent propulsion systems

Most batteries are of the Lead-Acid type which responds well to a broad bracket of charge and discharge rates, has a long life and is much cheaper than Silver-Zinc. Twenty-five years ago Russian cells delivered 8000 ampere-hours at the five-hour discharge rate: today, with only a 1.5 per cent increase in weight, there is no reason why they should not deliver 11 750 ampere hours — a 47 per cent improvement. That is about the limit — hence the larger hulls to accommodate more cells. There is battery ventilation and cooling to consider besides inspection and maintenance, so it is not practicable to stack cells directly on top of one another although they can certainly be arranged on two or more separate decks. It is true that Lead-Acid technology could be stretched further by rather revolutionary means: for example, an external reservoir of acid, with circulation into the cells during discharge, would increase performance usefully. But this would introduce undesirable and probably fragile complications: it is more sensible to investigate different kinds of battery associated with different kinds of generators.

Nickel-Zinc cells suffer the same disadvantages as Silver-Zinc — recharging difficulties, low cycle life and high cost. Sodium-Sulphur cells have a 50 per cent higher energy density than Lead-Acid but operate at 300°C while Lithium–Iron offers twice the energy density but operates at 400°C plus. Four times the energy density is claimed for Aluminium-Oxygen cells which show promise but there is some way to go before practical applications are possible.

In any case improved batteries do no more than increase submerged endurance: they do not by themselves eliminate exposure times. They are more important for burst speeds in conjunction with other air-inde-

pendent systems: the USSR must surely have explored possibilities as vigorously as Germany and Sweden.

Incidentally, energy can very conveniently be stored in composite flywheels. Only one firm[1] is known to have explored this possibility seriously but the potential, with an excellent space/weight-to-power ratio and full power instantly deliverable is promising; and there are ways of cancelling out the gyro couple (precession) which would otherwise make maneuvering impossible.

Fuel cells

Fuel cells for submarines have been seriously considered, discarded and reconsidered by turns since 1958. They are a practical proposition, proven in space, on land and in Deep Submergence Rescue Vehicles (DSRVs).

Fuel cells are compact with efficiency figures quoted as 70 to 80 per cent. They operate most efficiently at a constant current corresponding to a medium power rate: in terms of submarine propulsion this implies a speed somewhere in the eight to fourteen knot range and, naturally, this can only be maintained for as long as the fuel lasts — a week or more depending upon fuel capacity which in turn depends upon space available.

Fuel cells are not good for high-rate discharges: it is best to use a separate Lead-Acid battery for high-speed sprints or, quite possibly better, composite contra-rotating flywheels.

Closed cycle engines

Closed cycle (air-independent) engines have been a reality since the first German Walter design for the Type XVIIA *U-792* in November 1943. In a typical system an oxygen compound — usually concentrated High Test Peroxide (HTP) — is broken down by a catalyst to form oxygen and steam. The gases generated are then led to a combustion chamber where oil fuel is injected and ignited. Water is also sprayed in with the combustion products, increasing the volume of gas and reducing the temperature. The gas is passed to a turbine to provide power and thence to a condenser which separates the water from the gases, mostly carbon dioxide which dissolves in sea water when discharged overboard.

There are much better, and safer, closed-cycle engines available now. The underlying attraction is that, weight for weight or volume for volume, chemical fuels and oxidants can store much more energy than batteries —

SOME NON-NUCLEAR PROPULSION SYSTEMS

Diesel-electric propulsion is still usual for practically all SSKs. A German Type 206, which is a fairly typical small submarine (450-498 tons), has 1500 hp diesels and one 1800 hp main motor.

DIESEL ELECTRIC DRIVE

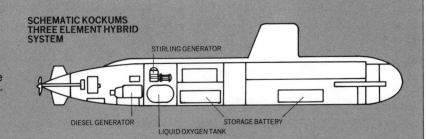

DIESEL-ELECTRIC/DRIVE GENERATOR(S)

ELECTRIC MOTOR(S)   DIESEL GENERATOR(S)   BATTERIES

The KOCKUM hybrid system for a 1000-ton submarine has a low power high-energy air-independent Stirling engine with liquid oxygen (LOX) storage, a battery for high burst speeds and a diesel for recharging the latter or transitting in low-level ASW areas.

SCHEMATIC KOCKUMS THREE ELEMENT HYBRID SYSTEM

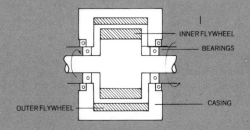

STIRLING GENERATOR

DIESEL GENERATOR   LIQUID OXYGEN TANK   STORAGE BATTERY

FLYWHEEL

A 'rechargeable' flywheel system (contra-rotating to avoid gyroscopic precession effects) would offer, with suitable transmission, power and instant acceleration with minimal complications in a hybrid system. The flywheels would best be constructed in a space-saving carbon fiber composite; and more energy would be available in less space than a comparable battery.

CONTRA-ROTATING FLYWHEEL FOR ENERGY STORAGE

INNER FLYWHEEL

BEARINGS

OUTER FLYWHEEL   CASING

STIRLING ENGINE

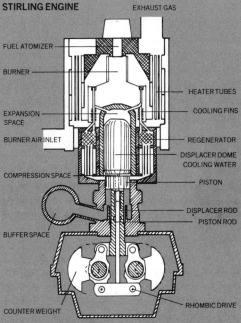

EXHAUST GAS

FUEL ATOMIZER

BURNER

EXPANSION SPACE

BURNER AIR INLET

COMPRESSION SPACE

BUFFER SPACE

COUNTER WEIGHT

HEATER TUBES

COOLING FINS

REGENERATOR

DISPLACER DOME COOLING WATER

PISTON

DISPLACER ROD

PISTON ROD

RHOMBIC DRIVE

BASIC HTP SYSTEM

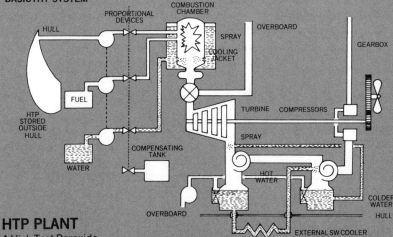

HULL

PROPORTIONAL DEVICES

COMBUSTION CHAMBER

OVERBOARD

SPRAY

COOLING JACKET

GEARBOX

FUEL

HTP STORED OUTSIDE HULL

WATER

COMPENSATING TANK

TURBINE   COMPRESSORS

SPRAY

HOT WATER

OVERBOARD

COLDER WATER HULL

EXTERNAL SW COOLER

HTP PLANT

A High Test Peroxide (HTP) plant is air-independent (see text), but much better and safer closed-cycle systems, albeit partly derived from the original Walter design illustrated schematically, are feasible today.

THE STIRLING ENGINE

The externally heated Stirling engine shows promise although a closed-cycle system which may be even better — and needs no snorkel is being produced by Maritalia, Italy. An SSK would run at low speed on the Stirling, using batteries (recharged in due course by snorkelling) for sprints.

The wartime Walter plant

There were high hopes in Germany, at the beginning of the war, for Professor Helmuth Walter's turbine-driven submarine powered by a highly concentrated solution of Hydrogen Peroxide known variously as Perhydrol, Ingolin or HTP. It was horribly dangerous stuff in a confined space but it did provide high speed for a limited period. The experimental boat V80 went to sea in April 1940 and supposedly operational boats began to follow two-and-a-half years later. None took part in the war. One of the latest, U-1407, a Type XVIIB, was brought to England where she became HMS Meteorite. The cynical

German badge was a shark and gallows angled against a wheel — the wheel offered a Hobson's choice between the risks of becoming food for the sharks if the boat was directed daringly or disgrace if prudent caution was employed.

High speed would have been handy for U-boats fighting the Battle of the Atlantic but it is doubtful whether the delicate machinery and HTP storage bags would have stood up to depth-charging.

Some little Soviet coastal defense 'Quebecs' of the fifties, had an HTP plant on their center shaft. Led by the Sakhalinsky Komsomolets they were known as 'cigarette lighters' by their crews: they were no more popular than the

Above: HMS Explorer in 1957 at London docks where, if the HTP plant had been started up, the customary fireballs might have caused some alarm.

British HTP boats Explorer and Excalibur, completed at Vickers in 1956 and 1958 respectively, and called — with reason — 'the two exploders'. Explorer, based on Meteorite, achieved 26½ knots on trials but not for long. Fuel stowage was a problem and it transpired that HTP propulsion was twice as expensive as nuclear power — one shilling and eleven pence three farthings a yard in old English money! Russia and Britain were agreed on one thing: HTP was not good news.

which is why an ordinary medium-sized diesel submarine can carry fuel for up to 10 000 miles (a far greater range, incidentally, than a frigate) while its battery, at an economical discharge rate, will only enable it to run submerged for 3–400 miles at best. Moreover, fuel of any kind can be stored in odd-shaped spaces where electric cells will not fit.

However, a closed-cycle system still has snags as well as benefits. The most encouraging contender is a small Stirling engine, developed by the Royal Swedish Navy and Kockums shipyard, which differs from a conventional engine in that heat is supplied externally and continuously to a working gas in a closed system. A regenerator reclaims energy by supplying, back to the cycle, much of the heat contained in the gas after expansion. The engine is integrated with a Liquid Oxygen (LOX) system.

Tests in Sweden have gone well, duly noted by the Soviet Navy. An operational submarine of 1000 tons would need two Stirling generator sets — each producing 70 kW — to float the electrical load at slow or moderate speeds allowing the standard batteries to remain charged and available for sprints.

Stirling development in Germany is said to aim for a higher output of about 250 kW per engine with a possibility of increasing this to about 600 kW. Whether an optimum non-nuclear system will involve fuel cells, ordinary batteries, flywheels and a closed-cycle engine or only a couple of these components remains to be seen.

However, the latest and simple Italian (Maritalia) GST system (see Chapter 1.10) is a very strong competitor for Stirling.

In all this, superconducting electric motors are firmly on the horizon and have very probably been a feature of at least a proportion of Soviet submarines for several years. The very low temperatures previously required (in the order of $-400°F$ to $-300°F$) are being raised closer to ambient: superconductivity will then become entirely practicable and, predictably, widespread in everything from small computers to large motors.

Some Soviet boats are observed to surface with ice forming around their after casings so cryogenics must still be involved at present. Superconductivity virtually eliminates transmission losses, reduces heat generation to zero and allows electrical units to be much smaller — thus making available more space for fuel, weapons or whatever.

Nuclear power

The fuel for a nuclear plant is U-235 — an isotope found in slightly less than one per cent of all Uranium — which has three fewer neutrons in the nucleus of its atom. An atom of U-235 splits when hit by a neutron from another atom, provided that it is slowed down or 'thermalised', giving off energy and radio-activity. Some of its neutrons shoot off and shatter other U-235 atoms which in turn give off energy, radioactivity and more neutrons in a self-sustaining chain reaction. The reactor is then said to be critical.

The core of a nuclear reactor produces the energy: it is composed of fuel elements, each of which is enclosed by a strong outer metallic case or cladding. The elements are surrounded and separated by pure water. This is not only the coolant (a rather confusing term because it actually takes up energy in the form of heat) but it is also the essential moderator for slowing down emitted neutrons so that, instead of flying off into nowhere, they are more likely to hit and split a nucleus on their way.

The fission process has been compared to throwing magnets at a steel wire mesh: if thrown too hard they sail through and do not stick. Control rods containing Hafnium, Cadmium or Boron elements absorb neutrons, acting like a sort of blotting paper, when lowered into the core to bring a reactor to sub-criticality.

The small core is enclosed in a large and very strong Reactor Pressure Vessel (RPV), pressurised to prevent water from boiling — thus permitting it to attain a higher temperature while avoiding very undesirable disturbances in the flow. Hence this type of plant is known as a Pressurised Water Reactor (PWR).

Impurities in the hot coolant water in the RPV become radioactive and cannot safely be used for generating power directly: the water is therefore circulated by primary coolant pumps (sometimes after more than one pass through the reactor) through a heat exchanger, which generates steam for a non-radioactive secondary loop supplying the main turbine(s), turbo-generators and associated condensers — a conventional steam plant assembly.

Most of the later reactor plants can operate at low or moderate power without running the coolant pumps which are apt to be the noisiest machines in the assembly: natural circulation within the RPV is enough.

A pressurised water nuclear plant usually responds immediately to an increase or decrease of power used without moving the control rods which permit or halt the fission process. If more energy (steam) is taken from the secondary circuit by opening a throttle valve wider the coolant (moderator) loses heat, becomes denser and slows down more neutrons: these collide with more atoms and instantaneously produce more heat until, very quickly, a balance is achieved at the new level of power required. If less power is demanded, the coolant (moderator) becomes hotter and less dense; fewer neutrons are slowed down to 'splitting speed' and again the process stabilises. It is all elegantly simple.

The reactor compartment containing the entire primary circuit is shielded by lead and polythene which generally accounts for between 20–30 per cent of the plant's weight.[2] This is where the early Soviet boats skimped to such an extent that radioactivity was measured by NATO 'surveillance' units and was seriously considered, for a while, as a means of ASW detection.

It is assumed that automated Soviet nuclear engine rooms in the later classes do not have to be manned. If that is so the weight of reactor-shielding could have been cut dramatically with marked benefits in other areas. One must hope, for Soviet sub-mariners' sakes, that the automation is reliable.

It is sometimes thought that only diesel-electric submarines can discharge swimmers, but most SSNs (and SSBNs for repair work) have the capability. However, the major benefits of nuclear power are obviously wasted in coastal waters while a large submarine is at greater risk than a comparatively small SSK or midget.

There are certain materials which, if pure, would not become radioactive in a reactor — hydrocarbons, helium, lead and bismuth. If any of these were used as a coolant together with some kind of moderator — graphite perhaps — direct power generation would theoretically be possible without the need for a secondary circuit.

This is presumably the system used in the 3700-ton 'Alfas' which have twin lead-bismuth cooled reactors supplying two turbo-alternators for a single superconductivity electric motor. The result from 47 000 shp is 45 knots in a fairly small hull. The 6400-ton 'Mike' is likely to have similar arrangement with 60 000 shp for a top speed around 38 knots. The 'Alfa' is 40 per cent faster and the 'Mike' is 19 per cent faster than 7000 and 5000-ton 32-knot American and British SSNs with PW reactors. The latter, in turn, are 28 per cent faster than the 25-knot 2670-ton French 'Rubis' class SSNs, the smallest in any navy with a 48 MW turbo-electric drive. There is a moral somewhere but it is not that fast submarines have to be big for speed alone: they just need to be slippery and have the right kind of power plant. The tragedy is that Admiral Rickover's dogmatic conser-

vatism, admittedly supported by problems with the liquid Sodium reactor in USS *Seawolf*, allowed the Russians to stride ahead.

A liquid metal reactor has quiet electro-magnetic coolant pumps (with no moving parts) and is compatible with a very quiet magnetohydrodynamic (MHD) generator. This device produces electrical energy by the motion of an electrically conductive plasma through a transverse magnetic field. One system apparently tried in Russia feeds a liquid metal heat-transfer fluid through the reactor where it is vaporised. The vapor (plasma) is ionized and passed through a magnetic channel at high speed where its energy is converted into electrical energy. The metal vapor is then cooled to condense it before being fed back again to the reactor in liquid form by an electromagnetic pump. The snag is that MHD substantially increases the magnetic signature of a submarine.

The MHD principle in reverse can be applied to direct thrust without a propeller, by a form of ripple motor, akin to the way in which a skate propels itself through the water. One credible theory suggests that such a motor could be contained in the mysterious pod perched on the tail fin of 'Victor III'

PRESSURIZED WATER REACTOR

The PW reactor is still by far the most common type, mainly because it was so very well proven in the USN from the outset and is elegantly simple. Coolant pumps, for long a predominant noise source in the plant, have been markedly quietened, especially in Western boats like the British 'Trafalgar'-class, and many modern SSNs and SSBNs do not have to run them at all at slow or moderate speeds, because natural circulation suffices.

British 'Swiftsure'-class machinery is compactly laid out, with two main turbines geared to a single shaft with an emergency electric motor.

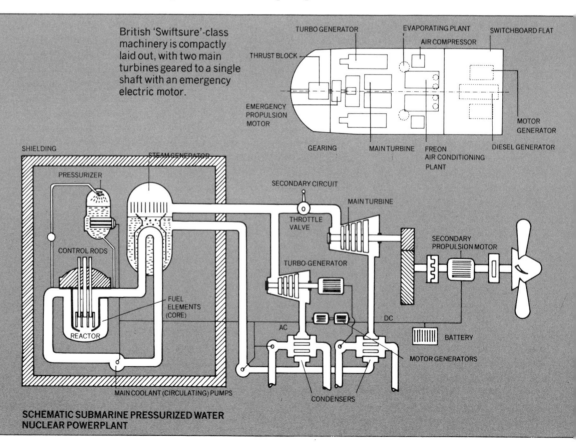

SCHEMATIC SUBMARINE PRESSURIZED WATER NUCLEAR POWERPLANT

'Sierra' and 'Akula' SSNs.

According to this, a pulsing magnetic field acts on a magnetic-fluid filled flexible sheath surrounding a water tube running through the pod. That sets up a travelling wave in the sheath. The resulting motion draws water in to the tube's venturi entrance at the forward end of the pod and expels it aft. The pod-motor should be good for a stealthy seven knots; but the system might conceivably be scaled up from auxiliary drive to primary propulsion, especially if the hull itself is motorized to ripple. In any event, jet propulsion of some kind is clearly predictable.

(For those who do not want to delve deeply into MHD principles, Fleming's right and left-hand rules indicate the general idea.)

Coping with failure

Reverting to less esoteric matters, a total coolant failure in any nuclear plant is disastrous and inevitably leads to a melt-down of the core. Western submariners are absolutely certain that their safety devices and back-up systems will never allow this to happen. The Russians said the same — until Chernobyl. They are notoriously relaxed about safety: serious accidents, human errors, action damage — or deliberate sabotage come to that — could cause havoc but one thing is sure: no kind of reactor can turn itself into an atomic bomb in any circumstances.[2]

Nor is it likely that the external pressure of water on a sunken submarine would result in radioactive pollution. Reactor Pressure Vessels (RPVs) are well shaped to resist external pressure even though they are constructed to withstand high internal pressure; and the metal in the primary circuits is stainless steel which is not likely to corrode. There was no published evidence of significant radioactivity around the wrecks of USS *Scorpion* (SSN 589) which was lost in 1968 in 10 000 ft of water or USS *Thresher* (SSN 593) which went down in 1963 and was found at a depth of 8400 ft. And there does not seem to be undue concern about radioactivity from the two reactors in the Russian 'Yankee'-class SSBN which was scuttled, following a fire on board, 763 nautical miles from New York on 6 October, 1986: she lies at a depth of 18 000 ft where the sea exerts 3.6 tons on every square inch. This odd event has other connotations noted in Chapter 1.8.

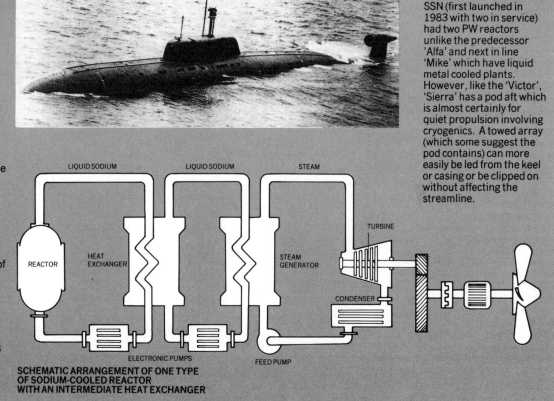

LIQUID METAL REACTOR COOLING

Liquid metal reactor cooling has significant advantages over pressurized water — a virtually silent pumping system, compactness and much more thermal energy available to the secondary circuit, when the latter uses superheated steam, because the coolant temperature can be several hundred degrees higher over a wider range. Moreover, it is compatible with MHD generation. However, thermal stresses demand metallurgical technology of a high order and a degree of risk at the test and evaluation stage, which evidently deterred the USN after the (1957) *Seawolf* experiment but which the Soviet Navy has accepted.

The Soviet 'Sierra'-class SSN (first launched in 1983 with two in service) had two PW reactors unlike the predecessor 'Alfa' and next in line 'Mike' which have liquid metal cooled plants. However, like the 'Victor', 'Sierra' has a pod aft which is almost certainly for quiet propulsion involving cryogenics. A towed array (which some suggest the pod contains) can more easily be led from the keel or casing or be clipped on without affecting the streamline.

LIQUID SODIUM   LIQUID SODIUM   STEAM

TURBINE

REACTOR   HEAT EXCHANGER   STEAM GENERATOR

CONDENSER

ELECTRONIC PUMPS   FEED PUMP

SCHEMATIC ARRANGEMENT OF ONE TYPE OF SODIUM-COOLED REACTOR WITH AN INTERMEDIATE HEAT EXCHANGER

Speed

Nothing except nuclear power can give the sustained high speed which is necessary for strategic deployment — a matter of great importance to navies where areas of activity are distant from home ports. It is the greatest pity that Australia, whose defense depends upon rapid deployment over vast ocean areas, will not countenance nuclear power: no other navy, for purely defensive purposes, needs it so plainly — yet politics and emotion (as well as economics) prevent the outstandingly competent Australian submarine service from acquiring attack-type nuclear submarines.

Tactically, speed allows a submarine to engage or disengage at will, especially if it enjoys an advantage over the enemy in that respect. It is what Admiral Lord Fisher meant when he said some 80 years ago that 'speed is armour'.

Unfortunately high speed is exceedingly expensive (although it can be lessened by 'slippery' techniques) and other attributes may well be prejudiced by its costs: an extra 15 per cent at the top of the scale adds tens of millions to the price — around 50 per cent is quoted and the cost curve is exponential after that. Furthermore, the fact is that a submarine is deaf, dumb and blind above a certain speed. For future boats, not yet at sea, 25 knots has been suggested as the maximum at which sonar can be expected to function with a reasonable degree of acquisition probability: and at present it is likely that the figure is often lower, especially in the Soviet fleet. Whether the expense involved in increasing from, say, 32 to 38 knots for an SSN or from 20 to 25 knots for an SSK makes much tactical difference is difficult to say. Certainly, from the Western viewpoint, cost-effectiveness appears doubtful if there is a danger of speed-money robbing weapon-money. At all events, Western submariners seem to agree that, if a question of priorities arises, keeping very quiet is more desirable than going very fast; but avoiding detection, an art that will be scrutinised later, is becoming more than a matter of not making noise. Other factors are gaining weight in the detection-advantage equation.

Given a weapon system with adequate range — which is surely the key to the problem — it seems at first sight that exceptionally high speed is hard to justify. What can a Soviet 'Alfa' do at 45 knots once it has reached its patrol area? It is no use careering

about in wartime at full power unless, as Admiral Reich USN has pointed out, an ordnance package can ultimately be exploded alongside the enemy. Straightforward geometry suggests that burst speeds in the order of 20 knots should usually be sufficient to gain an attacking position if a submarine has a sufficiently long striking arm to match current and projected sonar detection (and classification) ranges. However, geometry can over-simplify some situations as will be apparent later. Paradoxically, very long detection ranges imply a need for very fast submarines to exploit them.

But what one navy needs is not necessarily the same as another. This is evidenced in the continuing arguments about diesel as against nuclear power. SSKs and SSNs have different jobs to do, in differing environments as a rule, and it is not sensible to try and compare them on a like-for-like basis.

Not all submarines in all areas require long endurance at high speed. For those which do not, but cannot risk exposing themselves, there is an inexpensive nuclear alternative.

Hybrid semi-nuclear propulsion
It is entirely feasible to insert a low-power, low-cost nuclear 'plug' or section into an ordinary diesel-electric boat thereby providing all the submerged endurance it needs at low speed while leaving the battery (or flywheel presumably) fully charged for high attack speeds.

AMPS (nuclear-based Autonomous Marine Power Source) has been developed by the Canadian ECS group of companies. Originally conceived for commercial use under the ice it is practically unattended, commendably simple and inherently safe. The SLOWPOKE-type neutron source is the least that can sustain a chain reaction: a significant variation in the normal operating conditions automatically results in shut-down. If pumped cooling supply is lost, natural convective circulation takes over.

The nominal fission power of AMPS is 1.5 MW and the low-pressure primary circulating loop supplies a low-temperature Rankine cycle engine. Computerized automation does the work.

AMPS has exciting possibilities, especially for anti-submarine tasks. The plant does not compare in terms of power with a standard reactor but there are places where it might well suffice — in the Canadian Arctic for example.

Falklands deployment

British SSNs deployed to the Falklands in 1982 appear, from simple arithmetic, to have gone flat out (apart from brief excursions to shallow depth, to receive messages and check on navigation) all the way to the South Atlantic. If they had had power for an extra five knots they would have arrived 36 hours earlier — helpful perhaps but surely not worth sacrifices in other directions. On the other hand, the diesel-electric *Onyx* with a submerged speed-of-advance around eight knots did not arrive for three weeks after the nuclear boats. *Onyx*, as a more suitable vehicle than the SSNs for launching and recovering Special Boat Squadron (SBS) raiders, must have been sorely missed in the early days of the Anglo-Argentinian confrontation.

HYBRID NUCLEAR/ DIESEL-ELECTRIC PROPULSION

The Canadian ECS Group of Companies (from whom these drawings are copied) has offered to design and construct a nuclear 'plug' based on the nuclear AMPS (Autonomous Marine Power Source), developed for the commercial SAGA-N project: it should be relatively simple to insert the plug into an existing diesel-electric boat.

The AMPS system is broadly similar to the 'Slowpoke' plants (also developed in Canada) which have been operating safely and well since the 1970s for a variety of uses: 'Slowpoke' is essentially a neutron source in a 'swimming pool' type reactor. The fissile material is uranium zirconium hydride.

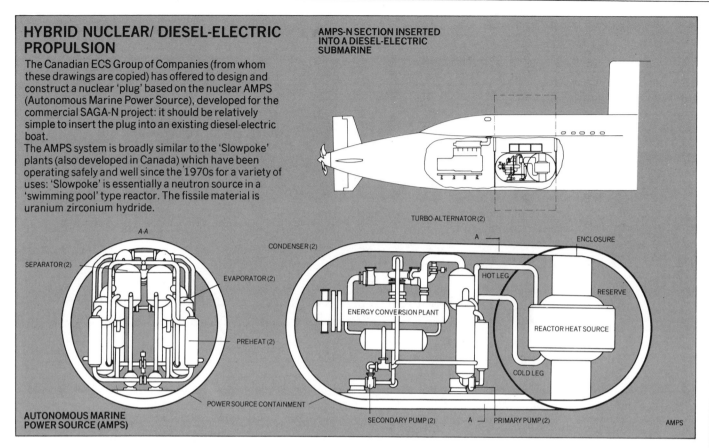

AMPS-N SECTION INSERTED INTO A DIESEL-ELECTRIC SUBMARINE

TURBO-ALTERNATOR (2)

A·A

SEPARATOR (2)
EVAPORATOR (2)
CONDENSER (2)
PREHEAT (2)
POWER SOURCE CONTAINMENT
ENERGY CONVERSION PLANT
SECONDARY PUMP (2)
PRIMARY PUMP (2)
A
A
ENCLOSURE
HOT LEG
RESERVE
REACTOR HEAT SOURCE
COLD LEG

AUTONOMOUS MARINE POWER SOURCE (AMPS)

AMPS

In light of Soviet submarine strategic and anti-shipping threats, Canada is intent on acquiring ten or a dozen SSNs for ASW patrolling in the Northeast Pacific, Northwest Atlantic and Arctic Oceans. A stated aim for as far back as 1975 was 'to conduct sub-surface surveillance, in conjunction with US forces, of shallow and deep water areas of the seaward approaches to North America, including the Canadian Arctic and the Denmark Strait, to provide a continuing intelligence picture of potentially hostile submarine activities'.[3]

Since then Canada appears to have become particularly anxious to retain her sovereignty in Arctic waters. The Government has taken exception to American transitter-trespassers *en route* to the North Pole; and, although rather less has been said publicly about Soviet sharks coming from the opposite direction, adversaries under the ice are reckoned to call for nuclear-powered submarines in response. However, it is surely worth investigating the practicality, for under-ice work, of employing ASW AMPS hybrids. A fair number of these relatively inexpensive craft might do just as well — perhaps better — in this very special arena

as a severely limited number of big and costly SSNs even if small hybrids are not adequate for defending Canada's interests in other areas.[4]

It does seem that alternatives to 'conventional' nuclear propulsion deserve, everywhere, more consideration than currently afforded. Some of them are especially attractive for certain ASW purposes by virtue of enabling submarines to be smaller — an increasingly important consideration nowadays.

END NOTES
1. Hicks Transmissions Ltd, Dolgerddon Hall, Rhyader, Powys LD6 5AD, UK. A preliminary study by Ray Hicks strongly suggests that contra-rotating composite flywheels (one inside the other) might prove very advantageous while being more economical than a battery in terms of weight, space and maintenance.
2. Reactor safety is comprehensibly and uniquely covered in *Submarine Warfare Today & Tomorrow* by Captain J Moore and Commander R Compton-Hall published by Michael Joseph in UK and by Adler & Adler in USA.
3. Canadian 1975 Defense Structure Review. This was superceded by the exceptionally well produced White Paper in June 1987 titled *Challenge and Commitment — A Defense Policy for Canada.*
4. See also Chapters 1.9 and 2.9.

1.4

SOUND, SONAR AND NON-ACOUSTIC INDICATORS

The aim in submarine-versus-submarine warfare is to gain the sonar range advantage. In the passive sense that means reducing radiated noise to prevent the enemy from hearing it and reducing self-noise to avoid interference with one's own listening ability. In the active sense it means lessening the chance of sonar transmissions being reflected back to the searcher.

Leonardo's sonar

'If you cause your ship to stop and place the head of a long tube in the water and the other extremity to your ear, you will hear a ship at great distance from you' — Leonardo da Vinci (1452–1519).

Fifteen years ago Soviet submarines were at a decided disadvantage. They were much noisier than most NATO boats; and NATO sonar was superior. Today the balance is more level and in a few years it could tip towards Russia: the trend is evident in the last chapter alone. As the Editor of *Jane's Fighting Ships* remarked in his 1987/88 foreword 'Since the commissioning of the first of this (the US Navy's "Los Angeles") class in 1976 the Soviet Navy has introduced four classes of nuclear attack submarines, at least three with an increased diving depth, all with a far higher power density than "Los Angeles" and a much superior armament... all the result of innovation and imagination... Because of conformism, conservation and complacency the US Navy will not have a radically new design of submarine at sea until 1994, USS *Seawolf*.' Hard words, but they ring true.

And by the time that *Seawolf* arrives at least a couple more very advanced Soviet types will be on the prowl.

The latest Russian boats are very quiet indeed because Soviet submariners fully appreciate that sound, of one sort or another, is the name of the underwater game. It is not much use cantering along with a load of weapons if everyone can hear you coming. And if an enemy *podlodka* is about, then *vam kryshka* (for you there is a lid) — you've had it. Surprise is still a submarine's main attri-

bute: there would be no point in going below the surface if it was not.

Russian submariners tackled the problem vigorously when they got the word. They took much the same steps as the Royal Navy which can reasonably claim to be the most silent Silent Service with its 'Trafalgar'-class SSNs (as quiet, at moderate speed, as the best 'Oberon'-class SSKs on electric motors) and the new 'Upholder'-class Type 2400 SSKs. Noise reduction is the mechanical aspect of surprise: but almost equally significant is the understanding of sound's behavior in water. The USSR has devoted a massive continuing effort to exploring the vagaries of inner space with no less than 117 oceanographic research vessels besides two or three auxiliary nuclear submarines (for under-ice work) and a diesel boat. This substantial fleet compares with a dozen oceanographic research ships and one diesel-electric submarine in the US Navy; and three oceanographic-cum-hydrographic survey vessels in the Royal Navy. France is no better supplied with only one purpose-built oceanographic ship but China, where the submarine force is being modernised, has 14.

The Soviet Union is not apt to waste its resources. It must know something that we do not.

The sea is a good conductor of sound but it is emphatically not a simple, homogenous medium: the propagation of sound in water is complex. Velocity varies with temperature, pressure and salinity; and consequently it also varies with depth, position and the season of the year. The result is a collection of refractive acoustic waves (bending due to changes in sound velocity as a function of depth or horizontal distance) and reflective waves (bending back due to interaction with the surface or seabed). There are relatively few conditions when the path does not bend in some way — sometimes horizontally as well as vertically — so refraction and reflection have to be allowed for. There is no guarantee that the radiated noise from a sub-

marine will consistently reach a given location but if the paths can be predicted they can be exploited advantageously — hence the marked Soviet interest in oceanography.

A simple picture of vertical ocean profile (never simple in reality) shows three layers of water, each with its own temperature or velocity characteristics.

The surface layer down to 50 or 60m is usually isothermal (temperature constant) because the water is well mixed by wind and waves: there is little or no bending here but the layer is cluttered by sea noise.

In the next region between 60 and

SOUND PROPAGATION

An ASW submarine aims to detect an enemy submarine while itself remaining undetected. Hence, it constantly tries to gain and maintain the sonar advantage — just as men-of-war under sail strove for the weather gauge. The key is to know, understand and exploit sonar conditions.

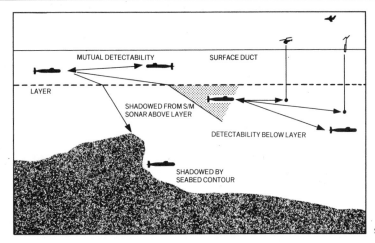

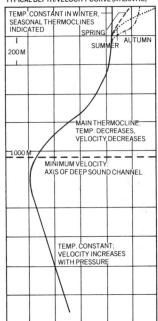

TYPICAL DEPTH/VELOCITY CURVE (ATLANTIC)

Above: This figure shows a fairly typical variation of sound velocity with depth in the Atlantic with seasonal variations in the upper stratum.

Left and below: The behavior of sound in water is complex and variable. Waves seldom travel in a straight line; but in a very simplified case, where there is a well defined layer, one boat can detect another at a fair range if both are in the same duct above or below the layer. Similarly, surface ship variable-depth sonar (VDS), sonobuoys or helicopter dunking sonar must be operated at the correct depth. Meanwhile, a boat may shelter behind a seabed contour.

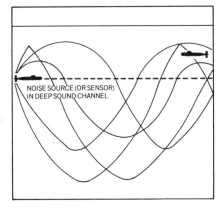

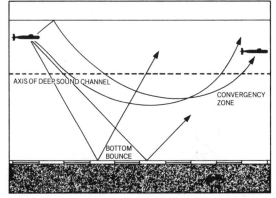

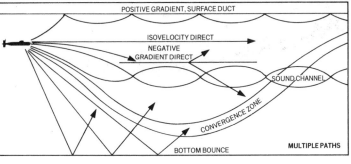

In practise the various sound channels are even more diverse than shown here; but they can be calculated quite accurately with known oceanographic data updated and localised by sound velocimeters. The latter, for giving the whole profile, are expendable and the number of measurements is limited.

1000 m, there is a negative gradient — temperature or velocity decreasing with depth, which bends sound downwards.

Below about 1000 m the temperature is constant and water pressure is dominant. Sound now travels faster because velocity increases with pressure. This region is called the deep isothermal layer. A sound wave finding its way into this deep sound channel — directly or by refraction — is trapped: it then travels horizontally for very great distances — perhaps thousands of miles.

Ducting or channelling can also occur between the shallower boundaries. If two submarines are in the same duct, detection possibilities are usually good; but if one boat is in one layer and one is in another the chances of detection are poor. It is therefore very important to know where boundaries and ducts are at any one time in a particular area and to make use of the deep sound channel, which most sound reaches eventually, if possible.

Bending can cause shadow zones where sound from a submarine does not penetrate and where it cannot be heard by a listening submarine even if both are in the same layer. But bending also forms 'convergence zones'

which lead to very long detection ranges. Convergence zones result when sound from a shallow submarine propagates downwards into deep water until (if it does not strike the bottom first) pressure overcomes temperature and refracts it upwards. When it approaches the surface it is bent down again to repeat the process until it dissipates. Convergence zones occur roughly 27 nautical miles apart (50 km). Contact can thus be gained at 27, 54 and 81 miles for a brief period (about 20 minutes on a submarine snorkelling at 10 knots) but may then be lost until it passes through the next zone.

If, on the other hand, a refracted ray strikes the sea bed it is reflected upwards by 'bottom bounce' and can therefore sometimes be received, like convergence zone signals, at longer ranges than by the direct path. Bottom bounce is applicable, in the main, to active sonar.

Signal processing techniques enable these paths to be used at various optimal depths according to conditions and depth of water and the submarine's own depth limit. None, save possibly an 'Alfa', can approach the deep sound channel but hydrophones — on a towed array — can be let down into it

BRITISH TYPE 2400 'UPHOLDER' CLASS SSK

The new Type 2400, so-called because that is its displacement in tonnes, has an exceptionally good weapon system, equivalent to an SSN with Ferranti-Gresham-Lion DCC fire control, Type 2040 bow sonar, Type 2024 or 2026 towed array and Micropuffs for passive ranging. Six bow tubes are for Tigerfish or Spearfish torpedoes, Sub-Harpoon missiles or mines. Twelve reloads (or more mines) can be carried.

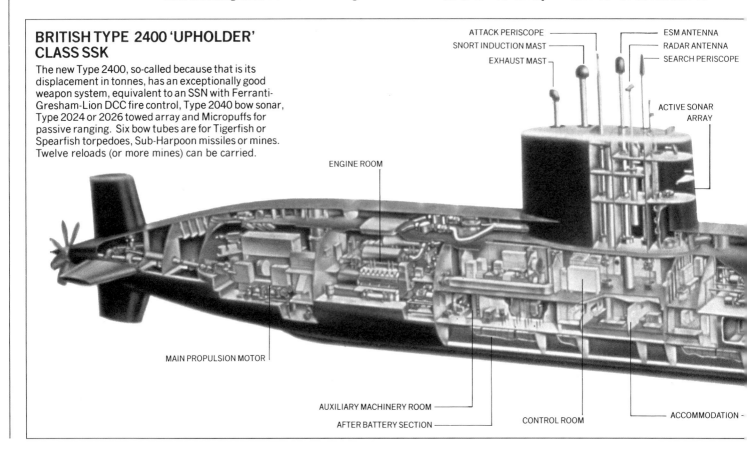

ATTACK PERISCOPE
SNORT INDUCTION MAST
EXHAUST MAST
ESM ANTENNA
RADAR ANTENNA
SEARCH PERISCOPE
ACTIVE SONAR ARRAY
ENGINE ROOM
MAIN PROPULSION MOTOR
AUXILIARY MACHINERY ROOM
AFTER BATTERY SECTION
CONTROL ROOM
ACCOMMODATION

while the submarine remains at a comfortable depth, searching above the channel with hull-mounted sonar and whatever part of the towed array remains above the deep channel.

The trick is to know what the sound propagation conditions are. The best oceanographic charts cannot forecast with complete confidence (except perhaps in fairly small areas of particular interest to an SSBN) so a submarine needs its own sound-velocity measuring device or bathythermograph. One type is attached to the hull but a hunter-killer can often not take time off to go deep and back again to the selected patrol depth. The answer is an instrument that can be dropped independently.

Meanwhile sensitive receivers on the seabed and preferably in the deep sound channel — SOSUS chains and the (not so good) Russian equivalent linked to shore stations — should be able to hear all sound from the surface downwards. And if there are enough of them identifiable, contact movements can be plotted quite accurately.

Underwater sound is attenuated by absorption and scattering, but it suffers far less attenuation than underwater light or radio waves. Attenuation increases rapidly with an increase of audio frequency and is less at low frequencies. For example, in a given area a 100 Hertz signal might propagate 150 nautical miles while one of the same intensity at 2000 Hertz would propagate only 50 nautical miles. Noting that a 100 Hertz signal has a wavelength of 14.6 m, a sonar receiver (hydrophone) has to be quite large to accept the long wavelengths (low frequencies) associated with long ranges and the especially interesting sound signatures which they reveal.

The underlying facts of life apply to both passive and active sonar. Passive sonar has predominated in recent years and will continue to do so for a while — perhaps indefinitely — but the quieting measures introduced in 'Typhoon' SSBNs, 'Oscar' SSGNs, 'Victor III', 'Sierra', 'Mike' and 'Akula' (Shark) SSNs strongly suggest that NATO SSNs will have to 'go active' at some stage. Isolated raft-mounted main machinery, dead water (or deadening material) between inner and outer hulls, decoupling hull coatings, natural circulation for reactors, less noisy coolant pumps, better shaped submarines, large propellers, pump-jet propulsors, ripple or jet propulsion enable the newer Soviet boats to be very quiet when they want to be. High speed must necessarily generate noise: floating machinery rafts have to be locked and even an ideal shape makes hydrodynamic noise. But hunter-killer boats must expect passive detection ranges to be very short if submerged transitters are not in a hurry.

The noise-band signature of a submarine consists of broad band noise amongst which, masked until plucked out by filtering and processing, are discrete lines or frequencies comprising narrow band noise. These can 'fingerprint' a type or even an individual boat.

Noise arises from three principal sources. Propeller cavitation — the formation and collapse of voids or bubbles along blade faces — was for long the most significant signal over a broad band of frequencies but it could be suppressed by going deep. Indeed, as already pointed out, the detection of any kind of emitted noise can still be avoided by a wily operator staying outside the layer of the sonic duct (if there is one) which the opposing vehicle's sonar is searching; or a submarine can hide acoustically in an area of high ambient noise — at the marginal ice zone (MIZ) for example or, more aggressively, in the middle of a convoy. A pump-jet — basically a rotor operating against a stator within

Small bang, long distance

In 1960 sound waves from a small explosive charge detonated south of Australia were received off Bermuda, after travelling a distance of 11 500 nautical miles (21 275 km), four hours later. Acoustic information passing through water at around 1500 m (4500 ft) per second (varying with temperature and pressure) is slow.

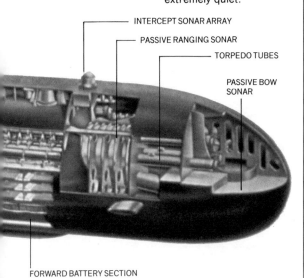

Automation and computerization enables the crew to be reduced to 7 officers, 13 senior ratings and 24 junior ratings with good accommodation which does not encroach on the attack center, sensors or weapon areas. The submarine is extremely quiet.

INTERCEPT SONAR ARRAY

PASSIVE RANGING SONAR

TORPEDO TUBES

PASSIVE BOW SONAR

FORWARD BATTERY SECTION

a shroud — markedly reduces the kind of continuous noise produced by propellers and does not give rise to 'blade rate' noise with regular beats which can be so helpful in determining a target's identity while at the same time indicating its speed. However, new types of single propeller — Soviet submariners favor seven blades although some boats have screws with five or six blades — are also effective in reducing cavitation and noise generally.

Modern propellers or propulsors (ie, pump-jets), let alone skate-like ripple motors, are unlikely to provide a significant noise source other than at high speed and nor are they likely to resonate or 'sing' in the revealing way that once they did. But cavitation is also caused by hull discontinuities and appendages; projections like hydroplanes may vibrate; and turbulence over the hull gives rise to hydrodynamic noise. These sources are related to speed and they, too, emit noise over a wide range of frequencies — that is, they are broad band.

If hull-insulation mountings are inadequate (as they frequently are) a different kind of noise, usually at very low frequencies — a few Hertz — is transmitted from internal machinery, gearing, hydraulic systems and other auxiliaries out into the water by excitation of the hull. For example, if a pump revolves at 3000 revolutions a minute it transmits energy (noise) at $3000 \div 60$ cycles per second or 50 Hz. This kind of low frequency noise can be identified as a distinctive signature by processing techniques (manual or computerized) which differentiate and display the narrow band signals for comparison with a library of intelligence data previously collected. Hence the continued mutual snooping and the intrusions, or even trespassing, by Soviet boats. Doppler shift associated with narrow band signals, corrected for own movement, indicates target rate of closing or opening.

On top of these discrete frequencies (and their diminishing harmonies) there may be quite brief noises (transients) arising from

CONJECTURAL MODERN SOVIET SONARS

Soviet sonar lagged behind Western equipment for a long time, but is now catching up on broadly similar lines while both self and radiated noise have been notably reduced in modern boats.

A bathythermograph and expendable velocimeter discharge tube (probably combined with a standard signal ejector), are certainly included but are not shown on the drawing. There is also very likely to be a high frequency Doppler navigation system forward.

The main bow and flank arrays are probably derived from selected British, American, German and Swedish technology, but a uniquely Soviet medium-frequency active fire-control sonar for rapid counterfire in a 'dogfight' is evidently incorporated.

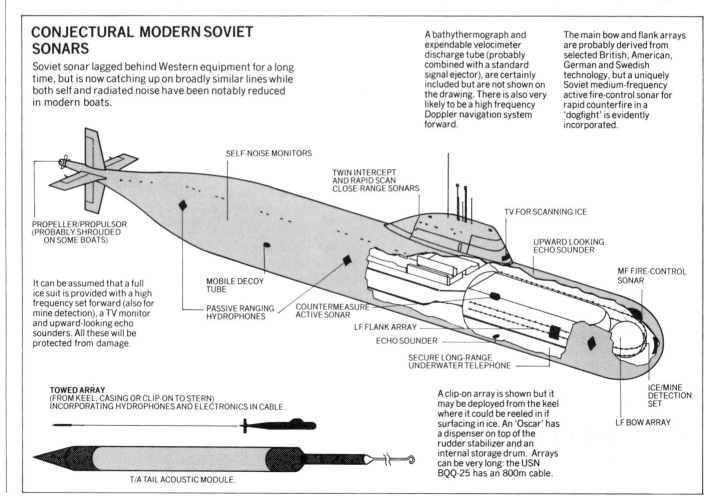

SELF-NOISE MONITORS

TWIN INTERCEPT AND RAPID SCAN CLOSE-RANGE SONARS

TV FOR SCANNING ICE

PROPELLER/PROPULSOR (PROBABLY SHROUDED ON SOME BOATS)

UPWARD LOOKING ECHO SOUNDER

MF FIRE-CONTROL SONAR

It can be assumed that a full ice suit is provided with a high frequency set forward (also for mine detection), a TV monitor and upward-looking echo sounders. All these will be protected from damage.

MOBILE DECOY TUBE

PASSIVE RANGING HYDROPHONES

COUNTERMEASURE ACTIVE SONAR

LF FLANK ARRAY

ECHO SOUNDER

SECURE LONG-RANGE UNDERWATER TELEPHONE

ICE/MINE DETECTION SET

LF BOW ARRAY

TOWED ARRAY (FROM KEEL, CASING OR CLIP-ON TO STERN) INCORPORATING HYDROPHONES AND ELECTRONICS IN CABLE.

A clip-on array is shown but it may be deployed from the keel where it could be reeled in if surfacing in ice. An 'Oscar' has a dispenser on top of the rudder stabilizer and an internal storage drum. Arrays can be very long: the USN BQQ-25 has an 800m cable.

T/A TAIL ACOUSTIC MODULE.

opening torpedo-tube bow caps, torpedo discharge or radical maneuvers which can warn a submarine that it is about to be kippered by another. Crew noise is also important: too much makes the sonar operator feel like being on the telephone in the middle of a rowdy party; and if the cook drops a load of plates at a critical moment he can abort an attack by warning the enemy.

About half the Soviet submarine fleet will be very quiet indeed by the mid-1990s. Meanwhile we can guess pretty well what sonar equipment Russian boats use to detect their quiet opposite numbers by reference to Western equipment.

There are various kinds of primary bow sonar in SSNs but all are low frequency (LF) active/passive, all rely on electronic beam-forming and steering with no mechanical moving parts, and all, especially in the active mode, demand a lot of electrical power.

The forward array is conformal, or spherical or cylindrical. Photographs suggest that the Russians have largely adopted the wrap-around conformal type. Typically, on either side of the submarine there is then a series of flank arrays (to give the longest possible baseline) and another array of specifically passive-ranging transducers (similar to PUFFS) at intervals along the hull.

The size and positioning of the forward area competes for space with weapon tubes so the latter tend either to be angled outwards or downwards or set well back from the bows in Western SSNs; but most Soviet boats seem to keep their tubes right forward with, sometimes, a couple external to the pressure hull.

Careful design delays the onset of noisy turbulence in the boundary area around the bow to keep the bow sonar in a quiet environment — hence the large semi-circular bows on the newer Soviet boats. But it is very advantageous to displace passive sonar right away from the submarine if possible: a towed array achieves this and provides a long base-line (for very low frequency reception and bearing measurement) which can be streamed astern or possibly dangled into the deep sound channel. The newest is the US Navy's Thin Line Array (TBX) — much longer than standard versions and able to cater for the extremely low frequency noise which Russian designers find difficult to iron out.

SSBN-towed arrays are usually reeled in and out: on SSNs and SSKs they can be clipped on with a special vessel when leaving harbor and unclipped on return.

A towed array reinforces the need for high speed. The extremely long detection ranges often obtained on less than ultra-quiet targets are not accompanied by an immediate indication of target range and movement. It can take a couple of hours to resolve target bearing and drift by which time a distant enemy may have sped off 40, 60 or 90 miles; and meaningful Target Motion Analysis (TMA) can take a lot longer — 10, 15 hours or more because the information is apt to be intermittent and fragmentary. Long legs are needed to intercept the target unless, of course, some kind of long-range air-flight weapon is available.

Sophisticated sonar

Besides the principal search equipment a sonar outfit includes active-intercept and torpedo-warning sets, mine-detection equipment, underwater communications and under-ice gear.

Western SSNs use their LF sonars for fire-control but most Soviet boats have an additional active/passive set in the medium frequency (MF) range (2–15 kHz) for shorter range fire-control snap-shooting: their Target Motion Analysis (TMA) ability with LF towed arrays may be relatively poor because they have not had long experience.

Although SSKs are excellent listening platforms they have less powerful sonar equipment because space and electrical supplies are limited; but the sonar is usually more than sufficient to match their comparatively low speed and endurance. Some SSKs do, however, have towed arrays nowadays which produce an almost embarrassing quantity of data. Sonar listening used to be compared to someone who was deaf using an ear-trumpet in a crowded room. By turning the trumpet in the required direction he could hear a specific speaker; now, with a much more sophisticated all-round hearing aid, he listens to what is going on in the street two blocks away as well.

But what of the submarines that cannot be heard? Must ASW units, SSNs especially, be prepared to use active sonar to a greater extent than hitherto? Cluster Guard anechoic tiles, together with the rounded and less reflective surfaces evidenced on modern Soviet boats, clearly anticipate the likelihood of this.

Submarines have almost always, until now, depended upon a covert approach for success. The only indication of a submarine's presence should be a 'flaming datum' — a weapon's arrival on target. Some of the older

SOVIET SEABED SOUND SURVEILLANCE SYSTEM (CONJECTURAL)

It is unlikely that Soviet SOSUS can fix the position of an enemy submarine detected to within forty or fifty miles unless, perhaps, the target is noisy for a prolonged period. However, very valuable indications of movement and approximate location can lead to prosecution by ASW air, surface or submarine units. Soviet seabed arrays are inferior to NATO, especially American, SOSUS installations which are continually improving. One problem is that, as in all ASW matters, so many non-submarine contacts are detected. Perhaps that is why the US SSN pictured here is going safely on its way while ASW forces search fruitlessly astern.

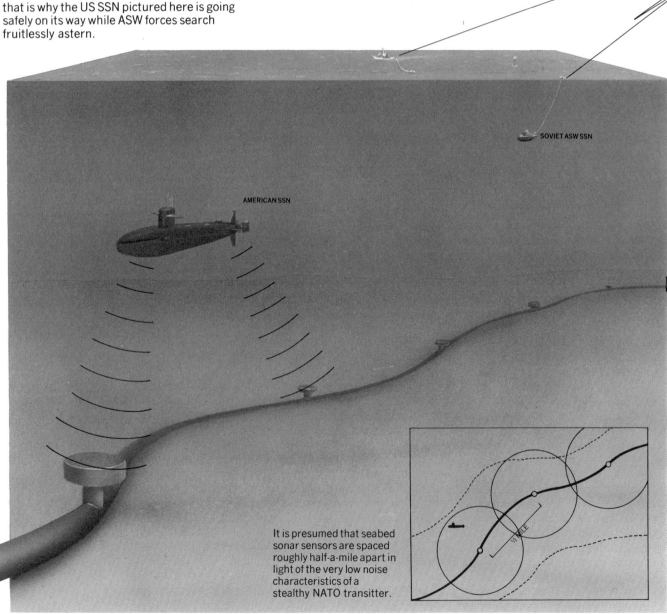

SOVIET ASW SSN

AMERICAN SSN

It is presumed that seabed sonar sensors are spaced roughly half-a-mile apart in light of the very low noise characteristics of a stealthy NATO transitter.

½ MILE

UHF satellite circuits and VLF broadcasts for submarines, control ASW units hunting for a contact indicated by seabed hydrophones.

The shore analysis, command, control and intelligence organisation sketched is purely conjectural but the system is probably based on these lines.

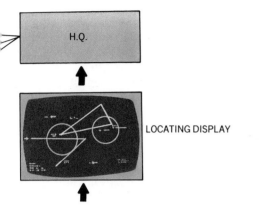

H.Q.

LOCATING DISPLAY

ANALYZERS

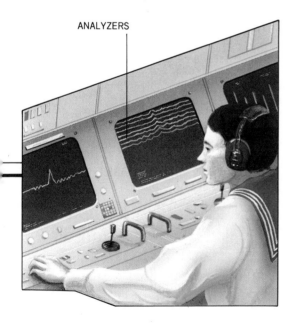

SONAR ROOM LAYOUT IN A SOVIET ASW FRIGATE

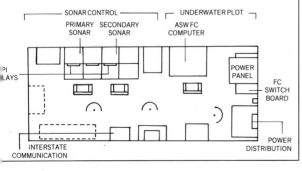

Soviet missile systems require a boat to surface and forego concealment in order to fire, albeit at very long range; and, of course, a diesel-electric submarine has to expose itself when snorkelling. But, in the main, submarines rely upon the sea to cloak their depredations until, for the enemy, it is too late. That means that ASW torpedoes must be very quiet: current Western (but not, apparently, Soviet) practise is to employ them primarily in the passive search mode and rather less often in the active or listen-and-ping mode. Presumably the active mode will be employed more frequently in future.

Submariners hate giving the game away. Making any kind of detectable noise or emission is anathema to them; but, sometimes, self-indicators have to be generated deliberately. For instance, an intelligence report might be so crucial that, where for some reason high frequency (HF) radio has to be used, the risk of the originator being located or even identified by listening stations has to be accepted; or radar, susceptible to electronic warfare (EW) collectors, may have to be employed. More commonly, an SSN may use noisy speed to attack or evade an enemy, or to deploy rapidly. Despite arguments in undersea society there are no hard and fast rules about sacrificing stealth by using active sonar in order to gain a particular objective.

An ASW submarine can certainly use active sonar briefly for localisation and fire-control, with a reasonable degree of security, if it has sniffed the target passively or been directed by external intelligence. Predictable ranges in good conditions by direct path are in the order of 30 miles and bottom bounce can be useful; given a known sound path it is reckoned that two transmissions are enough. Systematically investigating an area is another matter. Long-range active sonar used continually for search is going to be heard, and recognised for what it is, over a very wide expanse of ocean; and, because Soviet boats frequently operate in groups and co-operate with other ASW units, an SSN will be vulnerable to counter-attack unless it displaces itself between one transmission and the next.

It is clearly desirable for a submarine to regain its prime attribute — stealth — in these conditions. The most promising proposal is to make active sonar transmissions sound like something quite different — like ambient sea noise if possible. This is technically feasible and seems, without much

SUBMARINE INDICATORS

Although sonar, passive or active, is likely to remain the principal sensor for a long time to come, there are other indicators of a submerged submarine. At the surface or from above, they include radio and radar transmissions which are easily intercepted; active radar detection of a snorkel or masts; missile exhaust plumes; thermal scarring; a 'hump' from water displaced; turbulence and bioluminescence; and electrical fields set up in the water.

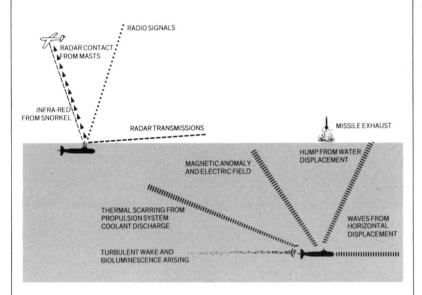

Blue-green lasers mirrored in space from a powerful shore transmitter could theoretically reveal submarines, albeit probably not when very deep, in the future although the huge cost might not be justified by problematical results.

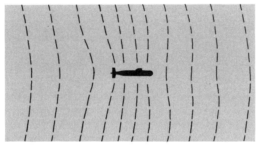

EARTH'S MAGNETIC FIELD DISTORTED – MAGNETIC ANOMALY

Magnetic anomaly detection equipment has by no means reached its full potential, and the detection of weak electrical fields is in its infancy. However, the permanent magnetic flux around any vessel (bottom drawing) is usually annulled by degaussing gear, and a titanium hull is non-magnetic.

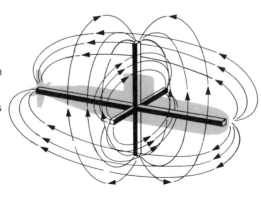

PERMANENT MAGNETIC FLUX OF STEEL (NOT TITANIUM) HULL – LARGELY ANNULLED BY DEPERMING AND DEGAUSSING.

doubt, to be the way ahead. It will be very costly, and software for the associated computer will be complex: it is not easy to simulate a burping whale or a flock of amorous shrimps, and noises in the sea itself change from place to place and day to day so it might be necessary to be able to alter the sound produced at will.

Alternatively, it is conceivable that certain critical locations could be ensonified by fixed seabed transmitters or by small explosive charges. A submarine towed array does not yet have an active component (although some surface ship versions do) but it could receive echoes from a remote transmitter and correlate the results if relative positions are accurately known. The submarine's own main active sonar could also transmit for the towed array to receive.

However, sound is not the only submarine indicator. Surface, airborne or satellite ASW sensors are capable of detecting various kinds of non-acoustic signatures — extremely low frequency (ELF) electric fields, magnetic anomalies and thermal scarring. A submarine generates an ELF field by reason of differing metals setting up a weak current in sea water; our old friend magnetohydrodynamics (MHD) creates an electrical field when water displaced by the hull moves across the earth's magnetic field; the latter is disturbed when a ferrous metal object passes through it; and waste heat produces a persistent and detectable scar.

Turbulent wake, bioluminescence (at night) and the hump caused by water displacement at the surface are also potential submarine indicators and they might be passed on by airborne or satellite sensors to an ASW boat.

If non-acoustic indicators are worth pursuing it would seem best for surface or air searchers to prosecute a contact directly and immediately because detections are bound to be fleeting.

On the whole it looks as though active sonar is the best solution to back up a lessening passive potential. It could well be advisable for fixed transmitters — an active SOSUS chain perhaps — to do the searching and relay information to hunter-killer submarines who will then have to make no more than spasmodic transmissions.

Meanwhile, the Russian submarines know better than anyone else where to look and where to hide, simply because the Soviet navy has dedicated such a vast amount of effort to oceanographical mapping.

1.5

SECONDARY SENSORS

Although the primary sensor today is sonar, periscopes are still important. Submarines, of whatever kind, never normally surface at sea and, besides needing a periscope for celestial navigation and terrestrial fixing, any captain still prefers to see a surface target before he shoots. Sonar analysis indicates the nature of a surface ship but identification is seldom certain: sorting out a prize amongst a mass of shipping can be a problem. Nor, in a limited war, is it helpful to attack an irritable neutral by mistake.

Periscopes have therefore been developed for all-weather day and night use. They have become sophisticated — and very expensive — items. At first sight they are not relevant to submarine versus submarine warfare but a submarine has to come to periscope depth occasionally for various reasons — and it has to keep a good look-out while it is there. Humiliatingly, SSNs have been attacked by ASW aircraft during exercises because the officer at the periscope has been schooled to sound and has neglected vision. Moreover, surface ships may well be involved in submarine ASW engagements because of the tendency — strong in the Soviet navy — for submarines to co-operate with other forces.

Nowadays there is usually one search (or general-purpose) periscope with a large head and one attack periscope with a small head to reduce the risk of detection during the closing stages of an attack. Fittings vary widely but modern Barr and Stroud periscopes embody direct range transmission, through a microprocessor, to the fire-control system with target designation letters and figures injected on to the eye-pieces and/or on off-mounted video monitors; bearing transmission is derived from an optical encoder in the crosshead and true bearing is displayed in the left eye-piece as well as remotely on some instruments; a laser range-finder can be added (accuracy plus or minus 10 m). The artificial horizon sextant includes a stabilised mirror coupled to the submarine's compass or inertial navigation system (SINS) and controls are kept simple, allowing a celestial sight to be taken within a few seconds. When taking sights there is pro-

vision for automatic removal of errors in the observed altitude caused by bending of the periscope or distortion of the boat's structure (some instruments can be used at speeds up to 16 knots although the wash is all too visible) and a print-out provides the observed altitude, bearing and time of observation. The top window and eye-piece can be heated to prevent ice forming and the submarine's high pressure air system provides for internal dessication.

A motor in the crosshead rotates the periscope without manual assistance by the operator; or it can be rotated and operated remotely from a Tactical TV Console (TTVC). Television/video screens are used extensively to display periscope images: they have the advantage of more than one person being able to study the target and a 'look' can be replayed for careful analysis without having to keep the periscope exposed.

Periscopes can also be equipped with Electronic Support Measures (ESM) antennae; a radio antenna is commonly fitted with whatever frequency coverage is required; and a camera is either permanently attached or one can be clipped to the eye-piece when needed. An image intensifier or thermal (infra-red) imager enables a target to be seen in dim or dark conditions: submariners tend to prefer infra-red optronics.

Modern periscopes are more than just an optical aid to the captain: they are sensors in their own right.

Electronic warfare

Electronic warfare (EW) is a vast and vital

Gin for the periscope

For three quarters of a century the Royal Navy cleaned top windows with wardroom duty-free gin — a commodity not available in American boats. Vodka was presumably used for Russian periscopes and doubtless, like the gin, it was not entirely consumed by the cleaning operation.

Early periscopes

Periscope devices were fitted in French submarines well before the turn of the century but they were very short: maintaining periscope depth was difficult in anything other than a flat calm. The first Inspecting Captain of (British) Submarines, Captain Reginald Bacon, invented a periscope with a 15 ft ocular tube for the Royal Navy's first Holland-type 'submarine boats': it lay flat along the casing when lowered and was raised on an elbow joint, meaning that it could not be put up and down at will. In the raised position it had to be stayed like a mast. However, it did enable the little boats to keep a satisfactory look-out submerged where the effects of sea and swell were less than in the virtually awash condition demanded by periscopes elsewhere.

The first submarines in the US Navy lacked a periscope altogether and it was not until after the initial five Adder-class (following USS *Holland*) were commissioned that an instrument was fitted to USS *Moccasin*, using the port forward ventilator for hull penetration.

Before that, American boats had to porpoise up and down to glimpse a target through thick glass scuttles set into the heavy, stubby brass conning tower (hence the

Left: A Holland boat in Portsmouth Harbour with stayed periscope c. 1904.

Below: Periscope viewing tube in *Holland I* (launched 1901) at RN Submarine Museum.

name): submarines were thereby called 'pig-boats' after the mariner's name for porpoises — sea pigs — and not as commonly supposed because of living conditions on board.

There was too little space in the early submersibles to revolve the eye-piece, particularly if the instrument was fitted in the conning-tower, so

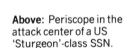

Above: Captain at the periscope in the wartime HMS *Tribune*.

the ocular box remained fixed in the ahead position while the operator rotated the upper part of the periscope tube by means of a handwheel. This had the effect of revolving the image so that it appeared upside down

Above: Periscope in the attack center of a US 'Sturgeon'-class SSN.

when astern and on end when abeam: although this would seem thoroughly confusing, commanding officers complained bitterly when the image was eventually righted — first by means of lenses (in HMS *A-10*)

and later by making the eye-piece and periscope rotatable together — because they could no longer judge relative bearing at a glance. Several of the diehards became 'lost in the box' when the new periscopes arrived — an affliction that is not entirely unknown in a darkened control room today.

subject with four distinct branches and several sub-divisions. The main branches are Signals Intelligence (SIGINT) comprising Communications Intelligence (COMINT) and Electronic Intelligence (ELINT); Electronic Support Measures (ESM); Electronic Countermeasures (ECM); and Electronic Counter-countermeasures (ECCM).

Already, Electronic Counter-counter Countermeasures are contemplated as a fifth branch and there is seemingly no end to this progression.

Signals Intelligence (SIGINT)

SIGINT is a very important form of intelligence-gathering associated with all types of warfare and many types of collector; but submarines are uniquely able to listen and record in sensitive areas without the overt provocation which would undoubtedly be caused by surface or air units. The same is true, of course, of sonar intelligence gathering: both are crucial to devising effective weapon systems and countermeasures as well as getting to know a potential enemy's capabilities and intentions. It is in the intelligence field that submarines repeatedly come to close quarters with the opposition's boats in peacetime.

Communications Intelligence (COMINT) is allied to code-breaking and/or assessing the implications of traffic intercepted; it is largely another name for spying and ELINT comes under much the same category. Both are processed ashore but, given the right equipment and personnel, a submarine can make use of SIGINT for its own immediate tactical purposes.

COMINT and ELINT collection methods are sensitive and highly classified: even on board they are confined to a small team who have 'need to know'; but their value reaches far out to cover practically every aspect of modern weaponry. For instance, if a submarine on a so-called surveillance mission records the precise terminal homing frequency of an anti-ship missile it will not be too difficult for the scientists back at home to produce a jammer. The same goes for the active frequency of a homing torpedo. Then a submarine may be lucky enough to take part, uninvited, in trials of the countermeasure: a counter-counter-measure will result — and so on. Submariners on all sides enjoy snooping and, as a bonus, it provides uniquely good training for war. The Russians are extremely proficient at intelligence gathering and have no scruples about trespassing or intruding: consequently, underwater near-misses and collisions can and do occur — so far, fortunately, without tragedy.

Electronic Support Measures (ESM)

Electronic Support Measures (ESM) are the product of ELINT. Conversely, ESM equipment collects ELINT but its tactical roles are warning, battle management and targetting.

Obviously, warning of ASW airborne units is a prime requirement for snorkellers and for the (relatively few) missile-launchers which have to expose themselves; but a submarine raising masts or periscopes for any purpose — navigation, communications or battle management and targetting by ESM — needs warning of incoming threats.

Russian submarines are exceptionally well supplied with ESM equipment and we can be fairly sure how the systems work.

The 'Warner' (probably incorporated with the search periscope as well as installed on a separate mast) must cover all enemy ASW aircraft and helicopter radar frequencies and automatically alert the watch to

a signal before it reaches the danger threshold — that is, before a signal is strong enough to return an echo from whatever masts are exposed in the existing sea state. This is easy, although cunning aircrews have been known to surprise a submarine by irregular emissions, sweeping only on the beam or detuning the radar.

Clockwise from top: HMS *Swiftsure* (SSN) with radio mast raised and search periscope embodying ESM; RACAL 'Porpoise' ESM antenna; Soviet 'Kresta' — an interesting ESM intelligence target; masts on a German Type 205 with 'Porpoise' ESM center.

The 'Searcher' is more complicated. A prudent Soviet captain will not want to raise the ESM mast for more than 20–30 seconds in a tight tactical situation. In that short time — over a wide bandwidth with all-round coverage — signal bearings, strengths and parameters must be noted, analysed and recorded. Which indicate targets? Which are electronic countermeasures? Which relate to sonar information? Which are dangerous? Ivan Ivanovich cannot answer instantaneously: a powerful computer, linked to a comprehensive ELINT library, is mandatory. The library in a Russian boat, constantly updated, needs to contain between 3–4000 emitter modes with frequency-agile radars amongst them: the ELINT gatherers are kept busy.

Supposing that a target is singled out electronically for attack, ESM bearings thereafter need to be accurate to within, say, two degrees; so it can be assumed that Soviet SSGNs and SSNs have a rotating dish reflector within the ESM antenna assembly below the omni-antenna — similar to commercial and freely advertised kits in the West. The whole assembly is, of course, covered with radar absorbent material (RAM).

Electronic Countermeasures (ECM)

Electronic Countermeasures (ECM) are not directly applicable to submarines except for the fact that SSGNs and SSGs want to know what countermeasures are being employed by the target(s). A surface ship employing ECM against incoming missiles may use active jamming and deception methods and/or chemical and mechanical passive methods. Ships under attack will also endeavor to shoot down missiles with anti-missile defensive systems. The launching submarine must select its missile counter-countermeasure (ECCM) mode accordingly but it may have to switch on radar for mid-course guidance. One task for an ASW submarine in the outfield could be to uncover a threat with ESM, report it immediately and bring the launcher under attack; or would it be better for the ASW submarine to stay at the best acoustic depth and rely on sonar? A good question and only one of many in battle management today.

Electronic warfare is part of the interception game: sonar-minded ASW submariners cannot ignore it. Nearly 30 years ago Vice Minister of Defense Marshal V D Sokolovkiy declared its role in Soviet strategy: 'to prevent the enemy from using electromagnetic emissions effectively while protecting one's own emissions from enemy ECM. ECM and ECCM are of the very greatest consequence; and electronic developments are of equal importance with the development of missiles and nuclear weapons which themselves could be of little use without electronic equipment'[1].

Very true: Russian submariners have taken careful note.

END NOTE
1. 'Soviet Military Strategy', by Marshal V D Sokolovkiy.

EW and the Battle of the Atlantic

During the last war, the German U-boat force lost the Battle of the Atlantic primarily because the Allies became able to detect submarines on the surface by airborne centimetric radar; and, towards the end they could detect them snorkelling. German radar warning equipment (ie, ESM) was not good enough. Moreover, high frequency radio direction-finding (D/F) equipment ashore and afloat could locate U-boats which transmitted messages amongst themselves, when operating in packs, or to shore control. Communications Intelligence, gathered from intercepting radio messages from shore as well as from U-boats themselves, contributed significantly to the Allies knowing where U-boats were operating because the enemy codes were broken; and intelligence of this kind was as valuable in the Pacific, against Japanese submarines, as it was in the Atlantic against the German boats. In fact SIGINT was so valuable

Above: U-71 attacked by two Sunderlands of 10 Squadron (Royal Australian Air Force) in the Bay of Biscay 5 June, 1942. The U-boat was a victim of electronic warfare which led the flying boats to her position; but in the event she escaped lethal damage.

that efforts to destroy Axis shore-to-submarine radio transmissions were deliberately halted.

Electronic warfare of one type or another eventually led to the majority of ASW attacks on U-boats.

1.6

NAVIGATION AND COMMUNICATIONS

A submarine can neither succeed in its mission nor be safe from friendly forces unless it navigates accurately. If that seems trite it must be remembered that boats out of position during the last war frequently lost attack opportunities, were all too often subjected to attack by their own ASW forces (including submarines) and ran into known minefields. Errors of 50 miles or so were not uncommon.

Besides operational dangers, bad navigation implies special grounding hazards for a submarine because, in effect, a nuclear boat has a draught of more than 400 m and the average SSK some 250 m. Unfortunately, this is not always kept in mind.

Gyro-compasses have improved and a submarine knows accurately which way it is heading; automatic plotting tables are less deceptive than they were due to more reliable logs; navigation satellite NAVSAT (or SATNAV) fixes and reliable radio aids like LORAN C and OMEGA are available — although they might be put out of action in war; sun and star sights can be taken through the periscope; and the seas are better charted so that, in many areas, accurate bottom-contour navigation is possible. This is a method favored by Soviet submarines who confidently career across the seabed at headlong speed with no more than an occasional echo-sounder transmission to check the route. Best of all, navigators are properly trained for the job — in contrast to wartime 'Pilots' and 'Vascos' (in the British Navy especially) who were pitchforked into their boats barely knowing the rudiments of coastal pilotage and dead reckoning.

Nuclear submarines of all kinds are equipped with SINS (Ship Inertial Navigation System) which senses movement by measuring and integrating accelerations relative to the earth. SINS is fairly accurate and two or even three equipments may be installed for cross-checking as well as redundancy; but, subject to the latest advances which include fiber optics and laser ring gyros which do not 'drift' like mechanical gyros, it is prudent to check and update SINS with a positive fix — a calculated position derived from external sources — when possible.

If SINS is fed with a known position at the start (the home port on departure, for example) the position thereafter is continuously known. In some boats the Latitude and Longitude is pounded out automatically every six minutes on an IBM typewriter.

An SSBN, more than any other type of submarine, must know very precisely where it is because unless its ballistic missiles are self-correcting in trajectory (which some are) they will not hit their targets. Satellite fixing by Transit Satellite System provides position to within 150 m; but it only works when a satellite passes overhead (transit) and there is an interval before the next satellite crosses. Soviet SSBNs almost certainly rely to a great degree on bottom-contour navigation in specific (and secret) areas which have been minutely charted.

The NavSTAR Global Positioning System (GPS) is now replacing the Transit network. GPS has a constellation of 18 satellites orbiting at an altitude of 17 500 km (10 937 miles): for the first time, a space-borne radio-navigation system will provide an all-weather 24-hour global service. Ten more satellites are being launched, apparently as in-orbit spares.

Each GPS satellite weighs 816 kg in orbit and transmits on 3 D-Band frequencies, one E/F-Band frequency and has a UHF satellite-to-satellite link. Continuous, three-dimension-

Deep draught

It is rather invidious to single out a particular boat but the sort of thing that can happen was instanced by USS *Skate* (SSN-578) on a simulated war patrol in 1959 when the Executive Officer, without informing the Captain or Navigator, strolled into the Control Room and ordered the boat deep to 700 ft for a 'Bathy' dip. Moments later the practically new nuclear submarine, which had successfully completed the second Polar crossing less than a year earlier, hit the bottom at seven knots. It was not surprising because a glance at the chart, too late, showed that there was only about 500 ft of water in that area. Yet the officers certainly knew how to use *Skate*'s advanced navigational aids — as evidenced by the Polar voyage. The Executive Officer simply forgot, for a moment, that the sea is not bottomless. Fortunately, no damage was done.

SINS (SHIP INERTIAL NAVIGATION SYSTEM)

SINS records every movement of the submarine relative to a three-dimensional gyro-stabilized platform coupled to accelerometers. The device works upon the principle that when a moving body accelerates, it leaves behind any free moving weight inside it. The force needed to bring this weight back to its original position is a function of the distance the body has moved.

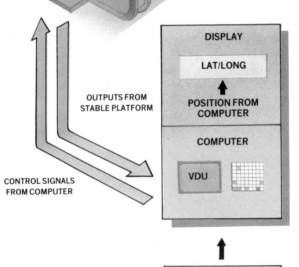

ROLL

PITCH

YAW

SINS MK 1 GYMBALS AT EQUATOR

If accelerometers are mounted in the North/South plane and in the East/West plane, the movement North or South and East or West is measured. The actual direction of movement can then be determined by integration, together with the speed and distance covered. Thus the actual course, speed and distance are known irrespective of tidal streams and currents.

THE DOPPLER ALTERNATIVE

A 500–600 kHz Doppler system, virtually undetectable, is almost as accurate, combined with a good but simple gyro, as SINS if Doppler is measured in relation to the seabed; but this is not possible in very deep water.

OUTPUTS FROM STABLE PLATFORM

CONTROL SIGNALS FROM COMPUTER

DISPLAY

LAT/LONG

POSITION FROM COMPUTER

COMPUTER

VDU

EXTERNAL FIX FROM NAVIGATING OFFICER

Latitude and Longitude are continuously computed and displayed either at set interval or on demand. However, although the latest models (notably Mk 2 SINS in US 'Ohios') are more reliable and accurate under all conditions than the early types, some degree of drift (error) can still occur. SINS is therefore checked or updated by external fixing (eg, by satellite) when possible; and where two sets of equipment are fitted one is compared with the other.

A useful by-product of the system is the ability to measure tidal streams and currents for oceanographical purposes, by noting the difference between a position calculated by Dead Reckoning (submarine Movement through the water without allowing for set) with SINS actual position on the chart.

al position-data signals are transmitted using two different codes. The code for military use employs pseudo-random encrypted signals and gives positional data accurate to within 15 m. The 'clear' code for other users provides accuracies in the order of 100 m. Signals from at least four satellites are needed for a really accurate fix.

The costly GPS satellites are intended for other purposes as well: data from them will probably update Trident missile-guidance systems after launch. Doubtless the Soviet GLONASS equivalents are also multi-purpose.

Meanwhile, SSNs and SSKs can navigate perfectly well for ASW operations without recourse to highly sophisticated aids — which is just as well because Soviet anti-satellite (ASAT) weapons may try (probably unsuccessfully, for some time yet) to knock orbiting birds out of the sky; and radio aids will be jammed if Russian submariners reckon that they themselves can do without them — which they can with virtually undetectable echo-sounders.

All in all, there is no excuse nowadays for a submarine navigator to get lost.

Communications

Admiral Gorshkov remarked feelingly a few years ago that the disruption of his control organisation would be equal to the destruction of Soviet naval forces in combat. Accordingly, he gave top priority to communication systems featuring automated, frequency-agile, high data-rate digitized techniques which, beside their obvious advantages, help to take error-prone personnel out of the picture.

The West spells out the control ensemble more fully as command, control, communications and intelligence — the familiar C[3]I — but it comes to the same thing.

Now, since Gorshkov's departure and with the complete integration of all Soviet strategic weapons under a single command, secure C[3]I assumes even greater importance for centralised control. Hopefully, NATO has contingency plans for exploiting this dependency by trumping the mastercard — communications; and, for sure, the USSR will do its utmost, probably before battle is joined, to disrupt Western radio circuits.

Assuming that there will be a mutual

Wartime astro-navigation

Sight-taking from the bridge in rough weather, before periscopes were equipped with sextants, was a miserable evolution. The navigator had to wrap his sextant in a towel to keep it dry (never mind about himself) while buckets of indescribable gash and garbage were hauled up the conning tower alongside him for ditching to minimise vulnerable minutes on the surface. He then had to use the oldest of old-fashioned haversine tables (unless he was lucky enough to be in the US Navy) to work out what was supposed to be a fix. In fact he was doing well if the plotted position lines came anywhere near to intersecting: more often than not, after an hour of laborious spherical trigonometry, a 'cocked hat'

five or ten miles across resulted and it was anybody's guess where the boat really was.

It has to be said that Quartermaster navigators, enlisted men in

American and German boats, were good at their job; they compared very favorably with officer navigators in other navies and were supplied, long before the rest, with

rapid reduction tables. Nevertheless, they would admit that, in the old days, a position triangle (cocked hat) could be large enough to contain the entire Sixth Fleet.

Above: Submarines used to be notorious for bad navigation. Here is *K.4*, one of the accident-prone steam-driven British K-class, 'on the putty' in 1917.

communications-wrecking program on a massive scale, Western submarine captains will be better placed than their Russian opposite numbers because they are expected and encouraged to make independent decisions — which are emphatically not encouraged in the Soviet submarine force. However, it is certain that no commanding officer, in any navy, will ever be permitted to launch nuclear strategic missiles without express orders from shore.

Transmitting information

It is relatively simple for a Soviet HQ to keep in touch with SSBNs because the majority will not be far away. SSGNs and missile-armed SSNs off distant seaboards are more of a problem as it is easier for an enemy to interfere with long-range communications. For that reason, American, British and French SSBNs, usually in remote patrol areas, need a very wide range of communication paths and frequencies. ELF, VLF, HF direct broadcasts, UHF, SHF and EHF[1] (jam-resistant) satellite links (SATCOM), and submarine blue-green laser (470–550 nanometers) communication satellites are all employed or envisaged. Despite its potential volume of data (100 million bits a second) a blue-green laser does not pass information all that rapidly because it has to be repeatedly directed over a wide expanse of sea to ensure striking the submarine; but it does have the great advantage of sending messages to a submerged boat without requiring it to deploy an antenna to the surface.

Needless to say, lasers are expensive. Indeed, communication systems, backed up by an airborne fleet of VLF/LF antennae, trailing TACAMO[2] aircraft (now called Hermes), comprise a substantial part of undersea nuclear deterrent costs. But the Kremlin has to be convinced that messages will always, somehow, get through to Western SSBNs: that is a crucial part of the deterrent package.

Very low frequency (VLF) teletype has long been standard for submarine reception because VLF can be received down to great depths via a buoyant antenna cable (trailing wire) or an antenna buoy streamed a few meters below the surface. VLF transmissions from shore (typically around 15 kHz) can theoretically be jammed and they are sometimes difficult to receive under the ice. Extremely low frequencies (ELF) are more reliable and penetrate much deeper into the sea: Russian communicators have set up

Pigeon post

Pigeons were extensively used for ship-to-shore communications by British submarines during World War I. Provided that they were not over-fed by pet-loving sailors they were secure, reliable and quick enough: a bird in trim flew at an average speed of 30 mph but due allowance had to be made for wind. On one typical recorded occasion in 1915 a pigeon was released from an E-class boat off the Dutch coast at 0930 hours against a 15-knot West-South-Westerly wind: it reached its loft on the English East Coast before noon, whence the message from its leg was taken to the Admiralty in London by car, decrypted and in the right hands by 1500.

SUBMARINE RADIO COMMUNICATIONS

Any submarine needs to receive messages from base or, occasionally, from other friendly units with the minimum of delay: intelligence about enemy movements is particularly important. Some breaks in communication are acceptable during normal SSN or SSK ASW operations; but an SSBN must be absolutely sure of constant, uninterrupted reception. Consequently, a number of alternative communication systems, in the hope that at least one will continue functioning whatever, are available to Boomers, Bombers and PLARBs; and some of these are also used by attack submarines who from time to time, albeit quite rarely, will wish to transmit messages themselves, preferably with minimal chance of interception by the enemy.

It is assumed that Soviet communications are much the same as Western systems, although with so many submarines they must need more channels in any one band; but now that the majority of PLARBs, if not all, operate so close to home they may be able to dispense with the TACAMO concept (see text and illustration) and rely on ELF for emergency call-ups.

Dummy messages, on all sides, maintain a constant flow of traffic on especially important frequencies (eg, PLARB command links) and help to prevent the enemy picking out a significant message, such as the order to launch missiles, which is anyway passed in secure code.

Communications, involving Command, Control and Intelligence (C[3]I when put together in current jargon), contribute markedly to the cost of submarine infrastructure.

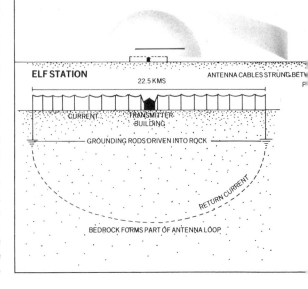

ELF STATION

22.5 KMS

ANTENNA CABLES STRUNG BETWEEN

CURRENT

TRANSMITTER BUILDING

GROUNDING RODS DRIVEN INTO ROCK

RETURN CURRENT

BEDROCK FORMS PART OF ANTENNA LOOP

VLF

The VLF band (3 to 30 kHz) can be received down to about 50 ft (15 m). To avoid submarines coming above optimum operating depth, a trailing wire or a loop antenna buoy is streamed.

ELF

ELF reception (300 Hz to 3 kHz) is assured down to 328 ft (100 m), but an improved antenna and receiving system will make 1300 ft (400 m) feasible.

LF/HF/UHF

HF reception/transmission needs a periscopic antenna and is thus normally depth limiting. The same mast serves LF reception and UHF links via satellite or with aircraft, but expendable buoys are used from deep.

TACAMO

Some shore-based aircraft are fitted as emergency command posts and TACAMO aircraft can broadcast on VLF with long trailing antennae.

OSCAR

Optical Submarine Communications by Aerospace Relay (OSCAR) will involve relay signals to a geostationary satellite which fires a laser (470-550 nanometers) at random into large ocean areas.

ELF wavelength is approximately 4000 km and the signal is guided between the earth's surface and the ionosphere. Water refracts the electric field, and signals propagate vertically downwards as shown. A principle aim of ELF is 'to enhance the capability of submarines to remain undetected' if the Soviets become capable of detecting boats deploying buoys or trailing antennae at relatively shallow depths.

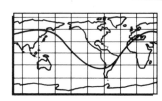

ELF achieves 'bell-ringing' coverage north of the solid line shown for American submarines.

IONOSPHERE

DIRECTION OF TRAVEL OF ELF WAVE FRONT ➡

WATER REFRACTS ELECTRIC FIELD

SIGNALS PROPAGATE VERTICALLY DOWN

RECEIVING ANTENNA

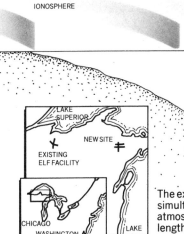

LAKE SUPERIOR

NEW SITE

EXISTING ELF FACILITY

CHICAGO
WASHINGTON

LAKE MICHIGAN

(NOT TO SCALE)

The existing USN ELF facility and the new site (operating simultaneously with the first to lessen the effects of atmospheric noise), are shown at left. Total antennae lengths are 45 and 90 km in 'X' and 'F' formations respectively.

several ELF transmitters, each with a very long antenna stretching for hundreds of kilometers, to cater for frequencies around 70 or 80 Hz. The US and British navies are following the same path, albeit on a rather less ambitious scale. ELF reaches far; it is invulnerable to Electromagnetic Pulse Effect (EMP) resulting from a nuclear explosion; it is nearly impossible, in practical terms, to jam; and it is unaffected by the abnormal propagation conditions which occur from time to time in the Arctic. Unfortunately, the data-rate on ELF is very low: an early trial involving USS *Tinosa* (SSN-606) suggested 0.03 bits per second so ELF can only carry short, simple messages — 'bell-ringers' — to alert deep addressees and call them up for a longer message on other circuits. It is probably not possible to pass Emergency Action Messages (EAMs) — missile firing orders — let alone lengthy operational instructions to submarines by this system.

Problems of detection

A submarine itself never transmits on high frequency (HF) long-range radio if it can possibly avoid doing so: enemy intercept and direction finding (D/F) equipment can too easily identify and locate the transmitter. Super and ultra high frequencies (SHF and UHF) are nominally limited to horizon range and can be used with relative impunity either direct to aircraft or via satellite to ships and shore; but they are not altogether popular with submariners either, because they imply breaking off in the middle of sonar tracking to come shallow and extend an antenna. One way round this is to eject, from deep, a small expendable radio buoy which continuously broadcasts a pre-recorded signal on arrival at the surface: when the addressee receives the message it transmits a coded group to silence the buoy which scuttles itself. Alternatively the buoy transmits only for a limited period. Either way the submarine will only know if the message has got through if receipt is acknowledged on a standard circuit.

Another kind of expendable tactical buoy is dropped by aircraft: by converting UHF to underwater sound signals and vice-versa a link can be established between the aircraft and a deep submarine.

UHF satellite communications have become extremely important for passing tactical intelligence to submarines, especially on ASW missions. A satellite stores messages and relays them at given times or immediately on coded command from the

boat concerned which can thereby choose its moment for coming shallow. The messages are compressed into a burst transmission automatically decrypted and typed out in the submarine. (Incidentally, the radio room in USS *Ohio* (SSBN-726) has three times as many receivers as early 'Boomers' and by itself costs twice as much as a complete Second World War fleet submarine).

All these channels, or something very like them, are available to the Soviet navy; but Soviet submarines have an extra through-water communication link which is reckoned to be useable at 100 miles or so, ten times the range of revamped Gertrude, the NATO underwater telephone, and a great deal more secure than wartime Submarine Sound Telegraphy (SST). It seems reasonable to assume that Gertrude's secretive Russian equivalent talks directionally in digits on low frequency carrier waves, hopping with agility from one to another in order to avoid a sustained detectable signal, and quite possibly sounding like ambient background noise. If so, precise synchronisation between speaker and listener is necessary but that should not be too difficult. Russian boats are almost certainly equipped with actively triggered IFF (Interrogation Friend or Foe) response units for use underwater and similar in concept to long-established Radar IFF.

A multiplicity of communication links is available to the Soviet submarine force but the complexity of a comprehensive system covering all tasks and eventualities for so many boats would send the average Western communicator into spasms'. Complexity is accompanied by a certain fragility as a rule and, however much automation is involved, physical and human weaknesses are inevitable. Moreover, history has another lesson here which has doubtless been swept under the Kremlin carpet. Communications are notorious for plain old-fashioned malfunctioning when most needed. They are subject to Murphy's Law — anything that can go wrong *will* go wrong. And it is sure that Murphy, under a variety of Slavonic and Islamic pseudonyms, applies his Law with abandon throughout the Russian Empire.

END NOTES
1. Extremely Low Frequency; Very Low Frequency; High Frequency; Ultra High Frequency; Super High Frequency and Extremely High Frequency — the latter being jam-resistant.
2. TACAMO — Take Charge and Move Out — aircraft are continuously ready to take over from primary shore-based radio stations to maintain a communications link with SSBNs.

Wartime communications problems

During the last war VLF was the only dependable link from shore to a submerged submarine. Reception was usually possible, at periscope depth, on a loop aerial which had to be roughly aligned with the bearing of the distant VLF station. That meant maintaining the optimum course for longish periods — maybe an hour or so — while a string of numbered messages were laboriously written down by hand. A momentary loss of depth resulted in blanks on the signal pad and made decoding (a lengthy job in itself) difficult if not impossible. Routines were typically broadcast every four hours and signals were repeated three times: it was therefore mandatory for a boat to read the routine at least twice a day. In rough weather, on an adverse course, the battery drained away with the trimming officer continually speeding up to keep periscope depth. Meanwhile, of course, enemy ships or aircraft might put in an untimely appearance.

1.7

SUBMARINE ANTI-SUBMARINE WEAPON SYSTEMS

I t is necessary to say a few things about weapons systems in general before going into detail. Firstly, it must be repeated that a submarine should, for the best results, constitute a complete, integrated weapon system in itself. In practice it is often nothing of the sort. The ideal smooth flow from command to weapon explosion on target is too often interrupted by material units which are imperfectly matched or by personnel who have too much to do, or who have too difficult a problem to solve with the means and time available.

It is, in some cases outside the USSR, quite common to award the design and/or production of one part of the system to team or company X, another to Y and yet another to Z, each with specific financial restraints and no liability for the total package — that is, the entire submarine. Alternatively, new components are bought off the shelf from X, Y and Z (based often enough in different countries) during the submarine's life.

There are considerable drawbacks to piecemeal procurement. An (admittedly simplistic) analogy can be drawn from a motor car. If a particular manufacturer is invited, for an agreed price, to produce an engine capable of 6000 rpm at a given horsepower he will probably be able to make exactly what is asked. But supposing that somebody else independently designs the steering system and someone quite different, maybe miles away, produces the wheels and brakes without regard for the whole vehicle, it is odds on that the car will be difficult to drive and a menace on the roads. And perhaps another little company which offers to build the exhaust system, for much less than its competitors, will come up with a so-called silencer which is inadequate for the engine and makes the car sound like a World War 1 tank.

Thankfully, that is not how reliable car manufacturers proceed. But it is not unlike the way in which weapons systems have sometimes been procured. The British Mark 24 Tigerfish torpedo was a case in point although the defense establishments and firms concerned were all in the UK. It is now, in the Mod II version, working — and working very well — thanks to Marconi (MUSL) who took over, eventually, management of the system from fire-control through weapon handling, discharge, weapon guidance, impact and fuzing and brought everything together.

It used to be said that a submarine captain was a one-man band at the periscope, using his crew as extensions of his own senses. That can no longer be so because several sensors other than the periscope, including sensors in smart weapons, now form what amounts to a full orchestra whose members must perform in perfect harmony. Agreed, the captain is still the conductor but he cannot possibly play or even supervise every instrument himself.

Harmony and continuity (principally involving interfaces when jargonized) are another difficulty. For example, it is quite usual to find that some fire-control units are digital while others are analog; and data-exchange mechanisms are frequently inelegant (to put it mildly) while inputs and outputs have to pass, like it or not, through a

Wet feet
Older submariners will recall that the order 'Dive, dive, dive' from the bridge down a voicepipe was changed to 'Dive the submarine' when on one feet-wetting occasion the order to 'Steer 355' was misinterpreted.

A national disaster

The German U-boat arm has been exceptionally practical in procurement matters, with excellent results for the most part, from before World War II. Yet even the exceptionally thorough schooling by Admiral Doenitz failed, in the first year of war, to ensure that the torpedoes ran at the correct depth or that magnetic pistols worked as they should: wartime conditions were not simulated on trial to the full. Most notably, an air pressure, resulting from HP air leaks, used to build up in a boat after a longish period submerged: this pressure insidiously worked its way into torpedo balance chambers, in effect strengthening the internal depth-setting spring against the external hydrostatic valve. Consequently, a torpedo 'thought' it was shallower than it really was and went deeper — too deep in many instances to hit the target or allow the influence pistol to function. That is why U-boat involvement in the 1940 Norwegian campaign was an abject failure. Out of 48 U-boats deployed, 42 engaged the enemy but more than 30 attacks failed simply because the torpedoes did not explode. 'The torpedo crisis is a national disaster', declared an appalled Admiral Raeder.[1]

central calculator. Sometimes, figures — bearings or whatever — have to be passed by manual drill or by word of mouth from one piece of equipment, reasonably accurate in itself, to another with a fairly substantial risk of wrong reception at a crucial moment.

Or perhaps the gyro-compass, hidden away but fundamental to the entire business, is not up to the job: it may precess after radical changes of course, invalidating the most meticulous fire-control calculations.

Furthermore, supposing that every component in the long chain from the submarine's sensor to the torpedo warhead's detonator has, individually, a high probability — say 90 per cent — of functioning correctly that does not, unfortunately, mean that the whole system has a 90 per cent probability of success. Unless everything is perfectly integrated the laws of aggregated chance dictate that the overall probability will be unacceptably low — just as it was initially with the Tigerfish system. And this is not apt to be revealed by standard exercises and inspections where everything and everyone is on top form for a brief period and 'cooking the books' is, understandably, the order of the day.

Very simple attacks on surface ships, using basic weapons, can still be conducted without an integrated system; but there is much less chance of a submarine-versus-submarine engagement being successful without every component and every man being welded into a harmonious whole. To take a seemingly absurd but entirely relevant example, if the engine room crew does not know what is going on and somebody drops a spanner on a bare steel deck at the *moment critique*, long hours of patient, stealthy tracking may well be aborted.

The smaller navies who are now enthusiastically going underwater may profitably reflect on this rather depressing philosophy and endeavor to avoid pitfalls into which major navies have stumbled. The Indians, for one instance, are reportedly buying equipment for their German Type 1500 boats from four different countries — including the USSR — advantageously, no doubt, with regard to price, but one has to wonder if it will all be compatible when put together.

It is best, nowadays, to choose a single trustworthy system-designer and start with a modular lay-out linked to a standard data bus — like a motorway with exit and entry points — and change modules in all submarines,

more or less at the same time, when it is quite certain that modifications or improvements are justified and that crews can cope with the new set-up. Operator and maintainer training has to be included in costings (and 'down time') whenever systems are revised: the Royal Navy's Submarine School has to run no less than 400 separate courses, significantly because of varied equipment.

Above all, any system must be tested in absolutely realistic circumstances.

Lessons of history

It is, by the way, wise to heed advice from the original operators if something is bought from abroad rather than taking a system at face value. The little Argentinian *San Luis* scored no hits during two approaches on the British Task Force in 1982 partly because the Captain — against express instructions from the Head of the German U-boat Arm — fired his fish from deep.[2]

In short, history suggests that submarine weapon systems are not necessarily as effective as the owners hope. It is impossible to estimate the probability of success in a submarine-versus-submarine situation: there are far too many variables. Nor is it realistic to think that each and every man, sensor, piece of machinery — or the main propulsion itself for that matter — will consistently function at peak performance: human and mechanical malfunctions are inevitable in the real world. In other words, a list of characteristics in military catalogues like *Jane's Fighting Ships* are optimal and are rarely all applicable at any one time: some allowance has to be made for the inescapable facts of life at sea.

It will also be remembered that only a proportion of submarines listed in an Order of Battle can be operational: overhauls/refits, maintenance, leave periods and shore training, to say nothing of defects and mishaps of one kind or another, cut deep into availability. Then, too, there is passage time to and from the patrol area to take into consideration. A broad rule of thumb is one submarine on patrol, one on passage, one in harbor and one in the dockyard: so four submarines may be needed to keep one in business. The figures look much better when nuclear power — meaning faster deployment — is put into the picture; but in the Soviet Navy, where maintenance is known to be poor and often suspect (not least due to severe weather conditions), it will be surprising if more than 25 per cent of the submarine fleet overall can be kept on station although, as in

MACHINERY RAFT

There are considerable difficulties in sound (and shock) insulating/isolating individual large machines from the hull, so the RN adopted a raft to carry all main machinery in SSNs from the 'Swiftsure'-class onwards. This is effective (although it apparently has to be locked at high speed) in preventing noise from reaching the sea; and doubtless Soviet designers have copied the idea. Some form of flexible transmission to the propulsion shaft would seem to be needed but details have not been made public.

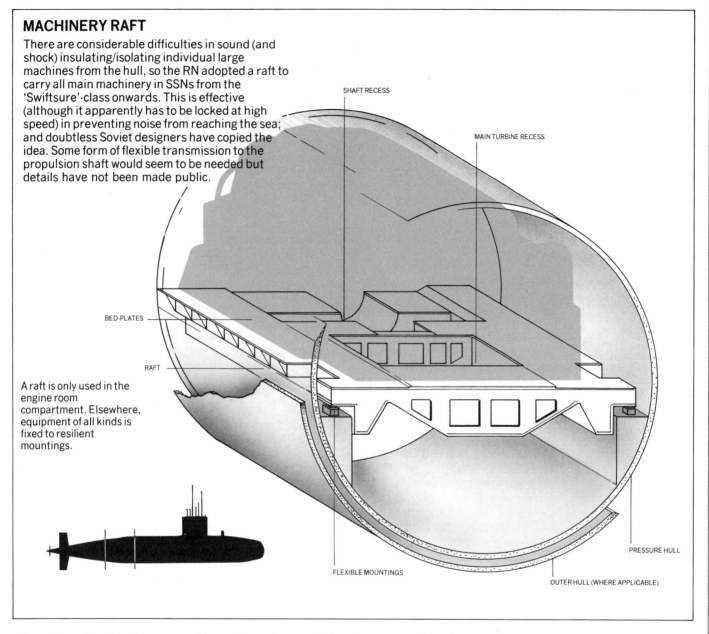

SHAFT RECESS

MAIN TURBINE RECESS

BED-PLATES

RAFT

A raft is only used in the engine room compartment. Elsewhere, equipment of all kinds is fixed to resilient mountings.

FLEXIBLE MOUNTINGS

PRESSURE HULL

OUTER HULL (WHERE APPLICABLE)

all navies, the Russians are able to 'surge' considerably more boats if the need arises. However, some of the boats surged are bound to lack performance; submarines despatched on patrol with inadequate maintenance and tired or dispirited crews run an above-average risk of being listed as 'missing presumed lost'.

During the Second World War for instance, Admiral Doenitz managed, at best, to keep 64 per cent of his U-boats operational — that is, preparing for patrol, on passage and on patrol.

The French have a two-crew system for their attack-type nuclear submarines to maximize time at sea but they are unique in doing so: in other navies only SSBNs have two crews.

To what extent does the Soviet Navy experience the sort of procurement difficulties evident elsewhere? We will be examining Soviet power and its associated problems later but it is worth looking at the main differences in procurement processes now: they include advantages for the USSR which are not, in the main, practicable in Western navies.

The most significant difference is the longevity of post-holders in Russia — given that they are not chopped short as a result of

Own goal

A 'Victor III', on intelligence operations, fouled the towed sonar array of USS *McCloy* (FF1038) off the American east coast in November 1983 and had to be towed to Cuba for repairs: the fate of the captain is not known. HMS *Superb* (SSN) reportedly lost her towed array in 1986 in circumstances which have not been made public. There have been sundry collisions at various times between Russian boats and other vessels — some of them submarines.

in-fighting or some political misdemeanor. We have already seen that Gorshkov headed the navy for 29 years: he was able to set his sights far into the future and carry his plans through to fruition. Engineer Admiral T G Kotov was the deputy Controller of Ship Production and Armament in the 1950s before being appointed Controller in 1966: he is still in charge. How long does an American or British admiral stay in a particular post? Two, three or four years at most, with very few exceptions. Worse, democratic administrations, and hence policies, change every four or five years with consequent stop-go-stop programs. Continuity is therefore a strong point in favor of Soviet procurement methods and Soviet five-year plans, unlike Western equivalents, mean what they say and are accountable at the end of each period: long-term planning has very definite goals and there is a painful reckoning if they are not met.

There is, of course, no commercial competition in the USSR: production is judged by results which are often exaggerated and this is undoubtedly a minus point. But a single organ, the hard-headed and long-serving Military Industrial Commission (VPK), oversees all aspects of procurement without having to return to the decision makers once the latter have agreed a project at Politburo level if necessary or, more usually, by joint decree between the Central Committee and the Council of Ministers. No shilly-shallying is permitted thereafter.

Units and components are standardized as far as possible in the Soviet fleet; and they are not changed in successive systems unless really necessary. One essential change in recent years has been a shift, in submarines, to micro-computers — something that is happening more slowly in Western boats where first-generation machines are still apt to take up an enormous amount of space and need cooling. HMS *Trafalgar* for instance, commissioned in 1983 as the lead submarine in the Royal Navy's latest class of SSNs, has bulky computers designed some 20 years ago — and other facilities including bunks, have had to give way to them.

So what have the Russians achieved with submarine weapon systems under an organisation that has frequently been criticised as ultra-bureaucratic but gets results?

We will have to revert to conjecture to some extent if we are to trace the probable course that developments have taken; but Soviet thinking is logical, and enough is

known to paint a reasonably clear picture.

Going back to 1958 when the initial 'November' SSNs emerged, the twin problems of self and radiated noise were nowhere near to being solved. However, at very slow speed, with only one reactor critical, the low-to-medium frequency conformal array bow sonar, perhaps covering 200 Hz to 5 kHz judging by external photographs, should have been able to hear snorkelling targets at ranges in the order of 20 miles and achieve active detection at 10–12 miles. Aural classifications depended entirely upon operators who cannot have been experienced: narrow band analysis lay some way in the future. Eight 553-mm (21-in) torpedo tubes forward (with 12 reloads) probably fired salvos either of 45-knot 5000-yd straight-running anti-ship fish (or possibly longer range pattern runners) and approximately 25-knot straight-running ASW passive-homing torpedoes. Two small 406-mm (16-in) tubes aft (with four reloads) were for last-ditch defense against surface ASW vessels; they were to be removed later and probably replaced by mobile decoy systems. The weapons, except for the pattern runners, were comparable to British and French torpedoes of the time but were astern of USN Mark 37 developments.

The hit probability against any but the noisiest, slowest submarine targets would have been extremely low (as Russian submariners grudgingly recognised in due course) and a 'November' SSN — a decidedly unintegrated weapon system — cannot for long have been considered an effective ASW platform. It would have been 'standing into danger' if it tried to tangle with NATO submarines were it not for the fact that they, too, had no effective ASW weapons.

Target motion analysis (TMA), fire-control and weapons were problematical on all sides until at least the mid-1970s — some would say the 1980s. Indeed, it would be rash to claim complete confidence in systems today simply because of the age-old difficulty in proving them under wartime conditions against wartime targets. Nevertheless, the advances have been dramatic, mostly due to computer technology.

Little seems to be known about Russian submarine ASW systems but we can get a shrewd idea of how they perform if we start with the questions facing Soviet submariners some 30 years ago and imagine how they would logically have answered them in relation to submarine-versus-submarine warfare.

The noise factor

It was quite obvious that NATO submarines enjoyed a substantial sonar range advantage — which is the basis of submarine-versus-submarine warfare.

It is difficult to say exactly when noise began to be suppressed in the Soviet underwater fleet but by 1980 the latest boats — 6300-ton 'Victor III' ASW SSNs (21 in service by 1985) were as quiet as the American and British designs of the 1960s which came into production during the 1970s. That is to say, the 'Victor IIIs' representing a leap forward from the earlier 'Victors', were comparable to the American 'Los Angeles' and the British 'Swiftsure' classes; and it can be supposed that they borrowed technology from both, thanks in part to the Walker-Whitworth spy ring.

Assuming that noise-reduction methods followed Western innovation, they included mounting machinery on a floating raft insulated from the hull (but locked down and less effective at high speed), flexible mountings for auxiliary machinery, carefully designed coolant pumps for the reactors (probably with the ability to dispense with pumps at low speed by employing natural circulation), de-coupling materials around the outer hull and double-hull construction which itself does much to prevent noise being transmitted to the sea.

How, the Russian designers asked themselves, can a prime noise source from propellers be removed? Cavitation was overcome by fitting some 'Victor IIIs' with a single large seven-bladed propeller which allowed comparatively low revolutions per knot. In others, tell-tale blade rate was partially overcome by two four-bladed screws mounted in tandem on one shaft, both rotating in the same direction. This solution cannot have been as satisfactory as the British pump-jet propulsor which underwent trials in HMS *Churchill* (SSN) from 1970 and was widely installed thereafter. American adoption is planned for the 9100-ton USS *Seawolf* (SSN) in the early 1990s. It is possible that the Soviet 7600-ton 'Sierras' (first-of-class trials in 1984) and subsequent boats have a similar pump-jet which may give way to pure jet propulsion.

Far left: HMS *Trafalgar* (SSN). Despite automated devices, a manual contact plot is still an invaluable aid to the command.
Left: Type 2020 sonar display console in HMS *Trafalgar*. This fairly new sonar, with a bow-mounted conformal array, has a computerized auto-tracking facility and, with Type 2007 flank array and Type 2046 towed array provides all-round passive coverage. It also incorporates a very effective computer-aided active capability.
Below left: Weapon space (5 tubes) and control console in HMS *Trafalgar*. A mix of 20 Tigerfish (future Spearfish), Sub-Harpoon missiles can be carried, besides weapons in the tubes, or a larger number of mines.
Below right: The end product of a successful submarine-versus-submarine attack as seen from the surface.

One of six Soviet 'Alfas', by far the fastest submarines in the world at 45 knots, with titanium alloy hulls, automated and computerized machinery (to allow a small complement of 40) and well armed with six bow tubes — but without any clearly defined purpose save as test vehicles or perhaps to dash out to hit a Strike Fleet approaching the Motherland and dash back again. The 'Alfas' do not seem to be tasked specifically for ASW operations, although their extreme agility should be advantageous in a mêlée.

All the 'Victors' (Types I, II and III) were given two small electrically driven auxiliary propellers on the after control surfaces for maneuvering in harbor and as a standby. British SSNs have a tiny 'egg-beater' which is lowered through the hull for the same purposes — reminiscent of the 'up funnel, down screw' arrangement in nineteenth century sail-and-steam warships.

Meanwhile, Soviet scientists occupied themselves with ripple motors together with well-shaped slippery and probably flexible outer hulls to make the best possible use, dolphin fashion, of super-conducting motors. If ripple propulsion could eventually be incorporated in the outer hull itself, and if super-conductivity could be taken to its limits, a small, fast, very deep diving and virtually noiseless submarine would result. Speeds of 50, 60 or even 70 knots were reckoned to be feasible by Russian studies conducted during the 1970s. As we know, the little Alfa — nicknamed *Zolotaya Ryba* (Golden Fish) by Soviet submariners because of its fantastic cost — has a top speed of 45 knots and its 'Akula' ('Shark' — platinum shark?) successor, more than twice the size at 8000 tons, is only a couple of knots slower. There is no doubt that the Soviet navy has very advanced and unconventional technology at its disposal.

The importance of sonar

Knowing that noise could be greatly reduced — as demonstrated by the West — low frequency passive sonars, especially towed arrays, could be developed rapidly before means of quieting were actually introduced. In the meantime Soviet tactics were mainly evolved around active sonar because American and British boats were so quiet and it was taking an interminable time to put narrow-band techniques to work. Apparently, Russian captains are still prone to

'go active' when they suspect that they are about to be goosed by a stealthy Westerner.

Soviet sonar used to lag behind Western equipment but it has probably caught up now. The British Flag Officer Submarines boasted in 1986 that 'we meet the opposition: they do not meet us'. That was true, then, in the majority of cases but near parity is expected today between the newest Russian, American and British boats. Nevertheless, although half the Soviet submarine force will be virtually silent, with excellent sonar, by the mid 1990s, the remainder will continue to be quite noisy and unsuitable for ASW work. There is nothing, in practical terms, that Admiral Chernavin can do to improve the older boats significantly.

The Soviet Staff must have concluded that only the good sonar platforms, a limited number of submarines, deserved equipping with top quality ASW sonar and weapon systems — the 'Victor IIIs', 'Sierras' (1984 onwards), 'Mikes' (1985 onwards), 'Akulas' (1985 onwards), and at least one new advanced class of submarine which has not yet been seen. The fast 'Alfas' are more suited to defensive interceptions, rushing out to attack the Strike Fleet, than to anti-submarine duties.

The ASW SSNs can operate anywhere; but modern, very quiet and much cheaper SSKs — 'Tangos' (1972–1982) and 'Kilos' (1982 continuing) — should be capable of barrier ASW operations close to home: they, too, deserved good ASW systems even if anti-shipping attack was their main original role as successors to the 55 ageing 'Foxtrots'.

Passive sonar classification had to be developed in parallel with all-round detection capabilities; so about a dozen ASW submarines, equipped with Hi-Fi recorders, were tasked for collecting underwater intelligence data. In distant areas this sensitive work appears to have fallen mainly on 'Victor IIIs' from 1980 and the intruders concerned have been commanded by highly trusted officers — one a Rear Admiral. The 'fingerprint' computerized library held in Soviet submarine sonar rooms can hardly fail to be comprehensive by now; and up-dating intelligence activities continue on a large scale. Of course, electronic and other intelligence is gathered at the same time. It was soon discovered that the gear required, together with the carefully screened intelligence teams, demanded a lot of space, secure from prying eyes: that could be a contributory reason for 'Victor IIIs' being two meters longer than

'Victor IIs', and, on at least one, for the additional curved structure forward of the sail. The fat 'Sierras' and 'Mikes' — two meters broader than the 'Victors' — should have no trouble in accommodating the necessary kit which is extremely useful tactically in addition to its primary purpose.

However, the main reason for increased size has undoubtedly been the room required by the multiplicity of weapons required to deal with all the specified targets.

ASW missiles

While low-frequency sonar with narrow band analysis was on the way, it was predictable that detections ought to be achieved out to the first convergence zone (with all the 'ifs' and 'buts' associated with target noise and sound channels), so it made sense to provide weapons capable of engaging submarines out to around 30 miles if possible. Active sonar, perhaps using bottom-bounce, should be capable of nailing a target at this sort of range and so should passive sonar — although experience was to show that it would take many hours, far longer than expected, to deduce target range and motion. In any case, by the time that a normal unguided torpedo arrived in a target area an hour or so later (assuming it had the legs to go so far) the data would be hopelessly stale. Consequently, Russian submariners copied the (now obsolete) American tube-launched nuclear missile Subroc.

The Soviet SS-N-15 'Subroc', fitted in middle generation SSNs, 'Tango' and 'Kilo' SSKs, is powerful; but Gorshkov recognised, even before USN admirals, that total reliance on a large nuclear depth charge is politically unrealistic. Accordingly, the complimentary SS-N-16, with a lightweight homing torpedo payload, was produced for the 'Victor IIIs' and followers — several years ahead of the US Navy's new stand-off missile Sea Lance carrying a Mark 50 ASW torpedo which is a much more effective type than anything available in the 1950s and 1960s.

SS-N-16 may be last in the line of Russian submarine long-range ASW missiles. With detection ranges becoming shorter there is little point in seeking a longer reach although the torpedo payload will need to be improved continually to keep pace with new submerged targets.

ASW torpedoes

At ranges much beyond a couple of miles, the chances of hitting a submerged target with free-running homing torpedoes can be discounted. The best gyro cannot steer closer than half-a-degree from the set course and a small error of that order may displace it enough — 50 ft per mile — to prevent target acquisition: more importantly, alterations of course or speed by the target — or imprecise calculations by the attacker — are almost certain to result in torpedoes passing outside acquisition range. However, at one or two miles a salvo of two unguided ping-and-listen homers may well be effective: the Russians have plenty of these relatively unsophisticated fish.

For medium or long-range shots — say from three miles outwards — a weapon needs to be steered and commanded in the water: wire-guidance is the only practicable method of control at present.

Typical wire-guided torpedoes

Tigerfish is an excellent example of a wire-guided weapon. The torpedoes can be kept in flooded tubes in the patrol state, ready to fire, with no maintenance for a year. They can swim out but in British submarines they are invariably discharged positively, by water-ram from an SSN or by high pressure air from an 'Oberon' class SSK.

The Russians are thought to have experimented with sonic commands but they cannot be two-way so it is presumed that Soviet ASW guided torpedoes broadly resemble Western equivalents. The Russian version is probably not as good as Tigerfish, which is claimed to be the quietest torpedo in the world, because wire-guidance was adopted quite late and Soviet submariners have therefore not had all that much practice with it; but it is fair to assume that the principles are not too different from our own.

Making that assumption, a Russian standard wire (which may be replaced with fiber optics) enables commands to be passed to the torpedo — speed, course, depth, homing mode and 'release' — and information can be sent back to the firing submarine.

A static reference is needed for the torpedo and its controller to work from. There are minor variations on the theme but the idea is to pay out wire, from the torpedo in one direction and from the submarine in the other, by means of a dispenser which allows the wire itself to remain stationary in the water.

In wartime, it will be the enemy's objective to cut the vital wire. He can hardly

Subroc

The US Navy's Subroc system was initiated in 1955 following (mainly unsuccessful) attempts at SUBAIR co-ordinated attacks and equally disappointing trials at the time with anti-submarine torpedoes. It took a long while — some 11 years which is not bad for the development of a totally new weapon — to solve the problems associated with submerged launch, rocket-motor ignition, precise airborne trajectory to the target's future position and underwater detonation at the end of flight. Unlike ballistic missiles, fired vertically, Subroc required an exit angle of about 30°.

Only a nuclear warhead (lethal or critically damaging at three to five miles) could be expected to compensate for inaccuracies at long range. Subroc had to be a nuclear weapon with no conventional alternative — with all the political and tactical limitations implied.

TIGERFISH ATTACK

After many vicissitudes, Marconi's Tigerfish is now one of the world's few really well peacetime-tested, smart dual-purpose weapons.

The attack sequence is straightforward and command orders are minimal: 'Stand by Tigerfish attack. Assume weapon readiness State One. Open numbers (whatever) bow caps. Fire'.

Two Tigerfish are normally launched, when within range and as soon as possible, 10 or 20 seconds apart, with

certain restrictions (not unduly inhibiting) on the submarine's speed, depth and subsequent man-euvering.

One torpedo is assigned to attack and the other is either held in reserve or given a different search depth. Both torpedoes are steered, more or less in parallel, towards the target. At long range they may be run at high speed until within a given distance of the target, when they are switched to low speed to avoid counter-detection and to give them the best chance of hearing the target themselves.

AZIMUTH CONTROL
DEPTH UNIT
GUIDANCE CONTROL

FORWARD BATTERY

TRANSDUCERS
AND HOMING
ELECTRONICS

MOTOR

WARHEAD AND
FUZE/DETONATOR

ROLL GYRO
STABILIZER ELECTRONICS

AFT BATTERY

INVERTER
RUDDER CONTROL UNIT

DISPENSER

The wire dispensing system is deployed during a short dead run. Each weapon is then controlled by a tracker who steers and

commands it from a display console, rather like a radar screen, which constantly shows torpedo and target position.

Tigerfish has an active search capability but the firing submarine endeavors to avoid using it because the enemy is bound to be alerted.

Moreover, Russian submarines have active jammers, as well as decoys, presumably tuned to the correct frequency.

When one of the torpedoes acquires the target it flashes a signal back to the tracker. The Weapons Control Officer

decides that the acquisition is solid and releases the weapon to home in (but he can regain control if necessary).

The weapon immediately steers itself, in azimuth and depth, towards the noise source and the impact/influence fuze system activates when within the kill-zone. At this point, hopefully, there is a loud bang!

do this himself; but if he hears transients like discharge noises, or the incoming weapons themselves, and fires a retaliatory salvo of deliberately detectable unguided homing torpedoes at fairly close range (which is a likely Soviet tactic) the original attacker may well be forced to take such violent evasive action that the wire will indeed be severed.

It must also be assumed that mobile or static decoys ('Nixies') can be launched from most if not all Soviet submarines. Self-defense will be discussed separately but the need for countermeasures and counter-countermeasures is becoming just as relevant below water as it is in the electronic field above.

Super 'smart' weapons

It would be better to avoid guidance altogether but that implies a truly intelligent and autonomous weapon with a wide search capability in its own right. Although it would necessarily be quite large the concept is by no means out of bounds. Several Soviet submarines already have two or four outsize 650 mm (25.6 in) tubes, primarily for 30-mile anti-ship wake-homing torpedoes, and there is no reason why still bigger tubes cannot be fitted externally if necessary. The exciting possibilities for robotic vehicles are examined in the chapter on midget submarines because that is what such weapons would really be: it will be rather surprising if Russian designers are not actively investigating them in the privacy of the White Sea.

On the Western side, there is competitive debate about whether the British Tigerfish (to be superceded by Spearfish) or the American Mark 48 torpedo (being supplemented by the ADCAP ADvanced CAPability version) is the best. Mark 48 ADCAP is, amongst other things, specifically designed to deal with Soviet double-hulls as well as with under-ice encounters. From published reports the forthcoming Spearfish will have similar, or better, capabilities and will be very fast at about 70 knots. Spearfish is marking a departure from conventional propulsion systems — usually electric or Otto fuelled — in being powered by a gas-turbine engine driving a pump-jet propulsor.

The snag is that smart weapons are exceedingly expensive: the Mark 48 ADCAP has been quoted at four million dollars a shot although the price seems to have come down a little lately. It is very doubtful if every submarine in any force can be loaded entirely with the latest weapons — and that certainly

applies to Soviet as well as Western boats. The result is apt to be a mix of high performance and comparatively low grade ASW weapons which makes submariners everywhere unhappy because fire-control drills become complicated, training and maintenance difficulties are introduced and a boat is robbed of its full potential. And already some quite different types of weapon are often carried as well as anything in the ASW torpedo and missile line. Land-attack cruise missiles (eg, Tomahawk and SS-N-21), specifically anti-ship torpedoes (although most ASW fish have a dual capability), anti-ship missiles (eg, Sub Harpoon or SS-N-9) and, coming along in the Soviet fleet, anti-air missiles (SAM).

Then there is the additional complication of warheads. Guessing again, 25 per cent of missiles carried in Soviet boats are nuclear, each warhead yielding 15 kilotons. Taking into account the variety of weapons in a multi-purpose boat (and it does not appear that any Soviet submarines confine themselves exclusively to ASW) the number of submarine targets one boat can engage in a non-nuclear shoot-out is limited. For example, if a 'Victor III' has room for 18 tube-launched weapons (for two 533-mm [21-in] and four 650-mm [25.6-in] tubes) it can hardly embark more than ten conventional ASW torpedoes and SS-N-15/16 missiles — less if it has a salvo of unguided defensive fish always at the ready. In other words, it probably only has enough weapons for four or five offensive

The Ferranti Integrated Submarine Command System (FISCS) is a combat suite comprising sonar, advanced tactical data handling and weapon control facilities. It is the shape of things to come and, with the known Russian predilection for computers, it must be assumed that a somewhat similar system is installed in the latest Soviet submarines. Despite protests from the moneymen (although such combat equipment is by no means gold-plated), it is impossible for a modern submarine to go about its business efficiently without a fully integrated weapon system with centralized displays. (Photo *Ferranti*)

No Solution, Captain

The wartime and post-war US Navy fire-control calculator included an encouraging but untrustworthy sign which lit up when it was happy and said 'Solution'. In fact, at some stages during an approach the number of solutions that fitted a particular set of inputs (even if these were individually correct) was infinite.

ASW engagements. Any SS-N-21 land-attack cruise missiles carried would still further reduce its ASW capability.

The question of nuclear warheads is not clear-cut. High explosive (HE) heads on smart torpedoes are quite small although, from the Soviet aspect with single hull submerged targets in mind, they are big enough — if they actually hit. But supposing an enemy submarine — Russian or NATO — is going fast, what then? If the homing torpedo is forced into a stern chase will it catch up? And if it does hit, whatever the circumstances, will it sink or at least disable ('mission kill') the target? The last question is especially relevant to tough 'survivable' Russian boats but the Soviet Staff is fully aware that enemy submarines are protected in other ways — speed, maneuverability, decoys, anechoic coatings and possibly sonic countermeasures.

Would it therefore be wise for both sides to equip ASW torpedoes with nuclear warheads as the Russians have long done for anti-ship torpedoes? These could, if suitably programmed, detonate by command, at a set range after active acquisition or at a set time after passive acquisition rather than necessarily on impact. But if nuclear heads are used, would they escalate the fighting to full nuclear warfare?

The answer to the last all-important question is probably 'No', especially if the nuclear yield is sub-kiloton. It is feasible to insert a nuclear component, when required, in a standard warhead without sacrificing much of the normal HE charge (300 kg on a Mark 48) if it is decided to fire the torpedo in conventional mode.

A sub-kiloton insertable nuclear component (SKINC) can yield as little as 0.01 kilotons, equivalent to 4000 kg of high-explosive or 13 conventional Mark 48 warheads. A mission kill would result at 35-40 m; an average steel hull would be ruptured at 12-15 m; and a titanium hull at 10–12 m. The protection of a double hull would be largely negated. If the yield is increased tenfold to 0.1 kilotons the distances are multiplied by a factor of about three, leading to serious damage at 110–115 m. The safe stand-off range for an attacker is reckoned to be ten times the 'mission kill' figure; and it is believed that a small SKINC warhead would not too greatly degrade the acoustic environment by 'blue out' — the neutralisation of sonar systems.

Naturally, the SKINC concept would ease the Soviet problem of weapon availability outlined above because torpedoes and ASW missiles like SS-N-16 could be converted from HE to nuclear or vice-versa quite quickly at sea. NATO might advantageously follow the same course: safe stowage of SKINCs should not pose any insuperable difficulties.

Target motion analysis and fire control

When Admiral Gorshkov formulated his ASW submarine policy, target motion analysis (TMA) by passive means was everywhere in its infancy. Passive sonar bearings were inaccurate (they still are at low frequencies) and had to be smoothed manually by plotting them on one side of a vertical transparent perspex board while drawing a smooth curve through them on the other side. Drawing a curve was definitely an art not a science — it remains the only method in non-computerized submarines — and the measurement of rate-of-change of bearing (bearing rate), the mathematical input required, was dependent upon the drawer's skill. Provided that the target kept a steady course and speed, a marked change of course and speed by the attacker generated a 'bearings only' fire-control solution after some time on the second leg, assisted by sundry rather esoteric plots and, of course, indications from sonar such as propeller revolution count.

The process, even with fairly accurate medium frequency broad band sonar, took quite a while and depended absolutely on a man with his crayon at the time bearing plot. Wire-guidance lessened the need for accuracy but a computer was the only way to achieve quicker solutions, particularly when the target was maneuvering in a tight, rapidly changing situation — a mêlée or dogfight. Unfortunately, very low frequency signatures — tonals — may often be intermittent and the information derived can be fragmentary from a towed array when the target is quiet. Tracking to the point of TMA is therefore much more prolonged than it formerly was despite computer assistance.

It can safely be assumed that Russian submariners installed fire-control computers for all weapon systems in boats from the 'Victors' onwards. Russians are computer-minded anyway, and there is no way that they could cope with the full range of sensors and mix of weapons without help from machines. Moreover, they are bound by tactical rules — Western submariners would argue too much so — and are accustomed to following doctrine implicitly. Most of them probably do just what the computer tells them and it is just bad luck if the beast is programmed wrongly.

It is well nigh impossible to program a machine in such a way that every conceivable three-dimensional problem is solved. And time and again post-attack analysis in the West has shown how dangerous it is to become mesmerised by figures on the face of a calculator. Commonsense, a feel for the situation, has to be applied: although the Russians are rational, commonsense is not their strongpoint — and who dares argue with a machine, programmed and approved by the Party, when a *Zampolit* is looking over your shoulder?

Offensive mines

There are several types of anti-submarine mines, nuclear as well as conventional, which can be laid by submarines in shallow or deep water nowadays.

All Soviet submarines, possibly including Soviet SSBNs, are capable of carrying a quantity of mines instead of — or in addition to — a torpedo/missile load; and it could be that double-hulled boats accommodate these deadly eggs in chutes external to the pressure hull where they would not be visible to outside observers.

Soviet submarine-laid 1000 kilo (AMD-1000) ground mines, laid on the seabed, are magnetic, acoustic (high and low frequency passive) pressure or combination influence types; and they are effective against submarines down to 200 m. All except the most secret pressure and combination variants have been widely exported to client states and Warsaw Pact countries. There are, in addition, two particularly unpleasant types of Soviet submarine-laid offensive moored mines. So-called rising mines are moored until they detect (passively)

Wartime submarine minelayers

Some figures from World War II are interesting. The Free French submarine minelayer *Rubis* laid 683 mines during 28 patrols between 1940 and 1944, claiming 14 supply ships, seven anti-submarine vessels and mine-sweepers, and damage to one supply ship and a U-boat.

German U-boats laid 327 mines off the Eastern American seaboard resulting in 11 ships sunk and damaged; but, aside from sinkings, seven ports had to be closed for a total of 40 days — an intriguing aspect of submarine deterrence which could be applied to submarine bases.

A total of 658 mines were laid by Allied, almost wholly US, submarines in the Pacific resulting in 27 Japanese ships being sunk or damaged beyond repair, and another 27 being damaged but repairable. Therefore, for each dozen mines laid, one was successful.

Above: It is impossible to tell that HMS *E.41*, seen sailing from Harwich in 1918, carried 20 mines in her saddle tanks; and, apart from the absence of beam torpedo tubes, she looks no different from her sisters.

Left: *UC-163* building (but not completed) in 1918. The Germans installed mine-chutes centrally, and invisibly, in the hull.

SOVIET ASW RISING MINE

This sketch of a Soviet offensive ASW rising mine is purely conjectural. The actual mechanism is not known, but some kind of encapsulation (viz. US CAPTOR) is clearly necessary together with a firm mooring, a computerized sonar sensor and a weapon control system. Intelligence indicates that the lightweight torpedo is jet-propelled and self-homing when it acquires a target; it could be steered initially, possibly by active sonic command, into a gathering sonar beam.

PASSIVE ACQUISITION

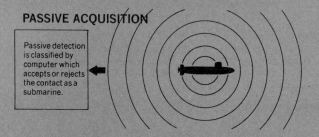

Passive detection is classified by computer which accepts or rejects the contact as a submarine.

ACTIVE ACQUISITION

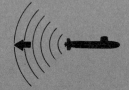

An active sonar beam is probably triggered when passive detection indicates a legitimate target.

It would be logical for a solid block to moor the device which itself must be buoyant; and it would be easiest to lay mines like this, with automatically detached parachute(s), from an aircraft. Water conditions must clearly be suitable for the sonar paths envisaged.

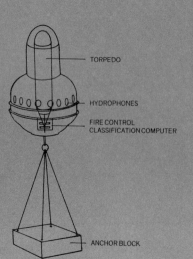

TORPEDO

HYDROPHONES

FIRE CONTROL CLASSIFICATION COMPUTER

ANCHOR BLOCK

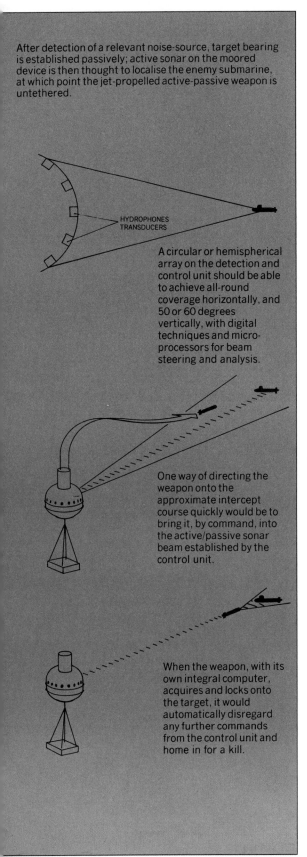

After detection of a relevant noise-source, target bearing is established passively; active sonar on the moored device is then thought to localise the enemy submarine, at which point the jet-propelled active-passive weapon is untethered.

HYDROPHONES
TRANSDUCERS

A circular or hemispherical array on the detection and control unit should be able to achieve all-round coverage horizontally, and 50 or 60 degrees vertically, with digital techniques and microprocessors for beam steering and analysis.

One way of directing the weapon onto the approximate intercept course quickly would be to bring it, by command, into the active/passive sonar beam established by the control unit.

When the weapon, with its own integral computer, acquires and locks onto the target, it would automatically disregard any further commands from the control unit and home in for a kill.

a pre-programmed target noise-source at which point the mine is untethered and driven upwards to its target by underwater jet propulsion under guidance from an active location device. The older version is designed for the Continental shelf and the newer is for deep water.

An even more sophisticated Soviet weapon senses the underwater electrical potential of its victim and is consequently known as the UEP mine.

'Risers' would be laid, as well as more conventional versions, around NATO submarine bases and across submarine transit lanes.

It can be expected that diesel-electric boats (SSKs) will deposit mines around European bases and at related choke points while SSNs (and perhaps SSGNs and SSBNs) might be deployed to lay deep-water mines further afield off the American coastline and wherever intelligence indicates that NATO submarines are likely to operate.

Offensive mining, like the employment of many Soviet submarines themselves, literally constitutes defense in depth for the USSR: the modern ASW mine could turn out to be more dangerous than any other anti-submarine weapon. It is to be hoped that NATO sees the threat in that light and is fully prepared but there is reason to think it is not — witness the difficulties posed by a modest mining threat in the Persian Gulf recently.

The Soviet Navy, including the submarine arm, has always been very keen on mine-laying albeit, until now, for close defense; but Western submariners have always hated a task which shows no immediate results and has frequently taken submarines into dangerous coastal waters while being forbidden to torpedo targets for fear of giving the game away. Submariners have also, in days gone by, tended to treat self-protection against mines rather perfunctorily, regarding wiping and similar activities to demagnetise the hull as a bore. It is said that, today, prudence prevails in matters of magnetic hygiene.

Nevertheless, it will be well to remember that nearly one third of the British submarines which failed to return from patrol during World War II were lost in minefields.

The US Navy CAPTOR (encapsulated torpedo) is the most advanced in-service Western offensive mine and it can be laid in deep water or under the ice-cap if required. CAPTOR embodies a Mark 46 Mod 4 lightweight homing torpedo which is released by a detection and control unit when an enemy sound signature has been recognised for a certain length of time. The predicted recognition range is about half-a-mile at which point an active-ranging/homing device is triggered. Soviet anechoic coatings would presumably degrade CAPTOR performance to some degree; and so, of course, would noise reduction. The sensor mechanism is programmed to disregard surface traffic but if this safety device were to fail when a friendly force was passing overhead the rather small 96-lb PBXN 103 explosive warhead would probably not do all that much harm to a major ship. Indeed, the warhead is on the small side for dealing with Soviet double hulls unless the CAPTOR/Mark 46 has a directional charge or unless the weapon also has a passive propellor-seeking capability with the idea of achieving a 'mission kill'. However, the effect of any mine would undoubtedly be very nasty under the ice.

Smart offensive mines have a limited life when laid, more likely to be measured in months than in years; and selective mine sensors have to be updated to match target submarine improvements and changes in sound-signatures — which is another good reason why continual underwater intelligence gathering is so important.

Integrated weapon systems

An astonishing amount of information comes in to a submarine's Action Information Organisation (AIO) from sonar, ESM, periscopic observations and intelligence messages. Some of it is interesting, some is not, but it all has to be sifted. When the time is ripe weapons have to be fed with the necessary inputs and there can be no delays or mistakes. Numerous contacts may need plotting simultaneously and own movements must be accurately injected into the system. Then there is a string of questions which constantly have to be answered. What is the best sonar listening depth? What speed can be ordered without risking counter-detection? Are there sonobuoys in the water? Has the towed array straightened out after the last turn? What is the meaning of this or that transient noise? Which narrow band windows should be searched? Which tonals indicate an enemy submarine? What is the priority target amongst them? Does it accord with a fleeting ESM emission analysed on the last excursion to periscope depth? When must the boat next come shallow to receive radio messages? What has happened to the contact which has gone silent? What kind of weapons must be brought to the ready state? Has the sound velocity profile changed since the last measurement? Does SINS need updating? Is the automatic plot indicating a more credible solution than the computer? Is a sudden transient indicative of a submarine close aboard? If so, can enough data be acquired for a snap attack? Should sonar go active? Is there a risk of physical collision? Could it possibly be a friendly submarine? Or mundanely, but importantly nonetheless, should the next meal be delayed? And so on.

The reasons for integration are obvious but a perfectly integrated weapon system embracing every aspect of submerged approach and attack, is still rare in Western boats: the systems which exist in many boats have grown around weapons with little regard to the total tactical problem and decision making involved. Integration is probably more common in modern Soviet submarines — whether or not it functions properly — because the crew quality is so poor that the human-factor has had to be removed from the chain where possible: machines talk to machines in unequivocal digital language.

British and American submariners fully appreciate the need for integration but both services suffer from the age-old submarine custom of making do somehow: the moneymen know that and they think, perhaps, that systems like US SUBACS or the British Submarine Command System (SMCS) moving towards a completely integrated Combat System are gilding the lily when they really are imperative. Submariners are not very good at stating their case: the silent services will have to be more vociferous if they are to get what they so urgently require. Meanwhile, the hodge-podge of assorted fire-control units and man-machine interfaces is slowly being rationalised and the boundaries of sub-systems are beginning to disappear, with yet more training every time one of the assorted packages is changed — which is one reason why the Soviet fleet attempts to make only major all-embracing changes and then preferably at long intervals.

END NOTES
1. A clear warning of this problem was given in the standard German U-boat Tactical Handbook in 1915, 25 years earlier — but history, which is the same thing as experience, was ignored or forgotten.
2. Very recent information from West Germany suggests, however, that the depth mechanism had anyway been sabotaged before delivery of the weapons. It is not known whether this allegation is justified.

1.8

SUBMARINE-LAUNCHED MISSILES

L and-attack and anti-ship missiles might seem outside the scope of this book but they have to be considered in some detail because submarine-launched nuclear ballistic missiles (SLBMs) are the greatest threat to humanity since the world began while submarine-launched cruise missiles (SLCMs) are arguably the greatest threat to surface ships as well as being very effective against shore targets. Hence, missile submarines are high priority ASW submarine targets and a missile-launcher's habits and habitat need to be known.

Strategic underwater missile systems

Politics, like it or not, dominate naval strategy and, when it comes to strategic underwater missile systems, it is politicians and not naval staffs that demand their creation, development and continuing existence.

A navy, any navy, is the servant and advisor of government. If a government wants a strategic nuclear capability its navy will rightly advise that missiles are best mounted underwater. Whether it is desirable or sensible for every government which now possesses nuclear ballistic missile submarines (SSBNs) to retain or advance that capability is another matter altogether and undeniably outside the present context. Nevertheless, it is impossible to resist making some points about the British Polaris/Trident force (four SSBNs — one on station) and the French *Force de Dissuasion* (six SSBNs — two on patrol and another available) because their activities are of interest to the Soviet underwater opposition. They are of concern to the Kremlin masters as well although not, perhaps, in quite the way that the UK and French governments might wish. Briefly then:

1. The strategic nuclear balance — a balance of power to use a more traditional term — is kept level by the USA and USSR. No balance can have more than two weights, one either side, and there must be some danger of upsetting the scales if someone else tips in a pennyweight.

2. SLBMs do not carry an ID card. The identity of a submerged launcher cannot be established positively at the receiving end. Hence, the first SLBMs, of whatever origin, which climb into space must almost inevitably trigger the computers which initiate Armageddon: the response can scarcely be other than global. Does Congress recognise this when it supports so-called independent nuclear deterrent forces overseas?

3. Although it is claimed that no Western SSBNs have yet been trailed to their secret patrol areas or detected while there, a really concentrated Soviet submarine ASW effort against one or two British and/or French SSBNs might well succeed. What then in a pre-crisis situation?

4. The possession of SSBNs by middling naval powers is absolutely bound to weaken realistic non-nuclear forces — and there is growing evidence of that in the Royal Navy despite claims by politicians to the effect that the SSBN force absorbs only a small percentage of the defense budget.

5. The British strategic submarine force is by no means truly independent. The Tridents will depend very heavily on American cooperation: for example, the missiles, but not the warheads, will be built and serviced in the USA.

6. Finally, would a fairly limited number of SLBM warheads (from one or two

SSBNs) penetrate future Soviet ABM defenses in sufficient numbers to constitute a deterrent in Soviet eyes? If so, why does the USN and Soviet Navy think it necessary to keep so many SSBNs at sea themselves?

Of course, the Soviet Defense Council wishes to see the UK and French SSBNs dismantled. No householder likes having a pile of inflammable material stacked up outside his back yard. But it is questionable whether the hard-headed team in Moscow really believes those forces to be a deterrent. When and why would the British and French heads of government give the order to fire observing that, whatever the circumstances, the order would be nationally suicidal while very probably leading to cremation of the entire planet? Naturally, the latter consideration equally applies to the two superpowers but they can justify the nuclear balance of power between them while, hopefully, removing weights from the scales on each side steadily and simultaneously.

So much for philosophy. Some would say that the whole concept of nuclear deterrence is decidedly odd anyway; but, while SSBNs still lurk in the depths, we need to see how they work and what attack-type submarines, on both sides, can do about them.

On the one hand, NATO claims that its SSBNs are secure and on the other, that Soviet SSBNs are vulnerable to ASW submarine search-and-attack operations. It sounds rather like having your cake and eating it. Can the advantage be entirely with the West?

Soviet SSBNs (PLARBs)

Taking all things into account — maintenance, manning, trials and transit time — it should be possible for General Maksimov to keep about 20 PLARBs (the Soviet acronym for SSBNs) constantly on patrol with well over 300 missiles carrying some 1500 nuclear warheads between them. Maybe twice that number of PLARBs could be surged forward in a state of emergency; and the average number of warheads per PLARB is increasing anyway.

The earliest type is the 10 000-ton 'Yankee'. One was lost in October 1986 following a serious fire and explosion in the missile compartment.

Seventeen 'Yankees' with SLBMs currently remain. Until late 1987, SSBNs of this elderly and quite noisy type patrolled off

Eastern and Western American seaboards, having to traverse US SOSUS chains *en route*. It would be surprising if American SSNs did not have a shrewd idea where they were: the 'Yankee' that went down was just about where it might be expected — 763 n miles from New York where it could cover cities east of a line joining Minneapolis and New Orleans. A 'Yankee', with six 533-mm (21-in) torpedo tubes (18 weapons embarked), was presumably supplied, therefore, with pentiful ASW weapons, decoys or 'nixies' and countermeasure devices.

Now, however, the 'Yankees' have been withdrawn to safe Soviet-controlled waters from where their missiles can reach European and Asian theater targets, thus compensating for the loss of SS-20 land-based missiles under arms control agreements.

'Yankees' carry 16 1300-mile SS-N-6 Mod 1 or 1600-mile Mod 2 or 3 missiles in two banks of eight vertical tubes: the missiles are liquid-fuelled, like the great majority of Soviet SLBMs, and the danger of that was dramatically illustrated by the 1986 'Yankee' disaster. Thankfully, Western navies chose solid fuel from the start. Each warhead carries two re-entry vehicles (RVs) which cannot be independently maneuvered: they are not accurate enough for a pre-emptive strike against hardened silos and must be intended for 'city-busting' in the elegant phraseology of nuclear warfare,

The solitary 'Yankee II' is armed with 12 SS-N-17 missiles — apparently unique to this PLARB — which are fuelled with safer solid propellant and carry a post-boost vehicle (PBV) for a range of 2000 nautical miles. Multiple re-entry vehicles (MRVs) or multiple independently targettable re-entry vehicles (MIRVs) were expected when the SS-N-17 was reported in the experimental stage; but, so far, it appears to carry only a single warhead albeit, presumably, with a megaton payload.

For some reason the SS-N-17 has not prospered since trials began in 1975 and it may still be regarded in the Soviet Navy as an experimental step towards a new type.

The missiles in the 39 (or more) 11 000 to 13 600-ton 'Delta' PLARBs, completed in four successively improved versions between 1972 and 1985, are liquid-fuelled but much more advanced.

The SS-N-8 — 12 in 'Delta Is' and 16 in 'Delta IIs' — have a range of 4250 nautical miles for the Mod I with a single RV and nearly 5000 n miles for the Mod II with two

THE SOVIET 'TYPHOON' CLASS

Some observers credit the 'Typhoon' with 40 000 tons rather than 25 000 tons, including a huge 40 per cent reserve of buoyancy resulting from the wide separation between outer and inner hulls. It has also been suggested that 'Typhoon' may be the battleship of the Soviet Fleet, able to operate worldwide and, besides its primarily strategic role, threaten enemy surface battle groups — a task which could itself be considered strategic. Two large hatches abaft the sail may well be for divers and/or small mini-submersibles. A 'Typhoon' is 170 m (558 ft) long overall, with maximum beam 23 m (75 ft) and surface draught 11.5 m (37 ft). Great attention has been paid to eliminating vortices and reducing drag by boundary layer control. Limber holes are not evident and they are probably replaced by relief valves. Very rapid pumps may fill the casing on diving and empty it on surfacing: 'Typhoon' can apparently dive quickly, despite its size, and it is thought to be extremely quiet when it wants to be.

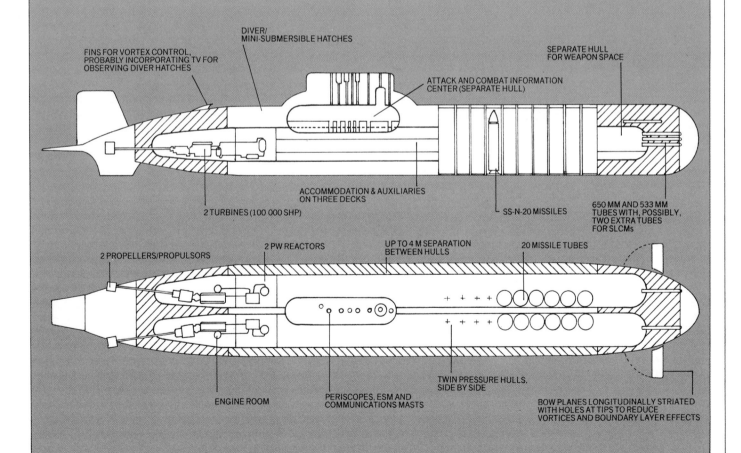

FINS FOR VORTEX CONTROL, PROBABLY INCORPORATING TV FOR OBSERVING DIVER HATCHES

DIVER/ MINI-SUBMERSIBLE HATCHES

SEPARATE HULL FOR WEAPON SPACE

ATTACK AND COMBAT INFORMATION CENTER (SEPARATE HULL)

ACCOMMODATION & AUXILIARIES ON THREE DECKS

2 TURBINES (100 000 SHP)

SS-N-20 MISSILES

650 MM AND 533 MM TUBES WITH, POSSIBLY, TWO EXTRA TUBES FOR SLCMs

2 PROPELLERS/PROPULSORS

2 PW REACTORS

UP TO 4 M SEPARATION BETWEEN HULLS

20 MISSILE TUBES

ENGINE ROOM

PERISCOPES, ESM AND COMMUNICATIONS MASTS

TWIN PRESSURE HULLS, SIDE BY SIDE

BOW PLANES LONGITUDINALLY STRIATED WITH HOLES AT TIPS TO REDUCE VORTICES AND BOUNDARY LAYER EFFECTS

Soviet 'Delta I', unlike 'Typhoon' not at all well configured for breaking upwards through ice. This 11,750-ton PLARB is 1000 to 1700 tons less than its three succeeding 'Delta' variants and considerably shorter at 139 m (456 ft). It carries 12 SLBMs instead of 16; but it is a powerful unit and, with the eighteenth of this type completed in 1972, it will figure in the Order of Battle for a few years to come. Maximum speed from two PW reactors and two steam turbines generating 35 000 shp is around 24 knots: the boat is relatively noisy (by modern standards), at all but slow speeds.

RVs. The CEP (circular error, probable — the usual measure of accuracy) is said to be less than a quarter of a mile under stellar-inertial guidance. This, with a megaton warhead, is significant with respect to hardened targets.

There is ample scope for bluff about missile capabilities and, indeed, about submarine warfare generally, but if that sort of accuracy is real (for the SS-N-8 and other new models) it could explain why the USSR seems willing to consider winding down its arsenal of accurate land-based missiles as a preliminary to a general reduction, on all sides, of ballistic missiles by a half and eventually to zero. That is, if various statements and reports of Soviet-American discussions so far have been interpreted correctly.

The 14 'Delta IIIs' carry 16 liquid-fuelled SS-N-18 missiles. Mod I has three multiple, independently targettable re-entry vehicles (MIRVs) with a range of 3530 n miles; Mod II, with a single megaton warhead, 4350 n miles; and Mod III, with seven MIRVs, 3530 n miles. The CEP miss-distance is estimated at 1500 m.

The three (or more) 'Delta IVs', the first of which was launched in 1984, are equipped for the recently developed SS-N-23 which is thought to deliver up to ten MIRVs with greater accuracy than SS-N-18 to a range of 4500 n miles. The new missile is expected to replace the latter in due course. Clearly, the 'Delta IVs' are high priority targets for NATO SSNs but they operate within (nominally) Soviet waters.

All the missiles in 'Deltas' are larger and longer than the SS-N-6 and 17 in 'Yankees' so,

to take the extra length, the 'Deltas' have a most distinctive raised section over the missile compartment amidships. It is this which reduces their top speed to the 24–25 knot mark, three or four knots slower than a 'Yankee'. Not that an SSBN normally needs high speed: its whole purpose in life is to remain quiet and undetected. But high speed could come in handy if a boat is threatened by anti-submarine forces.

The gigantic 'Typhoons', five completed since 1983 with probably another on the stocks and each displacing at least 25 000 tons submerged, are the largest submarines ever built and very different from any other SSBNs.

Twin pressure hulls are encased by the monster's outer hull and there is a separate hull above, 40 m long, for the operations and attack center. There is probably yet another hull forward to house the torpedo space where there are six 533-mm (21-in) and 650-mm (25.6-in) tubes — the latter, also fitted in 'Delta IVs', could hold encapsulated long-range SS-N-21 land-attack cruise missiles (which normally fit into standard tubes) rather than the large wake-homing torpedoes embarked in certain guided-missile boats (SSGNs) and the latest torpedo-attack type submarines (SSNs). Cruise missiles are impervious to defenses of the kind envisaged by the Strategic Defense Initiative ('Star Wars'), and are currently quite difficult to intercept by any means: as always, the Soviet Navy has opted for a powerful and plentiful mix of weapons with the object of defeating defenses.

Twin reactors and twin turbines, supplying 80 000 shp to twin shafts, should give a maximum speed, for rapid deployment and evasion, of around 30 knots — higher if Soviet investigations into boundary layer control (making the submarines 'slippery') have been as successful as predicted.

A notable change from tradition is the siting of the 20-missile tubes *forward* of the massive fin which, with the entire outer casing, is exceptionally well configured for breaking upwards through pack ice. The outer hull is well displaced from the pressure hull(s) to afford protection against ASW weapons and provide a very large amount of reserve buoyancy — about 40 per cent of total submerged displacement. Smooth and uncluttered, the monster is covered with Cluster Guard anechoic tiles to reduce active sonar reflections when being hunted; but 'Typhoon' is still a big target for ASW active systems and airborne magnetic anomaly detection equipment (MAD). At low speed on patrol she is quiet and hard to hear with passive sonar.

The forward position for the missile tubes has probably been selected in order to cope more easily, computer-assisted, with the massive and sudden changes in trim resulting from a rapid launching procedure: in 14 October, 1982 the first of class fired two missiles simultaneously during trials. Missiles in other classes are more commonly launched at intervals of 15 or 20 seconds. Salvo-launches might save three or four minutes although they seem unnecessarily dramatic. However, it is always desirable to get rid of missiles and depart quickly because, if having to break surface in the ice-field, a PLARB is vulnerable while exposed; and, anywhere, a ballistic-launcher's position can now be pin-pointed by satellites remarkably soon after firing although suggestions to the effect that it might be worth firing a nuclear ballistic missile at the launcher seem far-fetched.

If a 'Typhoon' does come under attack it will be a tough nut to crack: there is, as in most modern Soviet boats, strong physical emphasis on surviveability.

The 4800-nautical mile SS-N-20 missiles, with which 'Typhoon' is principally armed, are solid-fuelled with six to nine MIRVs. Thus, with the 'Deltas' and 'Typhoons', the Soviet Navy is able to target any part of the Northern hemisphere from under the ice or without ever leaving home waters: there is no longer any need to transit the risky passages through Atlantic and Pacific island gaps or run the gauntlet of US SOSUS surveillance chains.

United States Navy SSBNs

The USN currently has a total of 37 SSBNs[1] — Fleet Ballistic Missile (FBM) submarines or 'Boomers' — in its strategic fleet but, of course, only a proportion of them are on patrol: trials, training, replenishment, overhauls and transits to and from the assigned areas occupy a lot of time although, almost certainly, upkeep-related 'downtime' is less than in the Soviet navy and maintenance is much better. Ninety-four patrols were mounted in 1985, implying by simple arithmetic — perhaps too simple — that 15 to 18 'Boomers' were on station at any one time.

Two alternating crews, Blue and Gold, for each submarine ensure that seatime is maximised with 70-day patrols. All navies

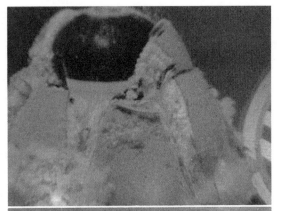

The Trident I C-4 missile (being replaced by Trident II D-5 in SSBN 734 onwards and which will also be deployed in the RN 'Vanguard' class) carries up to eight MIRVs (alternatively 6 MARVs) out to 4050 miles or, according to some sources, 4350 miles. The photographs show anti-clockwise from top: emerging from tube; clearing tube; first stage ignition; and commencement of flight trajectory.

employ the two-crew system for SSBNs.

Soviet submariners are, to say the least, a mixed lot and the older PLARBs, 'Yankees' especially, are probably crewed by conscripts who are not the pick of the bunch. By contrast, US Navy 'Boomer' crews have to meet an exactingly high standard of performance and are very well trained. The same is true of British crews; and that is fact, not chauvinism!

The bulk of the present FBM fleet is composed of 28 'Benjamin Franklin', 'Lafayette' and 'James Madison' classes which are broadly similar at 8250 tons submerged; but the 12 boats from USS *Benjamin Franklin*

Funding for 'Ohios' is massive. For example, SSBN 738 (thirteenth in line to be commissioned in December 1991) was approved at $1.256 billion in the FY 1986 program. A 6500-mile 14-MIRV D-5 missile, without vast development expenditure, costs (1988) about $67.8 million.

The size of the 16600/18700 'Ohio'-class SSBNs, although scarcely comparing with 'Typhoon', is indicated by these pictures. **Above:** USS *Michigan* (SSBN 727) building while USS *Phoenix* (SSN 702) is launched at left on 8 December, 1979. *Michigan,* second of the class numbering 10 at sea by 1989, was commissioned about three years later. **Right:** Simulated diving procedures in the control room of USS *Ohio* during pre-commissioning training October 1981. **Far right:** *Ohio's* missile tubes gaping open. **Above right:** The ballistic missile compartment in *Ohio* looking forward.

(SSBN 640) onwards are equipped with quieter machinery. A pressurised water S5W reactor and two geared turbines provide 15 000 shp for the single shaft with a maximum speed of 30 knots.

All these boats carry 16 missiles. The majority are equipped for Poseidon C-3 SLBMs which first became operational in March 1970, as the successors to Polaris A-3, with the same range of 2500 miles but carrying a greater payload of up to 14 MIRVs. There were about 300 Poseidon SLBMs available for operations by 1985 and the system is twice as accurate as Polaris A-3 — but the CEP has not been made public.

This raises a controversial question.

Patrol areas, times of sailing, transit routes and so on must be kept secret because they are crucial to the security on which an SSBN depends: but, if deterrence is really the aim, should not the full weapon capabilities be published for all sides to know?

Twelve FBM submarines were converted, between 1978 and 1982, for Trident I C-4 missiles taking eight 100-kiloton MIRVs to about 4050 n miles.

The guidance system for Trident I is smaller and lighter than that for Poseidon, thereby allowing more space for propulsion; but it has a valuable addition in the shape of a stellar sensor. The sensor takes a star sight and the flight path of the post-boost vehicle, which maneuvers to deploy re-entry vehicles after third-stage separation, is corrected by data from this to make good any errors in positional information at launch. Trident I is being equipped with Mk 500 MARVs (maneuvering re-entry vehicles) to evade ABM interceptor missiles and these are not terminally guided to improve accuracy. Boomers commissioned from 1989 will carry Trident II D-5 missiles with higher yield Mk 5 MIRVs.

A missile is normally fired from submerged with the submarine hovering or moving at a very slow speed; but launches are also possible from the surface, permitting boats in harbor (at much longer notice than the usual 15 minutes) to fire if the need arises.

The method of ejection varies in different naval systems. It is most often achieved by gas and/or steam although compressed air is used in some cases. For Poseidon and Trident missiles a small fixed rocket is ignited and its exhaust is directed through cooling water to the base of the tube. Expanding gases force the missile out and, when it has reached a specified height and distance from the submarine, the first-stage solid-fuel motor is ignited and then jettisoned after burn-out. The warheads are not armed, in any system, until this point or possibly later. There is no way that a nuclear explosion can be initiated in or near the firing submarine; nor is there the slightest possibility, in any navy, of an unauthorised or mistaken launch. The safeguards are absolute.

Firing depth, having pressurised the tubes and equalised internal/external pressure, is not unduly critical within quite broad limits for most systems.

The 'Ohios' are expensive at more than $1500 million apiece (1986 price) and that takes no account of shoreside infrastructure and support facilities. The crew is also large, and hence costly, with 16 officers and 155 enlisted men — and there are, as usual, two crews for each boat. Western navies are very slow to adopt the automation that must surely be available nowadays, as it certainly is in the Soviet fleet, and which would help to cut the heavy through-life outgoings of the personnel element. However, the 'Ohios' achieve more operational time by extending the period between 12-month overhauls to nine years: the 'Lafayettes' have to be overhauled for 22–23 months every six years.

Like all SSBNs the new Boomers have torpedo tubes forward (four in this case) which are primarily for defense but could prove very useful, against expectations, if the role was suddenly changed for some reason. Apart from the exceptional measures taken to reduce noise in their design there seems to be little if any adoption of the Soviet survive-ability concept in these or any other Western SSBNs.

Unfortunately, the fact that the US Navy managed to commission an SSBN fleet of 31 Fleet Ballistic Missile Submarines in the short space of four years (between April 1963 and April 1967) from four yards means that it is now facing block obsolescence; and there must be some doubts about the 'Ohio' building program while the USA and the USSR are debating the possibility of drastic cuts in the number of ballistic missiles deployed.

Meanwhile, it is just as well that the USN is following the Soviet path by equipping an unspecified number of nuclear attack-type submarines (SSNs) with strategic land-attack Tomahawk cruise missiles as part of their armament. Tomahawk's maximum range, for the nuclear warhead version, is quoted as 1350 n miles which does not begin to compare with 6000 n miles plus, unconfirmed but expected, for Trident II D-5 ballistic missiles; but SSNs are intended, to adapt the words of John Paul Jones, to go in harm's way. They do not require as much sea-room for security as the huge 'Ohios' which, like all SSBNs, operate on the totally different principle of avoiding ships and submarines whether friend or foe.

French SSBNs (SNLEs)[2]

France acquired her *Force de Frappe* (Striking Force) or, a more acceptable phrase today, her *Force de Dissuasion* arguably because General de Gaulle wanted to claim leadership of a *Europe des Patries*, without British competition, at a time when he thought the American nuclear guard for Europe was in danger of waning. Rejecting the American offer of Polaris in 1963 (which was to be on the same terms as Britain) de Gaulle decided to be truly independent: France, with her own nuclear weaponry, would lead Europe. The price was high.

It is difficult to see exactly where France now stands. She is not militarily in NATO (thereby losing certain invaluable training opportunities) but she maintains the Atlantic alliance; and she has lost pre-eminence in the EEC while, so far as valid dialogue with Moscow goes, she has largely given way to the West German and UK governments.

What is the purpose of the French SSBN (SNLE) Fleet today? One suggestion, to the effect that French *dissuasion* could interrupt a nuclear exchange, might seem too much like a pious hope to the Kremlin. Viewed from outside the country, one might suspect that, equipped with Gaullist thunder, France is stuck with a powerful but exceedingly expensive force — six SNLEs with two or even three constantly on patrol — which could be a little difficult to justify in the present context.

It is tempting to speculate not only on the purpose of the force but its practical problems as seen from Moscow. France does not seem to have such good support facilities

THE UK STRATEGIC DETERRENT

The first British deterrent patrol, by HMS *Resolution* Port crew (Commander M C Henry), was from June to August 1968. Since then one of the four British 'Bombers' has continuously been on station without (as claimed and believed) being detected by Soviet units. There have, however, been a few minor accidents to which HMS *Renown* seems to have been particularly prone in the past — a couple of groundings and a collision submerged with a merchant ship — and these have not been unknown in the US FBM force either, particularly around Ireland, involving navigational errors and fishing boats. None of these incidents was serious and none resulted in breaches of security although errors of this kind scarcely help to conceal SSBN movements from Soviet Intelligence.

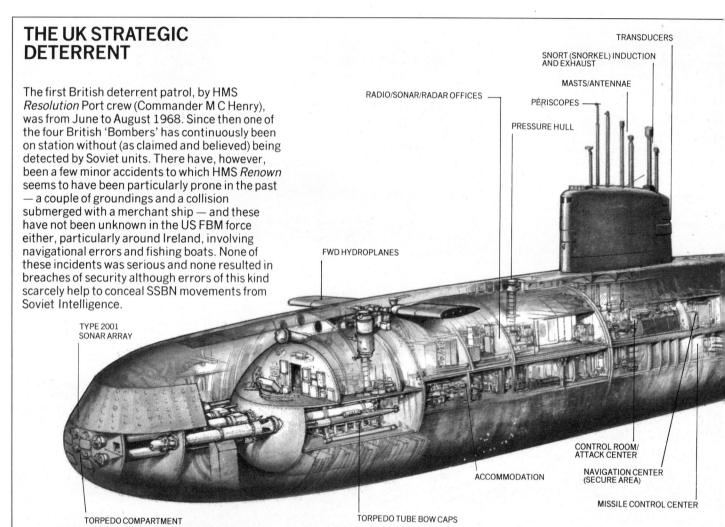

RADIO/SONAR/RADAR OFFICES

TRANSDUCERS

SNORT (SNORKEL) INDUCTION AND EXHAUST

MASTS/ANTENNAE

PERISCOPES

PRESSURE HULL

FWD HYDROPLANES

TYPE 2001 SONAR ARRAY

CONTROL ROOM/ ATTACK CENTER

ACCOMMODATION

NAVIGATION CENTER (SECURE AREA)

MISSILE CONTROL CENTER

TORPEDO COMPARTMENT

TORPEDO TUBE BOW CAPS

The advanced PWR 2 reactor (without fuel at this stage) arriving by barge at VSEL, Barrow-in-Furness, for installation in HMS *Vanguard*, due to commission in 1991 as the first of four new SSBNs to replace the existing 'Resolution' class.

as those available to the USA, UK and USSR. The 1500-n mile MSBSM-20 missiles (16 tubes in each boat) with megaton single heads, hardened against anti-ballistic missile (ABM) explosions, are now reportedly being replaced by 2500–3000-n mile M-4 missiles carrying six 150-kiloton heads (possibly MRV rather than MIRV); but, as Admiral Chernavin has doubtless noted, even the latter ranges are becoming a little restrictive in terms of sea-room and patrol areas — which is why, by 1994, it is planned to have the first of a new 15 000-ton class at sea with 6000-n mile M-5 missiles.

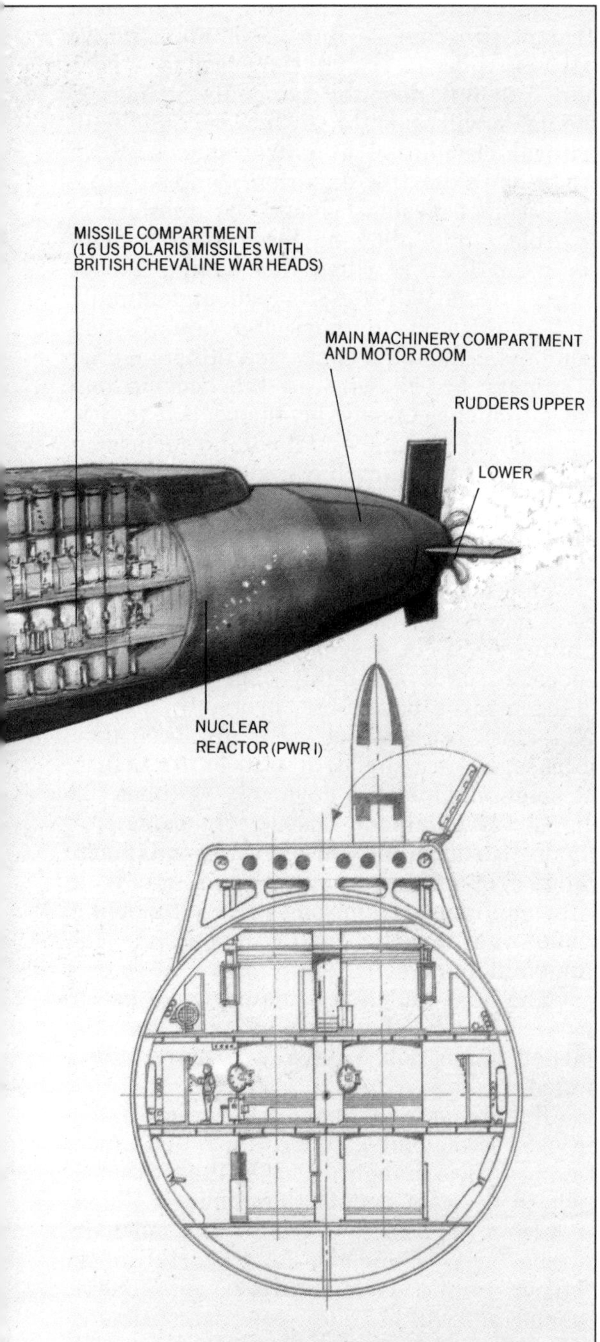

A few hints have emerged which suggest that France is considering a new approach for her submarine-launched missiles, presumably in the light of future Soviet (ABM) defenses. She clearly wants to be seen as remaining in the nuclear forefront but her political reasoning is not entirely clear. Incidentally, if a belief exists that strategic nuclear weapons are necessary to gain a place at the top table, West Germany, with no nuclear bargaining power of her own, achieved political parity with nuclear France and nuclear Britain towards the end of the 1970s. Industrial muscle, with high quality conventional forces to defend it in consort with the Alliance, was the reason for the Federal Republic being invited to join the elite. Her geographical position in the front line, host to NATO armies, certainly promoted Bonn's role; but West Germany's real strength lay in the Deutschmark which was neither being squandered on fantastic weaponry nor confused and over-stretched by unrealistic national nuclear demands.

With that passing thought, and mindful that strategic-missile submarines are wholly political by nature, let us look at SSBNs for the Royal Navy if only to guess what priority Soviet submariners afford them as targets.

British SSBNs

Political though it is, Britain's on-going acquisition of four new Trident SSBNs, to replace the ageing Polaris boats, can be examined objectively without taking sides. Party politics have fogged the whole issue and it is questionable whether British politicians in general, most of them immovably entrenched on one side or the other, have really thought the issue through in recent years. The Soviet Defense Council must be well aware of this; and things have changed since the United Kingdom first decided, in 1962, on a so-called independent nuclear policy. The USSR was then a fairly weak nuclear power: now she is immeasurably stronger than Britain while rapidly increasing her anti-ballistic missile (ABM) defenses. An objective observer might think, remembering that a nuclear launch by Britain would be suicidal, that Trident money could more advantageously be spent on many

MISSILE COMPARTMENT
(16 US POLARIS MISSILES WITH
BRITISH CHEVALINE WAR HEADS)

MAIN MACHINERY COMPARTMENT
AND MOTOR ROOM

RUDDERS UPPER

LOWER

NUCLEAR
REACTOR (PWR I)

Cross-section of HMS *Resolution* displacing 7600/8500 tons. The 'Vanguard' class will be much larger at 15 000 tonnes dived to accommodate 13.42 m, 130 000 lb Trident II D5 missiles.

more ASW submarines to help counter the threat from Soviet PLARBs.

It is impossible to say how many SSNs could be bought if Trident was abandoned (and the money is, anyway, deemed to be non-transferable) because it is not just the building costs that need to be quantified. Manning and infra-structure have to be considered in a complex equation; but, in theory, a score of advanced SSNs could be constructed without coming anywhere near the price of four Trident SSBNs and their support facilities. A total of £9.3 billion has been cited for the Trident project but never in history has any major weapon system failed to exceed the estimate — on average by 30 per cent — when the day dawns. Thus an ultimate cost of at least £11 billion (quoted by detached critics) is quite likely. (As an aside, figures of this magnitude are beyond the grasp of the average taxpayer. An amateur query amongst a dozen educated people established that not one of them knew, for sure, how many noughts there were in a billion — which should, in fact, be a milliard by current usage. They were appalled to learn that £11 000 million — £11 000 000 000 — is equivalent to a stack of £10 notes reaching 88.3 miles into the sky.

The four existing British Polaris 'Bombers' are broadly similar to the first American Boomers but have been continually updated with new equipment, Chevaline warheads and re-motored missiles since they first went to sea in the late 1960s; and the Chevaline system is currently having to be refurbished. The boats are now more than 20 years old, they have become impossibly expensive to maintain and the maximum missile range of about 2500 n miles is becoming too restrictive. Nor are the elderly Bombers as quiet as they might be.

A Chevaline-equipped missile has a penetration-aid carrier (PAC) rather similar to the American warhead bus, capable of maneuvering in space, fitted with a computer and a range of sensors to determine orientation. Warheads and 'penaids' are dispensed to confuse Soviet ABM radars which cannot distinguish between decoys and live warheads, thus hopefully saturating the defenses just as multiple warheads are intended to do. The Chevaline system is deployed at about 17 700 km/hour and the RVs re-enter the atmosphere at about 20 160 km/hour (5.6 km/second) — a speed which necessitates a protective coating against heat. Each real warhead is said to be hardened against electromagnetic

pulse (EMP) effect. It is possible that only those missiles targetted against Moscow, where the ABM defenses are especially strong, are fitted with Chevaline: three 'ordinary' 200-kiloton RVs are probably thought sufficient for other targets. However, Soviet ABM defenses are strengthening and spreading rapidly, some of them being mobile.

Assuming that the UK replacement Trident program — four 16 000-ton SSBNs each carrying 16 Trident D-5 missiles — goes ahead in full, despite arguments against it, the boats will undoubtedly be very quiet with natural circulation at patrol speeds. With American expertise, experience and backing, the Trident system should be thoroughly reliable while allowing more than enough sea-room for the single RN submarine on patrol. Soviet ASW SSNs will undoubtedly find it difficult to mark the new British Bombers although a concerted effort against a solitary SSBN, with all the eggs in one basket, might conceivably succeed if that is thought worthwhile; and it will be surprising if contingency plans have not been laid for covert minelaying and sabotage around the base in the Clyde area, possibly involving midget submarines as well as SSKs. (See Chapter 2.6).

Chinese SSBNs

Secrecy understandably surrounds the Chinese force consisting, probably, of four 'Xia'-class boats which, at about 8000 tons submerged, are similar in size to the British 'Resolution' class but have only 14 tubes for the CSS-N-3 ballistic missile which takes a single two-megaton warhead to a maximum range around 1500 n miles. There may be a later and improved missile variant following what was reported as a successful test launch in September 1984.

The next four 'Xias', now said to be on order, will probably have 16 tubes and the earlier boats could have two more tubes added.

If there are doubts about the advisability, or even desirability, of Britain and France having SSBNs in their armories there is some logic in the vast People's Republic of China acquiring an effective underwater nuclear missile force: China has no powerful allies and her situation is unique. However, Chinese submarines will have to race against time if they are going to catch up with Western and Soviet capabilities: in particular, it is hard to believe that Chinese SSBNs are anything like as quiet, yet, as the rest.

Tracks of dummy multiple re-entry vehicles heading for the US testing range near Kwajalein. The photograph illustrates the problem of trying to intercept a shower of warheads from one or more ballistic missiles, and underlines the desirability of 'Star Wars' weapons destroying missiles in space before MRVs, MIRVs or MARVs are released.

SLBM effectiveness and SSBN vulnerability

There are some interesting questions regarding SLBMs in all navies, the first of which is particularly relevant to the Soviets.

Nuclear warheads have a limited shelf life: it has not been said publicly what this is, but the Natural Resources Defense Council in the USA claimed in the 1987 edition of the Nuclear Weapons Databook (a controversial publication which the US Government says is 'not in the national interest') that America produces, on average, five new nuclear warheads a day, and at the same time withdraws four old warheads. These presumably cover the whole field of nuclear weapons but the figure gives some indication of the dating problem: total US nuclear-weapon production since 1945 has exceeded 60 000 and, during the Reagan Administration, the Department of Energy's budget to maintain weapons has risen from 3.4 billion dollars to 8 billion dollars.

In the face of such an expensive replacement requirement the sneaking suspicion arises that the Russians may not, across the board, be bothering overmuch to renew submarine missile warheads. Indeed, it is not beyond the bounds of possibility that some are actually dummies. After all, it is whispered that Britain considered concrete heads for Polaris at one time — seeing that nuclear deterrence can, in one light, be regarded as bluff anyway — but rejected the idea because the secret could not be kept in a more or less open society: credibility, the supposed basis of deterrence, would be bound to suffer. Things are quite different in the closed Soviet society and nobody on board a PLARB need know the status of missile warheads.

Just a thought, but it will be intriguing to see if efforts are made by the Soviet Navy to prevent by some means any foreign investigation of the 'Yankee' wreck which lies at a depth of three-and-a-half miles and which could be reached by deep-diving mini-subs. If Soviet activity is noted near the wreck, which is believed to be constantly watched by a surface vessel (and might be subject to NATO submarine surveillance periodically), it could be asked whether the intention is to check for radio-active leakage — which is conceivable from the warheads but unlikely from the twin reactors — or whether the warheads are being rendered safe from foreign inspection.

It is only sensible to assume that the majority of Soviet PLARBs are properly and fully equipped with the sort of SLBM characteristics openly published in the West. It has also to be assumed that a fair proportion of the missiles will take up their correct trajectory although there is good reason for thinking that some will not. There have been enough failures during carefully rehearsed test firings by Western and Soviet SSBNs to cast suspicion on the prospect of a 100 per cent correct multiple launch: the indications seem to be that 75 per cent is a more likely figure and even that could be optimistic.

Moreover, not one single ballistic 'bird' has ever been flown on a test wartime trajectory. Supposing that a 'Typhoon' assigns an SS-N-20 missile to a target 4500 km distant for instance, the apogee will be about 900 km: ballistic wind and air density corrections have to be applied although these are presumably less critical if the SS-N-20 has reliable stellar self-navigation facilities. The factors are changeable and must be added to the basic problem of predicting future target position which, so far as the missile is concerned, shifts with rotation of the earth (15° per hour) during the 22 minutes flight time.

Finally, despite claims that the ocean is being made to ring like a bell and despite Soviet suggestions that a revolutionary means of detecting SSBNs is on its way, the burden of counter-SSBN operations will continue to fall on ASW submarines for a very long time to come. SSBNs are unquestionably the most invulnerable ballistic-missile launching platforms; but, unfortunately, it is no longer rational to say that Western SSBNs are secure while at the same time claiming that Soviet PLARBs are vulnerable to attack by Western SSNs. What is sauce for the goose is sauce for the gander.

Cruise missiles

It is just possible to imagine nuclear ballistic missiles being targetted on a surface force even if their true purpose is to strike at territories. Submarine-launched cruise missiles (SLCMs), by contrast, have two separate, clearly defined roles — anti-ship and land-attack.

Cruise missiles are basically developed from the German wartime V-1 unmanned flying bomb but the modern versions are stealthy and much more sophisticated. Both the USA and the USSR mount a number of land-attack SLCMs in 'ordinary' SSNs. Each has a single warhead (nuclear or HE) and, having picked up a specific point of land, the

Salvage of a Soviet missile submarine

During the summer of 1968 a Soviet diesel-electric 'Golf'-class ballistic missile submarine (SSB) suffered a similar internal explosion and sank with all hands in mid-Pacific, where the depth was 16 600 ft. She was assumed to be carrying her full load of three SS-N-5 nuclear missiles at the time.

The story of the subsequent salvage of what was said to be only the forward (non-missile) section of the 'Golf' by the purpose-built *Glomar Explorer*, masterminded by the late Howard Hughes on behalf of the CIA for a fee of $350 million, is fogged by secrecy and understandably deliberate disinformation; but unless all the reports are utterly wrong Project Jennifer, as it was called, did demonstrate in 1973 that salvage is indeed possible at such an extreme depth, only 1400 ft short of where the 'Yankee' rests. The 'Yankee' may be partially buried but should be more or less intact (depending upon how hard she hit the seabed) because she was flooded when she was scuttled, equalising the pressure inside and out. She could, conceivably, be brought up together with her missiles.

The *Glomar Explorer* and a 'Golf' SSB are illustrated on page 113: refer also to text on that page.

THE TOMAHAWK CRUISE MISSILE

Despite inevitable teething problems Tomahawk, broadly equivalent to Soviet SS-N-21, is proving an exceptionally good SLCM and is being widely installed in USN submarines. A great advantage is that Tomahawk has nuclear and conventional HE variants.

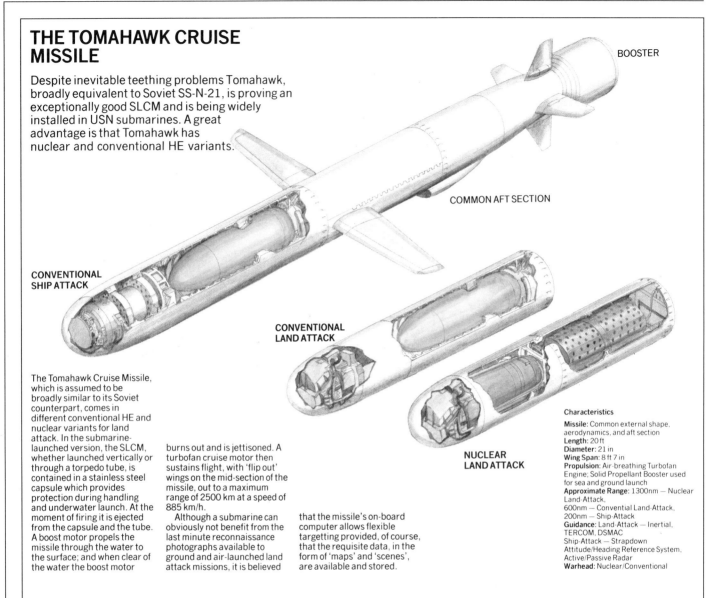

BOOSTER

COMMON AFT SECTION

CONVENTIONAL SHIP ATTACK

CONVENTIONAL LAND ATTACK

NUCLEAR LAND ATTACK

Characteristics

Missile: Common external shape, aerodynamics, and aft section
Length: 20 ft
Diameter: 21 in
Wing Span: 8 ft 7 in
Propulsion: Air-breathing Turbofan Engine; Solid Propellant Booster used for sea and ground launch
Approximate Range: 1300nm — Nuclear Land-Attack,
600nm — Convential Land-Attack,
200nm — Ship-Attack
Guidance: Land-Attack — Inertial, TERCOM, DSMAC
Ship-Attack — Strapdown Attitude/Heading Reference System, Active/Passive Radar
Warhead: Nuclear/Conventional

The Tomahawk Cruise Missile, which is assumed to be broadly similar to its Soviet counterpart, comes in different conventional HE and nuclear variants for land attack. In the submarine-launched version, the SLCM, whether launched vertically or through a torpedo tube, is contained in a stainless steel capsule which provides protection during handling and underwater launch. At the moment of firing it is ejected from the capsule and the tube. A boost motor propels the missile through the water to the surface; and when clear of the water the boost motor

burns out and is jettisoned. A turbofan cruise motor then sustains flight, with 'flip out' wings on the mid-section of the missile, out to a maximum range of 2500 km at a speed of 885 km/h.

Although a submarine can obviously not benefit from the last minute reconnaissance photographs available to ground and air-launched land attack missions, it is believed

that the missile's on-board computer allows flexible targetting provided, of course, that the requisite data, in the form of 'maps' and 'scenes', are available and stored.

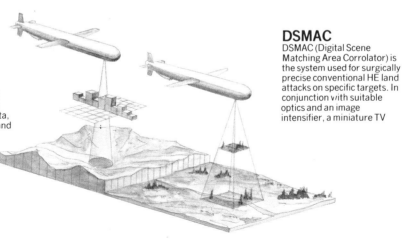

TERCOM

TERCOM (Terrain Contour Matching) allows a nuclear strike mission to be planned quickly by modelling missile performance and terrain data, analysing defense systems and selecting the appropriate TERCOM maps.

DSMAC

DSMAC (Digital Scene Matching Area Corrolator) is the system used for surgically precise conventional HE land attacks on specific targets. In conjunction with suitable optics and an image intensifier, a miniature TV

camera presents real-time video imagery to a processor: the latter, corrolating this video information, supplies final guidance corrections in the terminal phase of the SLCM flight to target. In other words, DSMAC compares optically sensed scenes of natural terrain and man-made installations with scenes stored in the missile's computer; and this discriminating information permits the guidance system to align Tomahawk for a precision strike.

The later USN 'Los Angeles' class are able to carry twelve vertically launched SLCMs and older submarines can carry four tube-launched Tomahawks each.

'bird' is guided by matching terrain contours with its own computerised map. The great advantages of an SLCM are that it is surgically precise and it can be employed in the nuclear or conventional mode. However, it is not just a matter of changing warheads: the vehicle itself is somewhat different in the alternative versions. Conventional SLCMs would be invaluable in limited war: if they had been available to Britain in 1982 they might well have cut short the Anglo-Argentinian confrontation.

The US Navy dropped its Regulus project when the program was overtaken by Polaris and did not revive the cruise concept until quite recently with Tomahawk. The Soviet Navy, on the other hand, followed a twin-track SLBM-SLCM path from the start. Successive improvements have led to the tube-launched SS-N-21 cruise, with a range of 1600 miles for 'Victor III' and later classes of SSN, and a larger SLCM perhaps associated with a totally new class of purpose-built land-attack SSGNs: SS-N-24 is thought to have a range of 2000 n miles or more.

The US Navy's 1350-n mile Tomahawk has performed extremely well during tests and an even more stealthy ground-hugging weapon is promised. The 'Los Angeles' class SSNs laid down before 1982 are able, or will be able, to carry 12 Tomahawks as part of the torpedo-tube launch load; and later boats of the class are equipped with 15 vertical launch tubes in the bow outside the pressure hull, thus not interfering with the torpedo and tactical missile capacity.

Tactical cruise missiles

Russian submarine-launched anti-ship missiles have been around a long time: the Soviet Navy has been alone in pursuing a continuous and extensive building program of anti-ship SLCMs in SSGNs while latterly equipping some ASW SSNs with land-attack cruise missiles — which may give a clue to where some of the ASW boats will operate in war. The distinction between tactical and strategic boats has become blurred although SSBNs must still be considered as purely strategic — barring the faint possibility of targetting large surface forces with ballistic missiles and even then the purpose could be deemed strategic.

By 1986 the Soviet Navy was operating a variety of tactical cruise-missile boats. The diesel-electric 'Juliett' and the nuclear 'Echo II' classes have to surface to launch their missiles: but with about ten of the latter now

equipped with the 270-n mile SS-N-12 (superceding the SS-N-3a which is probably limited to 50 miles for all practical purposes) these classes remain a notable threat, particularly if Airborne Early Warning (AEW) is scant in the area.

The 17 SSGNs of the 'Charlie I' and 'Charlie II' classes, with a submerged capability for 35-n mile SS-N-7 and 60-n mile SS-N-9 missiles respectively, are more of a menace, despite the shorter ranges, because they are less detectable when firing.

The huge 'Oscar' boats, five of which are probably in service by now, carry 24 340-n mile SS-N-19 missiles and, at 35 knots, are 12 knots faster than the 'Charlies'. The 'Oscars' could operate more or less at will on the bow of a Task Group. A 14 000-ton 'Oscar' is particularly well designed for surviveability with three meters or more between the outer and inner hulls, excellent sonar, ESM and radar, and effective quieting for all machinery. Counting the secondary armament of six 533-mm and 650-mm torpedo tubes (16 reloads) 'Oscar' is perhaps the supreme example of a comprehensive, fully

Above: USS *Grayback* (SSG-574) equipped with the twelve-ton Regulus II land-attack cruise-missile. This SLCM, said to be developed from Regulus I to ease its passage through the funding system but actually a totally new missile properly designated SSM-N-9, carried a nuclear warhead at twice the speed of sound to a maximum range of more than 1000 miles and had an excellent inertial guidance system. USS *Growler* was similarly equipped and so was the purpose-built *Halibut* (SSGN 587) commissioned in 1960.

Left: In the event *Grayback* was the only boat to launch a Regulus II (on 16 September, 1958) because efforts were switched to ballistic missiles: the 70 existing Regulus II 'birds' were used, mainly ashore, for training and evaluations. The last deterrent patrol by a US submarine carrying land-attack SLCMs (Regulus I) was conducted in 1964 by which time some 30 SSBNs were in service or nearing completion; but the abandoning of Regulus II lost valuable time for America in the cruise-missile field while the Soviets seized on the idea.

Top: Soviet 3000/3750-ton 'Juliett' SSG, built 1961-68, equipped with four tubes for SS-N-3A surface-launch anti-ship missiles with radar mid-course guidance, and 18 torpedoes for six 533 mm bow tubes. 'Juliett' is slow with a maximum speed of 12 knots on the surface and dived.
Above: A Soviet 5500-ton (dived) 'Charlie II'-class SSGN with 8 tubes for 60 n mile SS-N-9 anti-ship SLCMs, 14 torpedoes for 6 533 mm tubes, and a top speed of 24 knots from (unusually) only one PW reactor for one steam turbine developing 15 000 shp for the single shaft.

integrated and independent weapon system; but it can certainly coordinate its operations with surface and/or airborne units. The larger torpedo tubes are for wake-homers to supplement a missile attack on high value units (HVUs).

The USN, RN and certain other navies, notably Australia and Japan, employ the reliable and exceptionally well-tested Harpoon anti-ship missile which can be launched in virtually any sea conditions from tactically convenient depths. It is propelled at high subsonic speed by a turbo-jet engine out to a range of 70 or 80 n miles but in practice usually less. Like all anti-ship missiles it has a homing system designed to counter countermeasures: the latest developments are highly classified but the original system was an active radar-seeker which searched, locked on, and finally commanded an abrupt pull-up and swoop-down onto the target from above following a sea-skimming approach.

France, as always well up in the missile field, has the SM39, an adaptation of Exocet, with a range of around 30 n miles. The system is being installed in all but the first (*Rubis*) of the SSN (SNA)[3] fleet.

It would be logical, and characteristic, for the French Navy to develop exceptionally advanced anti-ship and land-attack cruise missiles in the fairly near future.

Long-range missile engagements require high-performance sonar and electronic sensors together with secure communications if they are to succeed. The Soviet aim is to coordinate missile launches — from subsurface, surface and airborne platforms — so that all the weapons arrive simultaneously in the target area. It is not an easy tactic to perform; and somewhere along the line ASW submarines ought to get wind of an impending attack from their sonar and/or ESM equipment aided by external intelligence.

The question for the defenders, of course, is where to station ASW SSNs in relation to a surface force. If they are too close they risk mutual interference; too far and they become so spread out that only chance will permit submarine-versus-submarine engagements. SSNs have been evaluated in the close and distant escort role but formal escorting seems, in general, to have been abandoned. In any case NATO SSNs would most economically and advantageously be employed where Soviet submarines are most highly concentrated. Although a fair number of enemy boats may well operate against a Carrier Group their density will not be high; so the most productive ASW operations will probably take place in choke points, as far forward as possible, where geography or minefields imply a reasonably dense enemy submarine population. The old adage of attack being the best means of defense is still valid — and the earlier the better.

END NOTES
1. 1988 total: it may well be reduced by Arms Limitation agreements, before or soon after, publication of this book, as well as by virtue of greater missile/warhead numbers in 'Ohio' SSBNs.
2. SNLE: Sous-marin nucléaire lance-engines.
3. SNA: Sous-marin nucléaire attaque.

1.9

UNDER THE ARCTIC ICE

Three American nuclear attack submarines, USS *Ray* (SSN-653), *Hawkbill* (SSN-666), and *Archerfish* (SSN-678) surfaced together at the North Pole during Exercise ICEX 86-1. HMS *Superb* (SSN), USS *Sea Devil* (SSN-664) and USS *Billfish* (SSN-676) repeated the demonstration a year later and something similar may well become an annual event.

The intention, with good media coverage, is obvious: although individual submarines — American, British and Russian — have appeared on the surface at the Pole and elsewhere in the ice-covered Arctic Ocean many times since USS *Skate* (SSN-578) first sat at the very top of the world on 17 March 1959, here is proof that the United States Navy, as well as the Royal Navy, can operate with force in what has come to be regarded as a Soviet bastion. Admiral James D Watkins, then Chief of Naval Operations, had given a strong hint in 1983 about future operations when he acknowledged that the US Navy was 'putting increased emphasis' on under-ice patrols to counter the 'strong interest' displayed by the Russians in deploying their submarines under the protection of the frozen waste. As Admiral Watkins remarked, it is 'a beautiful place to hide' and the Russians have been understandably coy about displaying themselves there: only the 'November'-class SSN *Leninsky Komsomolets* has been pictured (in 1962) at the Pole.

Incidentally, as remarked elsewhere, the Canadian government has shown resentment about American Arctic operations because of the possible implication that the submarines concerned have to pass through parts of the Northwest Passage which Canada claims as her own but which the USA regards as international. This appears to have strengthened the Canadian government's mind considerably in opting for an expensive SSN nuclear fleet.

It is not surprising that Soviet SSBNs favor the Polar ice-cap so strongly as a haven when missiles launched from forward Arctic patrol areas *en route* to American targets would give as little, or less, warning of their approach than from exposed areas off US coasts. But short flight times and protection for SSBNs (and possibly SSGNs) is by no means the only, or even the primary, reason for the Soviet Navy's anxiety to dominate whole vast areas.

A mercator projection affords no idea of the Arctic's importance to the USSR or, come to that, the United States and Canada; but a glance at the globe shows immediately how crucial it is to the defense of the Soviet homeland.

The Arctic naturally gained its importance only with the arrival of nuclear submarines: before that it was a barrier completing to the North, where Russia has 8166 nautical miles of Arctic coastline, the buffers to the West and South which have been established by satellite states, neutrals and water.

The technology of nuclear power has removed that northern barrier; and, in April, the edge of the Marginal Sea Ice Zone (MIZ) is less than 300 n miles from the Kola Peninsula. It would be surprising if the USSR did not feel naked and exposed to submarine attack by ballistic or cruise missiles from the Arctic Ocean.

Conversely, because another glance at the globe shows that the shortest distance between East and West lies North and South — that is across the Arctic Ocean — the threat to the North American Continent is also increased by nuclear power. Hence, the naval power that can control the depths beneath the ice cover of this virtually landlocked central ocean will achieve a dominant strategic position which can be used for deterrence or terminating war on favorable terms if deterrence fails. At present, the Arctic is something of a strategic vacuum, a kind of No Man's Land through which two great maritime powers are racing to establish precedence and control. Meanwhile, Canada, a deeply interested party, is evidently willing to devote substantial resources to re-establishing her rights and security in a part of the area as well.

The Arctic is therefore bound to be the scene of vigorous, urgent combat in war and highly competitive maneuvering in peace with the strong possibility of covert skirmishing if tension rises. It is paramount for all involved to learn everything possible about this strange and eerie region which only submarines can penetrate, where submarine-versus-submarine engagements (described by Admiral Gorshkov as 'battles of the first salvo') are inevitable if fighting breaks out and where close encounters during surveillance and exploratory operations are highly probable.

Soviet knowledge of the Arctic is bound to be more extensive than that of Western submariners while the Canadians will have to start there virtually from scratch with their projected fleet of nuclear boats. However, a great deal of information has been amassed since the 1960s by American and British boats, the latter including a few diesel-electric submarines which have penetrated quite far into the field and gained especially useful experience at the ice edge. The French, too, have mounted operations in the region, although not on a large scale, and the Chinese are now showing concern for cold waters.

It is a formidable task to chart an area the size of the United States, most of it under permanent pack ice, and predict environmental conditions at different times of the year. Only about one per cent of the Arctic ocean floor is adequately mapped on Western charts; but it can be assumed that at least the principal routes and a fair number of SSBN patrol zones are now accurately charted and annotated with comprehensive underwater warfare data for Soviet submarines.

Before analysing the peculiar characteristics of this future battlefield it will be as well to examine more deeply its strategic value to NATO. In most people's minds, and certainly in the great majority of articles on the subject, the Arctic is associated almost exclusively with the USSR, implying that Western submarines which venture there are more or less intruding into Soviet waters. Nothing could be further from the truth: the ocean is 'up for grabs' and there is absolutely no legal reason why Western submarines should not patrol it. The advantages of so doing are not immediately obvious — and, again, that is the fault of mercator projections.

While most strategists concentrate on submarine warfare in the Atlantic and Pacific Oceans and in the Norwegian Sea they forget the impact which a sustained Western submarine threat in the Arctic Ocean would have, psychologically and militarily, on the Red Banner Northern Fleet: this embodies a large proportion of the Soviet Navy's offensive power including 60 per cent of its modern SSBN fleet and 50 per cent of its total submarine strength.

The results of establishing a permanent NATO submarine force in the Arctic should prove manifold and markedly beneficial to the West. Soviet SSBNs and supportive-defensive general purpose forces — together constituting a kind of 'fleet in being' – would be rendered vulnerable to American SSNs which could use the now well-known Polar approach routes to the Northern Fleet operating area; the number of 'Northern' SLBMs available to the USSR, for first or follow-on strikes, might be reduced; early attrition of the Northern Fleet ought to contribute significantly to the possibility of early war termination on favorable terms for NATO; and the way would be at least partially cleared for projecting the full range of NATO naval power — Carrier Battle Groups, amphibious forces and cruise-missile submarines — against the Soviet mainland. In the meantime, the Soviet Northern Fleet would have to extend its defensive coverage along the whole northern flank and hence lessen its striking power elsewhere. The Soviet Supreme High Command would be faced with major force allocation problems by this effective variation of the deterrent concept — deterrence by division, the prevention of force concentration — turning the tables on the Soviet Navy which has itself been using its submarines worldwide for this very purpose for a long time.

All things considered, there is much to be said in favor of deploying a sizeable NATO submarine force on a permanent basis to this unpublicised ocean which has so far failed to catch the public or military imagination to any great extent. As a minimum we should

surely oblige the Soviet Navy to recognise that an Arctic force is a distinct possibility which has to be guarded against. Here, there is again scope for bluff. To repeat, bluff is something at which the Russians themselves excel and we could well emulate them.

But, self-evidently, Arctic deployment requires specialized equipment, expertise and knowledge. So what has in fact been learned about this claustrophobic setting for submarine-versus-submarine warfare?

The Soviet Union comprises more than half of the ocean's shores while Canada, Alaska and Finland virtually complete the circle together with numerous islands at the periphery. The approaches are shallow and, in places, tortuous but the central waters are land-free with depths ranging between 3–4000 m. The permanent ice-cap grows and shrinks seasonally while fairly constant and predictable water movements are determined by the great currents of the Pacific and Atlantic Oceans and by the earth's rotation.

Dangers of the ice
The floating raft of ice is at its maximum in April/May and at its minimum in September/October. The thickness varies from a few centimeters to some 50 m independently of the season. Expressed as a root mean square value the 'average draught' is about six or seven meters; but the figure is not very helpful and could be misleading because it is the differentials, caused by continual compression, traction and tilting of the pack, which concern the submariner. Ridges and dangerous 'keels' often abut onto gaps or

Joint American-British operations under the ice, culminating in a surface rendezvous at the North Pole, have seen conducted every year since the mid-1980s: the scene in May 1988 was similar to that above in 1987 but with different participants. **Left:** US SSN after surfacing through ice with sailplanes necessarily turned to the vertical position.

leads which are created, usually frozen over to a depth of a few centimeters, by the effects of wind or current on the raft of solid ice. The opening formed is known by its Russian name *polynya* which may be practically any size or shape: sometimes a *polynya* is large enough to accommodate a submarine, sometimes it is not; but it is these thin patches which a submarine tries to surface in if possible; and they are clearly revealed either by special ice-detector sonar, upward looking echosounders, assisted by *TV* monitors or, indeed, visually through the periscope in daylight because the water is astonishingly clear.

A *polynya* may often be discovered only at the last moment when the boat passes beneath it, especially if it is bordered by keels: if the submarine cannot stop quickly enough it must execute a 'Williamson turn' —

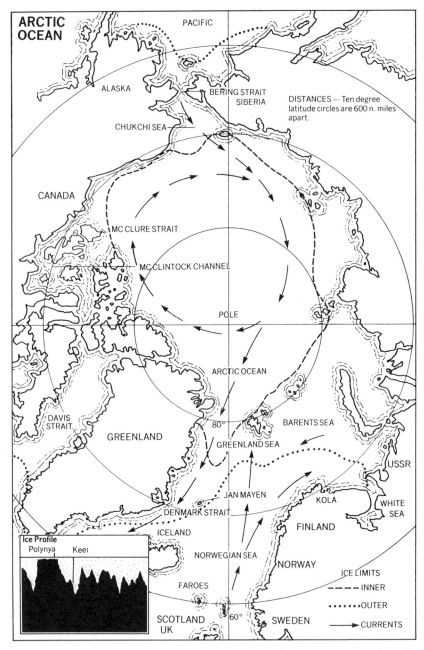

Above: The Arctic Ocean showing inner and outer limits and the most significant currents. **Inset:** schematic ice profile with a *polynya* and adjacent keels.

are generally good: the sound velocity profile (SVP) is usually positive all the way down because the ice is a wholly effective shield against solar heating and the water is thoroughly mixed by currents. The positive gradient produces the characteristics of a deep sound channel — normally only found at depths of 1000 m or more in the open Atlantic — with its axis at or near the surface. Sound, aided by the cylindrical spreading common to the more usual deep sound channels, can travel great distances with no thermoclines to deflect it, very little ambient or biological noise and no surface shipping to interfere. On the other hand, occasional gross salinity variations have dramatic effects on vertical and horizontal sound paths; noise is attenuated by the vertical surfaces of 'keels'; and the irregular underside of the pack causes sound in the sea to be reflected randomly. Active sonar transmissions, whether from a submarine or a torpedo, are obviously bound to suffer from heavy reverberations.

Ambient noise at the ice edge — the MIZ — is high by contrast, varying in degree with meteorological states which cause greater or lesser grinding, collision and melting noises.

A missile submarine on station, as opposed to a transitter, may therefore be able to hide under a *polynya* or a thinnish patch — possibly resting with slight positive buoyancy against the ice above if it is not too thin — behind the protection of surrounding keels; or it may select an area of high masking noise at the ice edge. Either way, it is doubtful whether weapons and sensors designed for open ocean operations are as well suited to under-ice encounters. The Arctic is a very difficult environment for acoustic homing torpedoes but it is assumed that the USN Mk 48 Mod 4 ADCAP and British Spearfish torpedoes have been given means of overcoming the problems to some extent. Fortunately, those problems are shared by both sides and, on the whole, it seems unlikely that Soviet submarines — which are generally on the defensive in the Arctic — have any better ASW equipment than their Western counterparts. However, it could be that some Soviet submarine computer software is specifically designed for dealing with the difficulties.

Communications are sometimes adversely affected under the ice, particularly for Western boats whose VLF transmitters are very distant, but much less so for Soviet submarines whose shore transmitters are relatively close. It is impractical to deploy a communications buoy although trailing wire

a 60° alteration of course immediately followed by full wheel in the opposite direction to bring the boat back to the opening on a reciprocal track.

Icebergs, calving from Greenland's glaciers at the rate of about 12 000 every year, constitute a danger when the currents take them southwards down the Davis and Denmark Straits because they can project 400 m below the surface: a transiting submarine may find it impossible to go beneath a berg and it can take hours to find a way around it.

Sonar conditions under the solid icepack

antennae for VLF reception can be streamed effectively, because ice propagates radio signals well; but the submarine must be virtually stopped beneath keels so as to allow the buoyant wire to find its own way up between them. Russian boats probably enjoy fairly reliable VLF reception in most places and, anyway, at least one Soviet ELF station is already fully operational: ELF signals, although very limited in content, are unaffected by ice to all intents and purposes and they are not subject to ionic interference — Polar-Cap Disturbance (PCD) — which upsets VLF signals for days at a time during periods of high sunspot activity. The new American and forthcoming British ELF shore stations will improve matters for NATO boats even if the messages can be no more than alerting bells.

In other words, good conditions — meaning reliable command and control — are pretty well assured for Soviet submarines throughout the Arctic Ocean but continuous C^{3}I for Western boats is less certain.

Needless to say, a submarine cannot itself transmit messages unless it breaks through the ice. Submarine-to-submarine underwater communications are possible out to a certain range, just as they are in the open ocean, but messages may well be blurred by reverberations. Computers in Soviet boats are probably able not only to unscramble coded underwater messages but also to clarify distorted signals.

Very accurate navigation (associated with accurate missile delivery) is possible by bottom-contour soundings and the Soviet Navy has, doubtless, minutely relevant charted areas of the Arctic seabed.

Inertial navigation systems (SINS) are not continuously reliable to the necessary degree, by themselves, in Soviet PLARBs: their readouts are presumably updated by radio aids, using the floating wire antenna, but Western aids like OMEGA and LORAN C are not good enough for ballistic boats in the Arctic. Satellite navigation requires an antenna above the surface.

Most PLARBs would prefer to surface through thinly covered *polynyas* or in leads at the ice fringe because, although strong enough to avoid damage, the flat topside over the missile compartment on 'Deltas' implies a possibility of bringing up heavy blocks when surfacing through thick ice. Blocks could present a problem when trying to open missile doors and hatches although listing the boat — which is advisable in any event for a

surface launch to avoid the possibility of fall-back — might help to shift the weight: there are guide rails around the casing for crewmen's safety harnesses if men have to come out and help. Delay is then inevitable but that would not be a stopper to PLARBs of any type sheltering beneath the ice; and the delay might not be longer than the assumed readiness-time of 15 minutes for the missiles themselves.

It is simple for Soviet submarines to reach the Arctic Ocean: the ice edge is no more than a day distant from the northern ports and, although there are some extensive shallow patches which are best avoided en route to deep water, it should be fairly plain sailing for them. It is also easy enough for NATO submarines if they decide to risk a passage through the Denmark Strait (which may be mined) and the Norwegian and Greenland Seas. However, it is more likely that US SSNs will transit — for reasons of time and the avoidance of Soviet opposition — through the Bering Strait and Chukchi Sea (the western part of the Northwest Passage) from the Pacific or through the Davis, Barrow and McClure Straits (the eastern part of the Northwest Passage) from the Atlantic.

The Straits are navigationally constrained and there are constant hazards of grounding and collision with ice. The use of high frequency ice-detection active sonar, with a bearing accuracy in the order of plus or minus two degrees, cannot be avoided for much of the way; and this is liable to counter-detection by enemy submarines if they have established patrols along the lengthy passages. Sonar conditions are poor initially because of marginal ice activity, but they improve rapidly as a transit progresses towards the Polar region. The classification of any possible contact is, naturally, simple: everything other than enemy submarines is eliminated from the question. But a transitter is at a considerable disadvantage compared with an SSN on patrol: not only does he have to reveal his presence by active sonar but he has to advance at best speed while, from time to time, maneuvering radically to avoid navigational hazards — all of which implies that he is quite likely to be discovered by passive means.

Whether or not the transitter can be successfully attacked is a different matter: chance will play a large part in that and a degree of risk will have to be accepted. A large number of American SSNs — perhaps most of the 637 'Sturgeon' class and several

The first attempt

In 1931 the gallant Australian explorer Sir Hubert Wilkins attempted to reach the North Pole in the rickety old ex-USN submarine *O-12*, rechristened *Nautilus* at a ceremony which Lady Wilkins concluded by emptying a bucket of ice over the bow.

The boat was fitted with a hydraulically cushioned bowsprit and a guide-arm like a trolley car for sliding, with positive buoyancy, under the ice: Wilkins reckoned that the submarine would automatically bob up to the surface when it came to a *polynya*. *Nautilus* was also prudently equipped with three vertical drills to bore air holes through the pack from beneath.

The submarine was obsolete and in poor shape to begin with; and the appointed skipper, Sloan Danenhower (a former submariner but now a partner in the firm of Lake and Danenhower) lacked practically every ability required of a submarine captain. As Wilkins mildly remarked, 'he was not always of a character conducive to maximum efficiency'.

The *Nautilus* repeatedly broke down on her way across the Atlantic and the crew did not relish the idea of venturing under the ice where reliability would be paramount. In fact they were thoroughly frightened.

When the boat paused at Bergen for stores somebody sabotaged the stern planes hoping, presumably, to bring the project to a halt. Wilkins, determined to a fault, was not going to give up. Stern planes would not, he said, be needed because the boat would be sledding along under the ice and under control: in case the guide-bar failed the upper surfaces of the hull has been made smooth and

of the 688 'Los Angeles' type, following the 'Nautilus', *Skate*, *Sea Dragon* and *Sargo* pioneers — have accomplished under-ice missions successfully. So have a good many British boats. There have been some close calls but, so far, no disasters.

The first SSN to navigate to the Arctic through the Bering and Chukchi seas was USS *Nautilus* (SSN-571) which passed under the geographic North Pole on 3 August, 1958. The shallow route into the deep North Canadian Basin was blocked repeatedly by ice ridges extending as much as 80 ft down from the surface even in summer. Time and again Commander Bill Anderson was forced to double back and try fresh routes before he reached the Arctic Ocean proper. On one occasion, the submarine, which measured 50 ft from keel to top of the sail, had to pass under an 80-ft deep ridge in just 142 ft of water leaving only six feet of clearance above and below. This was during the first attempt to penetrate and, because the sonar equipment could not detect ice keels until they were nearly overhead, Anderson wisely discontinued the mission and returned to Pearl Harbor to be fitted with better equipment before making a second and successful voyage to the Pole. When Commander Jim Calvert followed in USS *Skate* (SSN-578), actually surfacing at the Pole on March 17, 1959 during his second voyage, the transit was also, to say the least, exciting — and it has never ceased to be so since. Nevertheless, the routes are now known and they are feasible.

However, it would be decidedly dangerous to send a submarine to the Arctic, even if properly equipped and hardened, without thorough and extensive training. A first requirement is to learn how to hover and descend or rise vertically — no easy matter for a submarine displacing several thousand tons although some form of computer-assisted trimming is sometimes available nowadays, particularly in Soviet boats. When pitching is the problem there is, in fact, nothing to beat the old-fashioned custom of ordering crew members (the fatter the better) to run forward or aft as necessary. Trimming aside, the team has to become familiar with the traces which ice-detection sonar and upward looking echo-sounders (fathometers) produce and understand very clearly what they and the television pictures signify. Ice detectors can be tested during rehearsals, albeit not very satisfactorily, by passing under another submerged submarine simu-

lating an ice keel. Then there are heating appliances to be tested, high-latitude navigational equipment to be checked, fire damage-control procedures and a host of other drills to be practised. All this takes time: a submarine cannot be deployed under the ice at a sudden whim.

Most Soviet boats destined for under-ice operations have more than one propeller and this seems a wise precaution in case of damage. The little 'egg-beater' emergency propeller which can be lowered through the pressure hull in Western SSNs is probably sufficient to get them out of trouble at slow speed.

An SSBN or SSGN under the ice field has to surface in order to fire its missiles but an SSN on transit or patrol should not normally need to surface at all unless it is imperative to make a radio transmission or, less likely, to check navigation by radio aids or satellite: nevertheless, it would be very rash for an SSN not to know how to come up in an emergency.

The technique is to control upward rate very carefully, with no forward movement, so that the ice is rapped sufficiently hard to crack it but not hard enough to damage the sail and hence the periscopes, antennae and other indispensable equipment. It is perfectly possible, as first demonstrated by USS *Sargo* (SSN-583) in January and February 1960, for a standard SSN to break through two feet of solid ice. However, it was found then that, quite apart from deep keels, the ice was extremely uneven and when the submarine surfaced an enormous undetected block, five feet thick and measuring 15×20 ft, was resting on the after casing. The block weighed 13 tons but fortunately did little harm. The first British SSK to penetrate really deep under the pack, the diesel-electric HMS *Grampus* (in company with HMS *Porpoise*) had a similar experience when surfacing in a supposedly large enough *polynya* in 1963. The casing was badly dented and so was the bow sonar dome — but the damage could have been avoided if the commanding officer (the author as it happens) had not impatiently blown main ballast when part of the boat was still caught under the surrounding ice.

Finding a thinnish patch is difficult enough but maneuvering up and into it is greatly complicated by current and ice movement which can relatively displace, shrink or eliminate a *polynya* in minutes; and when the submarine is finally on the surface the ice pack may close in very quickly, threatening to crush the outer hull or superstructure and making it difficult to break loose and submerge vertically out of danger.

The limiting thickness of ice, for breaking through safely, is probably about three feet nowadays for hardened submarines although it is almost certainly more for specially shaped boats like the giant Soviet 'Typhoon'. But the possibility of an undetected miniridge a few feet away, resulting in an extremely heavy and damaging block being lifted, has to be remembered.

When the echo-sounder and detection gear suddenly show that there is very little space between the ice overhead and the bottom emergency measures, never much favored by submariners, may have to be resorted to — fast. Blowing main ballast for a few seconds with main vents open, resulting in temporary positive buoyancy (countered, if necessary, by almost immediately flooding and then blowing a negative tank) has proved one way of avoiding rapidly shoaling water without hitting the ice overhead — but it is a nerve-wracking pastime. The rudder-angle may well have to be limited, perhaps to three or five degrees, in order to avoid the possibility of pitching caused by large helm orders; but if more rudder *has* to be used — to avoid a keel ahead — blowing and flooding ballast tanks may again be necessary.

Mines under the ice are a man-made hazard and a singularly unpleasant one. The prevailing lack of minesweepers compared with the multitude of submarine minelayers is nowhere so marked as in the Arctic. There is, in fact, no way yet of neutralising mines below the ice-field: they remain a menace until either their life expires or they claim their victims. Although not much is apparently known about the performance of systems like the American CAPTOR there is little doubt that smart mines of some sort would work in the environment and ordinary ground mines — laid, of course, by submarines — would be just as effective as in the open sea. In deep water it is not impossible to conceive mines being suspended from the ice. Soviet and Western submarines will seek to keep their Arctic routes and patrol areas secret; but here again the West is at a disadvantage because NATO submarines must at some stage pass through choke points, some of which are very narrow.

ASW submarines by themselves will be hard put to patrol an area three times the size of the Mediterranean. Are there any other ASW systems which can supplement their searches? It is theoretically possible to plant SOSUS-type chains on the seabed and link them with transmitters on the ice surface but it has to be remembered that the pack moves — at an average rate of 5000 m a day depending on the season — and that could raise substantial difficulties. It is also possible to hang acoustic sensors below the ice and monitor them from the air or from satellites: it is believed that submarines have been associated with experiments of this kind. But how long will an aircraft or helicopter survive in the Arctic against opposing forces? And what ASW unit will prosecute a contact gained? Presumably the answer to the last question is an ASW SSN because it would be impossible even for monitoring V/STOL aircraft or helicopters to put weapons into the water in most areas; but close co-operation between airborne ASW platforms and ASW submarines is notoriously fraught with danger for the latter and without constant tactical communications and precise relative navigation — both of which are dubious — that danger would be greater than usual.

It will be surprising if Soviet submarines on the surface in leads, *polynyas* or at the ice edge do not have an anti-aircraft missile at the ready; and because surfaced submarines are so hard to see amongst the ice it may be that aircraft will come off second best in the detection and attack game. So, all in all, it looks as though ASW submarines will have to do the job as best they can without much support.

It has been said often enough that a submariner's greatest enemy is the sea itself: with unpredictable ice re-inforcing that already powerful enemy's strength the Arctic Ocean is totally relentless and always challenging. It was no accident that Admiral Chernavin, as a Captain Third Rank, made his name under the ice; that Captain Yuriy A Sysosev, later Commander-in-Chief of the Pacific Fleet, was made a Hero of the Soviet Union for surfacing the *Leninsky Komsomolets* at the North Pole in 1963; or that Captain First Rank Arkadiy P Mikhalovskiy, who took an SSN from the Kola to the Pacific via the Arctic in the same year, eventually relieved Chernavin as Commander of the Northern Fleet. Heroes all — and, although they might modestly decline the title, so are the American, British and French submariners who have taken their boats into what are undeniably dangerous and still largely unexplored waters.

rounded so, in his lone view there was no reason to think there would be any problem.

Unfortunately there were several problems.

Firstly, one of the drills jammed in the partially raised position: so much for the smooth upper hull form. Secondly, Danenhower either did not understand trimming or was scared into maintaining an absurd amount of positive buoyancy — 30 tons in fact. Efforts to slide at speed under a floe were spectacular but abortive.

Reluctantly, Wilkins gave up. Thankfully, the crew set course for Bergen. The explorer died just before the object of his dreams was realised by USS *Skate*. Jim Calvert reverently scattered Sir Herbert's ashes at the Pole.

1.10

RE-EMERGENCE OF THE MIDGETS

Numerous alarms and excursions in Scandinavian — mainly Swedish — waters since 1962 (some say ten years before that) are a sharp reminder that very small submersibles can penetrate harbors and inlets where their bigger brethren cannot, or dare not, go; and a special branch of the Soviet Navy has about 200 of the little beasts. When Sweden openly accused Russia of submarine incursions plaguing its 1670-nautical mile coastline, the Soviet Premier retorted: 'Present your proof if you have any. Then we can talk about violations'. It was a significant remark implying how exceedingly difficult it is to catch tiny submarines in coastal waters.

General Bengt Gustaffson, the Swedish Supreme Commander, presented Prime Minister Carlsson with a paper listing 40 contacts with foreign submarines (no specific mention of size) in Swedish waters between April and September 1987 alone. Another high-ranking officer declared: 'We found, for example, fresh bottom tracks in Eastern Coastal waters this summer in the middle of a sensitive military installation. The Russians may want us to believe that we've got giant prehistoric centipedes here, but they certainly make peculiar noises that tally with noise-prints of Soviet submarines in our archives'.

Sweden is not alone as a target. Late in 1985 there was an unconfirmed report of unidentified midget activity off Brazil; there have been mini-submarine tracks in San Francisco Bay similar to those found in the Herfsjardeng, Sweden; and, despite official denials, Japan (notably Hokkaido which, of course, is in the front line for invasion from the North) has suffered incursions as well as South Korea. Apart from alleged Soviet activity, the West German government has blocked the export of a four-man midget to North Korea but doubtless there will be other willing suppliers. Iran has started to build a miniature submarine fleet which is expected to number a dozen craft before long; Libya is keenly concerned with midgets; and it is

rumored that other countries bordering the Mediterranean are showing renewed interest in so-called human torpedoes.

While the maritime world concentrates its thoughts on the strategic implications of giant nuclear submarines, a threat has been quietly developing at the very bottom of the submarine size-scale. Sooner, rather than later, it will have to be seriously addressed: the midgets, so successful during the last war, have re-emerged.

Speculation about Soviet midget incursions is supported by remarkably few hard facts; or, rather, not much information has been made public — which usually means that not much is known. Midget submarines are easily kept secret and hidden: it may be that the best way of gauging dwarfish underwater warfare today and tomorrow is to glance briefly at some major midget achievements of the past; establish the reasons for success and failure; try to determine how the lessons learned could be applied now with the benefit of present-day technology derived, in part, from commercial mini-subs; and see what wartime designs were promising for further development.

During the last war there were three kinds of mini-submersibles — chariots, human torpedoes and more or less independent midget submarines. None of them engaged in anti-submarine warfare but

Suicide spelled failure

Except in the Imperial Japanese Navy, where most sneak craft were in effect suicidal, human torpedoes were mis-named. In their most successful Italian and British form they were indeed modelled on torpedoes but they were not suicide craft: the war-heads were detachable and fastened to target hulls — the targets, of course, being moored or anchored in harbor. The Italians, in the lead with these initially, delivered some devastating attacks. Most notably, three two-man *Maiali* ('pigs') crippled the 30 000-ton British battleships *Valiant* and *Queen Elizabeth* (together with a valuable tanker and destroyer) in Alexandria harbor on 21 December, 1941: the balance of power in the Mediterranean was thereby upset, by six men riding three pigs, in the space of a few minutes. Elsewhere pigs and very similar British 'chariots' were responsible for in-flicting heavy losses at minimal cost to the attackers in terms either of men or *matériel*. In fact, the *Decima Flottiglia Mas*, which incorporated

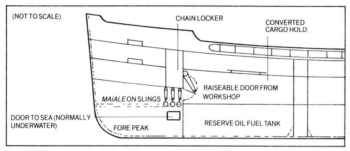

(NOT TO SCALE) CHAIN LOCKER CONVERTED CARGO HOLD RAISEABLE DOOR FROM WORKSHOP *MAIALE* ON SLINGS DOOR TO SEA (NORMALLY UNDERWATER) FORE PEAK RESERVE OIL FUEL TANK

SPAIN COMMERCIAL ANCHORAGE ALGECIRAS GIBRALTAR HARBOUR OLTERRA

the *Maiali*, enjoyed the lowest personnel/combat loss ratio of any front-line Italian unit.

In contrast to longer range operations, when pigs and chariots were transported by normal submarines in watertight containers, Italian *Maiali*-men used an extra-ordinary base at Algeçiras, in neutral Spain, for their raids on

Gibraltar harbor just across the bay. Right under the nose of the British Consul, a large square was cut below the waterline of the salvaged wreck of the Italian merchant ship *Olterra*, while listing the ship for pretended careening, for the secret exit and re-entry of the pigs; and secret support facilities were constructed inside

Top left and right: The secret exit and re-entry hatch for 'pigs' cut into MV *Olterra*'s bow and revealed only when the ship was finally brought up high in the water, after discovery, when her work as a chariot base was finished.

the vessel. *Olterra*'s function as a base was not suspected by the

Bottom left: Schematic diagram of the internal arrangements for the secret base in *Olterra*.
Bottom right: Algeciras Bay showing where *Olterra* was berthed opposite the important British harbor at Gibraltar only a few miles away.

British during some 20 months of operations from the tanker.

British post-war exercises showed clearly that submarines in harbor were just as vulnerable as the major vessels which suf-fered their attentions in wartime; and there is ample reason to think that submarines at their berths, particularly Boomers and Bombers, will be attacked by the mini-monsters or the combat swimmers which they can carry.

Boats lying alongside are still the most tempting targets but technological advances tomorrow, if not today, should enable midgets, in new guises, to extend their activi-ties to the open sea and under the ice.

The peculiar use of *Olterra* is not just of passing interest. Soviet Staffs are the most avid absorbers of useful historical ideas: they

may well have adapted the ploy to present needs. It is reasonable to guess that some of the numerous Hammer-and-Sickle merchant ships which ply their legitimate trade around the world — all under naval-political control — are equipped with hatches below the waterline and facilities for some type of mini-ature submersibles. Large trawlers would be ideal but they have become so notorious as intelligence-gatherers that the GRU might prefer to employ ordinary cargo vessels, although the latter are also apt to bristle with antennae. It is relevant that some British Merchant Navy apprentices were recently shown around a Soviet merchant ship at Port Said: they noted with interest that ladders led down to a hold well below the depth of the

Suicide riders
Launched mainly from large parent submarines (who were themselves exposed to undue danger during these operations and suffered substantial losses thereby), *Kaiten* was often used as an ordinary torpedo at short range (at least one American ship was sunk by that method) although the final version was capable of an independent sortie at 40 knots for 14 n miles, or 50 miles at half that speed: it carried up to 1800 kg of explosive in the head — about four times the weight of a normal warhead and enough to sink or inflict crippling damage on the largest ship.

ship indicated by the draught marks. Local pilots must have been puzzled by a Russian captain insisting on keeping to the 9-meter channel when, on the face of it, the 6-meter channel would have been safe enough!

A ship would not necessarily have to anchor or go alongside to discharge and recover submerged craft: it would not be difficult to devise arrangements for doing so underway at slow speed on the Ro-Ro ferry principle. It might therefore be prudent to suspect any Soviet vessel as a prospective midget-mother when at or near a port of particular interest to the GRU.

A characteristic of chariots, as distinct from midget submarines, is that the operators have to wear breathing sets and are exposed to pressure. They are not ideal, as the British discovered on Norwegian operations, for cold climates. Nevertheless, Yugoslavia has already sold a number of one-man 'R-1' and two-man 'R-2' types (perspex-hooded but free-flood) to the USSR; at least two have gone to Libya; and Sweden has acquired a couple which are assumed to act as the 'loyal opposition'. Soviet useage is more likely to be for probing Baltic harbor defenses than for serious warlike operations for which well-wishers in warmer climes like Libya, are better placed.

For navigation, an 'R-1' *Mala* ('little') chariot has a gyro-compass, echo-sounder, an electric clock and sonar: greybeard charioteers find it hard to believe that one man can use sonar effectively to navigate, but its employment does in fact accord with reported Swedish intercepts.

An 'R-2' can carry 250 kg of limpet mines or equipment — a formidable load. Although the Soviets may be using 'Mala' for some of their Baltic intrusions one would think that vehicles with a rather greater capability, as suggested later, are needed for important clandestine missions·or actual attacks. It is said that the Yugoslavs themselves are not enthusiastic about the craft; but in May 1985 the Yugoslavian Navy commissioned the first of a new 80/90-ton four-man 'Una' class which carries aqua-subs, mines and eight combat swimmers.

The chariot concept has also re-appeared in Western form as a Swimmer Delivery Vehicle (SDV) and the 134/150-ton 'Piranha' coastal submarine proposed by Vickers (VSEL) is designed to carry a pair of multi-purpose chariots secured amidships below the surface waterline: the craft would be manned through a lock-out chamber while

SMALL HARBOR-ATTACK CRAFT
Albeit more capable, by virtue of improved technology, Swimmer Delivery Vehicles (SDVs) in the USN and elsewhere today are similar to WWII Italian *Maiale* and British Chariots. In turn, the British Navy owed much to the original Italian design during the last war.

The Italian Navy took, therefore, the lead in covert underwater assault operations against ships in harbor during both World Wars. It could well be that the latest midget designs — very small submarines proper rather than simple human torpedo types (although modern *Maiale* could still be effective) — will again put Italy in the forefront, as exemplified by the Maritalia company, for operations of this kind against enemy submarines in their 'nests'. That is where sheer logic suggests they are best attacked, if possible.

the boat is submerged. There is no way of telling from the surface if any Soviet or Soviet-linked submarines are similarly equipped. Chariots slung externally would be a considerable hindrance to the performance of a modern Soviet submarine but would not inhibit an ageing, noisy 'Whiskey' or 'Romeo' overmuch.

There is, however, no need to transport chariots by submarine or even by a converted merchant ship in areas where no special watch is being kept. A small fishing vessel could conceal one or more under tarpaulins on deck and· hoist them out by derrick, or one could be slung underneath the keel. It has all been done before.

Human torpedoes
Experience is decidedly against something on the lines of the one-man Japanese *Kaiten* true human torpedo: it was complicated, individually idiosyncratic, difficult to operate and

Far left: Net-cutting exercise. (Photo *RN Commando Association*)
Top: Italian two-man *Maiali* at Venice 1944.
Above: Charioteer being dressed.
Left: British charioteers alongside a tethered craft.

(whatever the High Command may have said) there was no hope of survival if the pilot succeeded. However dedicated a man may be it is, to say the least, hard to control a complex torpedo in three dimensions with the surety of death not far away.

The quite complex engineering and training required to reintroduce *Kaiten* would preclude its use by small bands of avowedly suicidal fanatics; and it is highly improbable that larger organizations with Western mentalities would wish to revive the idea. Having said that, it would be quite easy and inexpensive to convert, crudely, an old-fashioned torpedo with a standard warhead and extremely simple controls such that a bareback rider, with the weapon awash, would have nothing to think about except steering straight for the target.

This kind of Kamikaze weapon would appeal to Muslim death-and-glory extremists and be more effective than a motorboat armed with missiles: a hit on an infidel Sixth Fleet ship, a tanker for choice perhaps, would result in the perpetrator going straight to Paradise. Alternatively, something on the lines of the German *Neger* — basically a one-man torpedo body for the pilot with a free-running torpedo slung beneath it — would be quite simple to reconstruct.

Midget submarines

Midget submarines proper were built, by the hundred, in a wide variety of shapes and sizes for the navies of Japan and Germany between 1939 and 1945. All were armed with torpedoes and some of the designs were excellent, especially the well-equipped long-range Japanese *Koryu* (Scaly Dragon). They had very little impact on the war because the naval Staffs seem neither to have appreciated their full potential, nor to have directed their operations with imagination. Training for the crews was also woefully inadequate and, anyway, the best craft arrived, in the main, when the war was practically over.

One kind of midget, the German amphibious *Seeteufel*, calls for especially close attention. The 'Sea Devil' was only an experimental model at the end of the war and its existence was thought to be a well-kept secret. Admiral Heye (wartime commander of the *Kleinkampfmittel* Small Battle Unit Force) was quoted in 1949 as saying that the type was 'strongly believed to be unknown to the Soviets'; but that belief was almost certainly unjustified, since tracks photographed on the seabed in Sweden and reported off Brazil match the final (and broader) design of the amphibian's caterpillar traction.

The 'Sea Devil' was designed with an engine that could be coupled either to a propeller or to a caterpillar undercarriage adopted from a tank. It had a crew of two and could carry torpedoes or mines, a machine gun and a rocket or flame-thrower. In Heye's words:

'I consider the "Sea Devil" a promising weapon for use in Commando raids. It is independent of mother craft and base personnel, can land on foreign shores, commit acts of sabotage, and evade pursuit ashore or afloat. It can

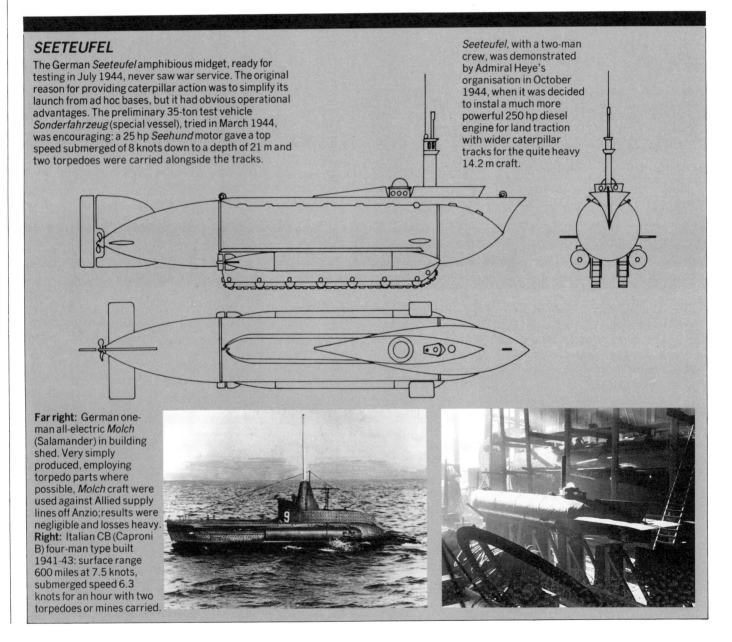

SEETEUFEL

The German *Seeteufel* amphibious midget, ready for testing in July 1944, never saw war service. The original reason for providing caterpillar action was to simplify its launch from ad hoc bases, but it had obvious operational advantages. The preliminary 35-ton test vehicle *Sonderfahrzeug* (special vessel), tried in March 1944, was encouraging: a 25 hp *Seehund* motor gave a top speed submerged of 8 knots down to a depth of 21 m and two torpedoes were carried alongside the tracks.

Seeteufel, with a two-man crew, was demonstrated by Admiral Heye's organisation in October 1944, when it was decided to instal a much more powerful 250 hp diesel engine for land traction with wider caterpillar tracks for the quite heavy 14.2 m craft.

Far right: German one-man all-electric *Molch* (Salamander) in building shed. Very simply produced, employing torpedo parts where possible, *Molch* craft were used against Allied supply lines off Anzio; results were negligible and losses heavy. **Right:** Italian CB (Caproni B) four-man type built 1941-43: surface range 600 miles at 7.5 knots, submerged speed 6.3 knots for an hour with two torpedoes or mines carried.

be taken to site by a mother ship equipped with a large crane. With an engine of higher output than that of the experimental boat, a speed of 8 to 10 knots can be obtained. Speed and radius of action could be further increased by installation of a closed-cycle engine.'

A 'Sea Devil' today would not necessarily need to climb completely out of the water: from a shelving beach, frogmen could haul ashore heavy packages of equipment and explosives which swimmers could not carry from further out. When hounded by helicopters and patrol boats the craft could rest on the bottom, if necessary, until the furore died down. Hydrographic and sonar conditions in the Baltic favor intruders of this kind.

One current Soviet version of 'Sea Devil' is the tracked *Argus*, a non-military edition of which appeared in the late 1960s on board the civilian research ship *Vitzaz*. A military type is said to be carried by the two 'India'-class rescue submarines (one in the Northern Fleet and one in the Pacific) which may also embark the unmanned *Zuuk* equipped with underwater cameras and TV. However, a tracked vehicle, similar to 'Sea Devil' but improved, could certainly be embarked in surface vessels as conjectured in Chapter 2.6.

Another midget, the British X-craft, also deserves a careful look in retrospect because it was the most versatile and independent of them all, albeit normally towed (submerged) by a standard submarine to the operational area at an average speed of nine or ten knots. It was very heavily armed with two two-ton delayed action mines ('side-cargoes') and/or limpets.

An X-craft, 45 ft long and 6 ft in diameter, was a perfect submarine in miniature. Everything was scaled down — battery cells, periscopes, valves and handwheels — so that taking command of one was rather like being given a toy-train set for Christmas. But they were emphatically not toys. Training was long and rigorous; the commanding officers and crews were carefully selected; and nothing was left to chance although the towing arrangements proved less than satisfactory in some cases and the one complication — the electric periscope hoist — gave trouble. The diesel engine properly belonged to a London omnibus: just as dependable rumbling throatily up a Norwegian fjord as on the streets of the metropolis, it typified the

thoroughly tested, simple, robust construction of the whole craft which cost, allowing for inflation to 1988 prices, about £250 000.

As a broad basis for a current design an X-craft would seem, in most major respects, to meet Soviet operational requirements. There was an exit and re-entry lock (the 'Wet and Dry Compartment' combined with a rather hazardous WC) and cutting equipment was provided for a diver to clear a way through nets. With a modern, higher capacity battery a craft on these lines should be capable of seven or eight knots fully submerged for one hour, or three knots for 150 n

Japanese triumph

Only one Japanese midget achieved a major success and it was the exception which proved the rule. On 30 May, 1942 a Type A 'fly' commanded by Lieutenant Saburo Akieda was floated off the large submarine *I-20*, ten miles north of Diego Suarez at the northern tip of Madagascar. Other 'flies' released at the same time from a group of three submarines broke down or lost their way; but Akieda, with crewman Petty Officer Masami Takamoto, was by

far the most experienced operator, and he successfully navigated the long treacherous channel leading to the inner anchorage used by the British fleet.

At 2025 hours, a torpedo struck the battleship HMS *Ramillies* on the port anti-torpedo bulge just forward of 'A' turret. The bulge plating was holed for 30 ft×30 ft and the outer bottom for 20 ft×20 ft. The damage assessment was that 'fighting efficiency was seriously impaired' and the battleship was out of

Above: *Koryu* midgets, assembled at Kure, had immense potential with top speed 16 knots, max depth 100 m and two torpedoes; but they could not show their paces.

action for nearly a year — an interesting reflection on the double-hull protection policy and the effect of non-sinking damage, that is, a 'mission kill'.

A few minutes after *Ramillies* was hit, the 6993-ton tanker *British Loyalty* went down to Akieda's second torpedo.

Midgets magnificent

X-craft were originally intended for putting the giant German battleship *Tirpitz* out of action. 'The Beast', as Prime Minister Winston Churchill called her, lay 50 miles up a Norwegian fjord, threatening Russian convoys from a supposedly impregnable lair where other units could not reach her: but on 22 September, 1943 two four-man craft (out of six despatched) penetrated the anti-torpedo nets and laid their charges beneath the target.

    Tirpitz never went to war again and the two American battleships which had been keeping guard in the Eastern Atlantic, together with major units of the British Home Fleet, were released for action in other areas where they were badly needed. In other words Operation

Source, as it was called, was a resounding strategic success.

    Besides other attacks on ships in harbor, X-craft scouted the Normandy invasion and, on D-Day, a pair of them acted as navigational beacons for the incoming armada. They also — significantly in today's context — cut the seabed telephone cables linking Saigon, Hong Kong and Singapore.

Clockwise from top left: HMS *Minnow* (post-war X-craft) in 1957 with author behind C-in-C; wartime X-craft building; *X-23* after marking SWORD beach on D-Day; HMS *Stickleback* control room looking forward to W&D compartment.

miles. An ability to snorkel is desirable and that is possible — albeit easier for a rather larger boat like the coastal 'Piranha' (26.6 m long) with a deeper snorkel depth; but even on the surface, trimmed down, a midget would be hard to see or pick out on radar at night. And any sensible captain will make the best of natural cover such as outlying rocks and promontories.

It is not necessary to contemplate a more sophisticated type of engine: anything like the oxygen-diesel system in the US Navy's *X-1* (launched in 1955) is best avoided. As the Officer-in-Charge remarked of *X-1* after a fire: 'High concentration unstabilized hydrogen peroxide has no place in a fighting ship'.

In fact the stuff *can* be handled safely — but it is certainly dangerous in a midget. However, the diesel engine could advantageously be made more powerful to give, say, eight or nine knots on the surface. In that case it would be helpful to have a short engine induction/exhaust mast (like a miniature snorkel) aft and it looks as though that is what the Iranians have done recently with what otherwise appears to be an ordinary wartime X-craft. There was considerable interest shown in obtaining historical X-craft plans from the RN Submarine Museum a couple of years before Iran started building their first craft — very probably with the anonymous help of A N Other from Europe.

Further modest improvements over the wartime type for wholly independent operations could include atmosphere control; simple sonar and a secure echo-sounder; a radio transceiver; basic built-in cooking arrangements (the old craft had only a carpenter's glue-pot which served as a double-boiler); and automated steering/depth controls for a long passage. None of these facilities need be in the least complicated and they are virtually available off the shelf. Limpet mines are easily acquired and side cargoes are not difficult to construct. Given a crew of four or five, two of which should be trained divers, a craft would be capable, with the crew working watch and watch, of transitting at least 250 n miles, carrying out the assigned mission and returning without support.

A parent vessel would be required for longer distances: it could be a converted merchant ship, as already suggested, or a submarine. One or two midgets could be carried on the deck of a nuclear or diesel submarine with connecting hatches (which were

Above and left: USS *X-1* was launched at Jakobson's Shipyard, Oyster Bay, Long Island on 7 September 1955. An advanced, if rather hazardous, open cycle oxygen-diesel reciprocating engine powered the 35.1/36.3-ton craft submerged (with battery back up) but *X-1* was not a success and her active life was short.

fitted for *Kaiten*) and the pair of Soviet 'India'-class diesel boats, already noted with regard to midgets, are equipped to carry two Deep Submergence Rescue Vessels (DSRVs) so the mating technique is well established in the USSR, just as it is in the US and Royal navies.

Soviet intentions

What are the 200 assorted midgets said to be in Soviet service doing now? And what do they intend if tension mounts?

Guessing the Kremlin's purposes is a chancy business but, apart from exercises in a realistic environment, commonsense suggests in peacetime the landing of agents from midgets; assessing and measuring harbor defenses (notably those protecting SSBN bases) for future penetrations; and tapping underwater communication cables. In a crisis, *Spetsnaz* teams (who form the combat part of midget crews) might work with *Osnaz* signal-interception experts to gather intelligence from seabed or sub-seabed communication lines, cut them, or even feed false messages into them. It will be recalled that the X-craft which cut the Far Eastern cables forced the Japanese to revert to radio communications — which Allied code-breakers could intercept.

In war — anywhere — midgets would doubtless seek to attack ships and submarines at their berths with limpets or ground mines. Torpedo attacks by midgets seem less likely in harbors and anchorages; but the possibility of very small submarines entering the fray in coastal, or even open, waters cannot in future be discounted — especially in light of predictably increasing active sonar use to detect large quiet SSNs.

Soviet midget crews

Spetsnaz is the Russian acronym for *spetsialnoye naznachenie* meaning special purpose; and *Spetsnaz* units are just that. Sometimes called *reydoviki* (raiders), diversionary or special reconnaissance troops, their primary mission is sabotage in every sense. This includes preliminaries such as subversion and intelligence-gathering (economic as well as military) before embarking on clandestine punitive expeditions in peace or assassinations and destructive operations in a wartime scenario.

The whole *Spetsnaz* force is thought to number around 20 000 men and women (some reports say 30 000), many of them linguists and all at the peak of physical training: in fact some take part in the Olympic Games and other international sporting events. The majority are two-year conscripts commanded by career officers and warrant ranks. It is not known how many are attached to the navy but it certainly has a sizeable share of this elite band. At a guess, the submarine service has about 2000. The conscripts are not allowed any leave during their period of service and all *Spetsnaz* personnel have to swear an oath of loyalty. The punishment for disloyalty (eg, jeopardising the secrecy and deception which cloaks the entire organisation) is death, very likely in dramatic and unpleasant circumstances witnessed by the transgressor's comrades. Only the highest ranking officers know the scale of *Spetsnaz* activities which range far wider than, for example, the British SAS or SBS who are also adept at keeping their business to themselves even when embarked in a submarine.

Each Fleet has an Intelligence Control

(RU) which reports to Naval Intelligence which is in turn subordinate to the Fifth Directorate of the Main Intelligence Control, *Glavnoe Razvedyvatelnoe Upravlenie* (GRU). In the Baltic, where the largest gathering of midgets appears to be, the RU is headed by a Rear Admiral whose Department Three recruits and trains *Spetsnaz* personnel. The midgets themselves are presumably operated by a senior specialist officer responsible to the Fleet Commander's Chief of Staff (Vice Admiral V A Kolmagorov in 1988). Midget bases are separated from the principal naval ports and guarded from ordinary naval personnel although *Spetsnaz* officers and conscripts wear normal naval uniforms, usually those of the Naval Infantry, and are billeted near Naval Infantry barracks.

Spetsnaz provides combat divers, swimmers, raiders and secret agents for the midgets: these are really supernumaries so far as the crew is concerned although they doubtless help with watch-keeping on passage. The crews proper can hardly be other than long-term professionals seconded from standard submarines.

Soviet midget characteristics

It would make sense for the Soviet Navy to have three kinds of midgets at present — a simple training craft on the chariot principle (eg, 'R-1' and 'R-2'); an amphibian intelligence gathering/agent-landing vehicle; and a general-purpose attack craft. It is the last type that concerns us now because of its ability to attack submarines in harbor or lay mines in submarine base approaches; but it would be very surprising if the development of a new kind of robotic midget designed for sea-going operations, with a particular eye on under-ice ASW, is not also well underway.

All we can do is to conjecture firstly the Soviet Staff Requirements for a GP craft (initiated, perhaps, in the late 1960s) and secondly for a robotic type formulated in about 1985. Some helpful clues emerge from a dozen small Russian submersibles which we know about — Deep Submergence Rescue Vehicles (DSRVs) of two kinds; Remotely Operated Vehicles (ROVs); underwater repair monitors and sample collectors; and research craft which may well have more of a military capability than their name suggests. So, supposing the Staff to have followed what seems to be a logical need, the formal Requirements paper for the GP midget submarine might have read something like this in, say, 1968:[1]

MOST SECRET:

DISTRIBUTION RU CODE GSP ONLY
GENERAL PURPOSE MIDGET SUBMARINE

Objective

Consequent upon Polit directives the Head of GRU has specified a requirement to infiltrate special units into foreign countries; to gather intelligence in, and close to, crucial inshore areas, choke points and naval harbors for future operations; and to intercept communication lines. Concurrently, a requirement is foreseen, in the event of crisis or war, for neutralising submarines, important ships and facilities in ports and anchorages where defenses are strong against attacks from the air.

Means of Meeting the Objective

Taking into account the wartime experience of all navies concerned (which removes the need for a tentative Staff Target) and adhering to the War Principles of Offense, Economy of Force, Maneuver and Initiative, Combined Aims, Surprise and Deception, the Staff Appreciation is that a miniature submersible will best meet the stated needs.

Operating Areas

Provision must be made for operating worldwide.

The Baltic will be the primary source of operations against the United States, NATO, neutral European countries and in the South Atlantic. The Far Eastern Fleet will be responsible for activities against US military facilities, command and control headquarters at Subic Bay, Yokosuka, Guam, Pearl Harbor and on the American West Coast; and against Japan with particular regard to installations affecting control of the Tsugaru and Soya straits. The Black Sea Fleet will undertake tasks in the Mediterranean, Adriatic and Dardanelles.

Bases

Operational and training bases must be secret and sufficiently removed from normal naval bases.

Range

Only exceptionally are midgets expected to transit to and from a target zone independently. Some merchant vessels and submarines (in addition to the Rescue type) must be adapted for covert transport, launching and recovery. This is the subject of a separate Staff Requirement.

Hence the independent range of any midget is not a governing factor in design.

Weapon Systems

Although great advantages can be seen in constructing very small torpedo-firing submarines on the lines of the German Type (1944) XXVIIB 'Seehund' 13.7-ton U-boats, no practical way can be devised at present for sending them into action in sufficiently large numbers to swamp enemy anti-submarine escorting forces at sea as intended by the Nazi U-boat Arm: this concept has therefore not been added to the objectives which did not, in any event, consider it. Nor is it considered that torpedoes fired into well-defended harbors would be significantly effective despite forthcoming American developments along this line.

Limpet mines and ground mines (high explosive and nuclear) with variable delays and capable of being triggered remotely at any time after being laid, are therefore selected as the alternative or combination weapon systems.

Armament

Two ground mines (released from inside the craft) each carrying at least two tons of HE or up to five kilotons of nuclear explosive plus 12 standard limpets for positioning by divers. The mine cases should each be capable of carrying 20 limpet mines instead of HE or nuclear explosive if required.

Oil ignition devices for use after a successful attack are to be carried internally for discharge through the submerged signal ejector (listed under Self Defense below).

Hull

Non-magnetic, glass-reinforced plastic acceptable. Control room forward. Hull to be faired with minimal projections. Periscope housing but no conning tower as such.

Dimensions

No greater than 15×2 m (not including external mines).

Density

Standard saltwater range (Baltic), but must also be capable of operating in freshwater and compensating instantly for fresh or low-density patches: 1000-litre rapid flood/blow safety tank in addition to standard negative tank.

Crew

Four including a diver (GRU to recruit and train in co-operation with area Submarine Brigade Commander).

Assault Swimmers/Special Forces

Space for two *Spetsnaz* personnel in addition to crew.

Exit and Re-entry Lock

Standard but with additional hatch below for parent submarine connection.

Range and Endurance[2]

A. 1000 miles snorkel at 6 knots (snorkel limited to fair weather) or on surface at eight knots or better. Standard diesel.
B. 150 miles at five knots submerged on battery or 300 miles at three knots.
C. Burst speed 15 knots submerged for 45 minutes (to no less than 50 per cent battery capacity).

Habitability

Unimportant, but special forces embarked must not be unduly cramped. Chemical WC.

Air Purification

Oxygen generator and carbon dioxide scrubber sufficient for 60 hours total submergence with six personnel on board.

Navigation and Controls

Automated or semi-automated with immediate reversion to direct physical control when required. Hover-assist trimming if possible. NATO radio navigational aids (from commercial sources). Secure echo-sounders (standard) for navigation and (upwards) for target indication.

Compasses

Aircraft/helicopter type — electrical gyro and one precision air-blast (30-minute duration) with a plus or minus five degrees magnetic compass for emergency use.

Shock Resistance and Diving Depth
Compatible with standard diesel submarines. Minimum safe depth 350 m. 1.5 safety factor.

Noise Reduction
No cavitation at periscope depth (propeller/propulsor at 3 m) below 3.5 knots. Resilient mountings for all machinery with particular attention to air purification. Anti-sonar coating over the whole hull; sound insulation around main machinery space.

Self-Defense
No weapons but two mobile decoys (standard external launchers) and submerged signal ejector for chemical decoys, exercise flares and oil-ignition stores.

Diving Apparatus
Self-contained closed-circuit oxygen re-breathing sets. No automatic safety release gear. Limit of 9 m prolonged-working depth acceptable. Divers to be armed with dart guns.

Net-cutting
Diver-portable net-cutting gun to be stowed externally. Guards around propeller/propulsor.

Viewing
A. Main periscope telescopic/periscopic: head diameter less then 3 cm; monocular, selectable magnification ×6 and ×1.5; ranging by graticule only. Image intensification desirable but not at the expense of top-optics head diameter.
B. Non-raisable wide-angle image-intensified periscope 50 cm above casing level for night viewing on the surface and for use underwater when submerged.
C. Non-raisable, protected faired periscope right forward for conning through nets and obstructions when submerged.
D. Scuttles (with deadlights) for side and upward viewing by commanding officer in control room forward. Laminated glass suitable for relaying and amplifying external diver's speech without a direct link; capable of withstanding shock as for hull.

Sonar
Passive listening in 10 kHz range. Directivity plus or minus two degrees.

Communications
A. HF transceiver (voice and CW) with raisable elbow-joint whip antenna.
B. VLF/LF receiver and automatic recorder with antenna incorporated in hull.
C. Underwater telephone (standard).

Self-destruct
Internal charge with time delay up to one hour.

Additional
To be fitted for but not with:
A. Taut wire measuring gear.
B. Grapnel for locating cables.
C. Underwater searchlight, diver portable.
D. Bacteriological/chemical warfare dissemination equipment.

Robotic ASW midgets

The indications are that ASW torpedoes by themselves will not be smart enough to compete with all the future underwater targets and that, anyway, force multipliers will be needed by both sides to fill the inevitably wide gaps between standard submarines through which hard-to-detect transitters may pass.

The best answer seems to lie in robotic midgets or initially, maybe, ROVs[3] which will be rather like large homing torpedoes with a good active/passive search capability of their own and a heavy payload.

Some of the suggestions for such vehicles read like science-fiction; but (British) Scicon's proposed Patrolling Underwater Robot (SPUR) has real possibilities for the future even if it may not be able to develop its comprehensive potential before the end of the century. Conceptually, SPUR will have a wide radius of operation at 12 knots with drop-tanks and a maximum speed of 50 knots for suicide attacks if so programmed. It will be able to navigate autonomously, primarily by comparing depths and underwater terrain with a digital hydrographic data base. Control appears to be envisaged, in the first instance, from shore or surface ships using

Scicon's Patrolling Undersea Robot (SPUR)
SPUR is an exciting and feasible concept although not yet developed. Small robotic vehicles would have great advantages for under-ice work, attacking enemy submarines and for intelligence gathering. The on-board computer would be of the order of 10 Gbytes and 20 mips. Artificial intelligence would be used to assist functions which SPUR needs to perform autonomously, mostly in the field of tactical decision making. Typical of these are route planning to implement initial patrol orders; depth selection with regard to targets and environmental factors; target classification; contact holding maneuvers; attack maneuvers; communication routines; navigational routines; and fuel usage calculations.

MODERN MARITALIA MIDGETS

Lacking positive intelligence about the latest Soviet midgets (although the conjectural requirements for the 1970s generation are probably not far off the mark) it is relevant to look at the most modern Italian Maritalia designs which are very advanced: hopefully, the Soviet navy has not yet progressed so far but it would be prudent to assume that it is only a matter of time.

The unique propulsion system, with gaseous oxygen stored in a toroidal pressure hull (acronym gst) for an Anaerobic Diesel engine, allows the submarine to remain fully submerged (no snorkelling) for an entire transit/mission with great operational flexibility. No exhaust is discharged to sea. The system had undergone successful tests for more than 20,000 hours underwater by early 1988.

PANOPLY
A gst midget can carry one, or a combination of several, of the following options depending on task and variant employed:

- 4 lightweight torpedoes (wire-guided and/or active/passive homing)
- 2 heavyweight torpedoes
- 12 ground mines (each 150 Kg HPE) in torpedo tubes
- 2 mine dispensers for total 20 ground mines (each 600 kg)
- 2 swimmer delivery vehicles (2 combat swimmers for each) and two 600 kg charges; or 2 SDVs, each with a 300 kg charge and 4 limpets

- 2 mine delivery vehicles (2 combat swimmers each) and total 10 600 kg ground mines;
- 2 commando delivery vehicles for total 16 commandos;
- twin 7.62 mm pressure-resistant retractable machine guns
- one pressure-resistant retractable 20 mm gun

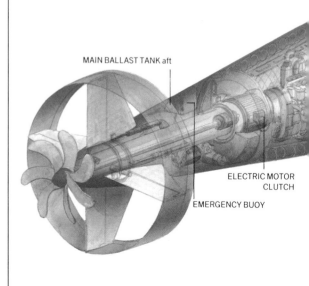

Prt ANAEROBIC DIESEL GENERATOR

MAIN BALLAST TANK aft

ELECTRIC MOTOR CLUTCH

EMERGENCY BUOY

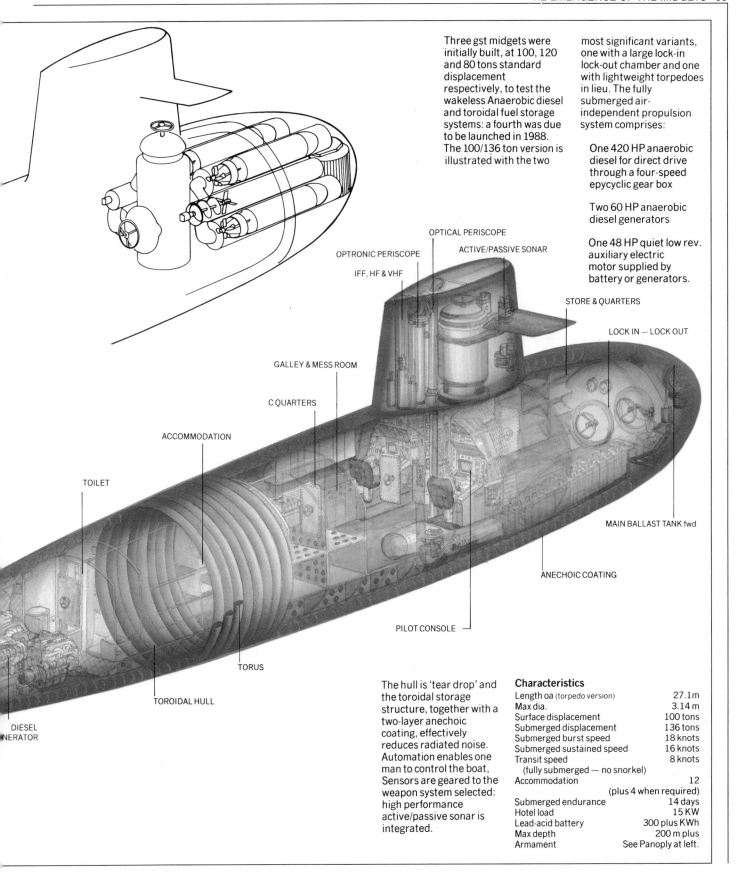

Three gst midgets were initially built, at 100, 120 and 80 tons standard displacement respectively, to test the wakeless Anaerobic diesel and toroidal fuel storage systems: a fourth was due to be launched in 1988. The 100/136 ton version is illustrated with the two most significant variants, one with a large lock-in lock-out chamber and one with lightweight torpedoes in lieu. The fully submerged air-independent propulsion system comprises:

One 420 HP anaerobic diesel for direct drive through a four-speed epicyclic gear box

Two 60 HP anaerobic diesel generators

One 48 HP quiet low rev. auxiliary electric motor supplied by battery or generators.

OPTICAL PERISCOPE

OPTRONIC PERISCOPE

ACTIVE/PASSIVE SONAR

IFF, HF & VHF

STORE & QUARTERS

LOCK IN — LOCK OUT

GALLEY & MESS ROOM

C QUARTERS

ACCOMMODATION

MAIN BALLAST TANK fwd

TOILET

ANECHOIC COATING

PILOT CONSOLE

TORUS

TOROIDAL HULL

DIESEL NERATOR

The hull is 'tear drop' and the toroidal storage structure, together with a two-layer anechoic coating, effectively reduces radiated noise. Automation enables one man to control the boat, Sensors are geared to the weapon system selected: high performance active/passive sonar is integrated.

Characteristics

Length oa (torpedo version)	27.1m
Max dia.	3.14 m
Surface displacement	100 tons
Submerged displacement	136 tons
Submerged burst speed	18 knots
Submerged sustained speed	16 knots
Transit speed (fully submerged — no snorkel)	8 knots
Accommodation	12 (plus 4 when required)
Submerged endurance	14 days
Hotel load	15 KW
Lead-acid battery	300 plus KWh
Max depth	200 m plus
Armament	See Panoply at left.

Top: The French Navy adopted *Seehund* for a while after the war but discarded them in 1955, a couple of years before the Royal Navy disbanded its X-craft unit. The 11.9 m boat displaced 12.3 tons with two torpedoes slung externally. Range was 500 miles at 7.7 knots on the surface, 63 miles at 3 knots submerged or 19 miles at 6 knots.
Above: *Seehund* Type XXVIIB5 U-boat mass production: 285 units were delivered between September 1944 and April 1985.

totally unmanned nuclear powerplant than any Westerner. Nuclear or not, whoever brings a robotic midget project to full fruition will radically change the nature of submarine-versus-submarine warfare.

Torpedo-armed midgets

The excellent wartime German 14.7-ton Type XXVIIB U-boat *Seehund* really arrived too late (although 285 units were built before Germany surrendered) but it was credited with sinking or damaging about 100 000 tons of shipping between January and May 1945. If *Seehund* had come earlier in the battle, and if adequate working-up facilities had been available, ASW defenses might have been swamped by large groups making co-ordinated attacks.

There are no indications in open press of a *Seehund* in the Russian armory, but supposing this type to be modernised and suitably. equipped, it might today have a valuable, if limited, anti-submarine role. If such a beast is re-invented it will be exceedingly hard to uncover in coastal waters through which submarines have to pass, often along well defined and shallow lanes that tend to inhibit stealth and result in the monsters being relatively easy to ambush before they vanish into the ocean depths. It is the sort of idea that would appeal to the Chinese whose submarines were strongly supported by Chairman Mao because he visualized them as guerilla fighters.

Wartime lessons learned

It has to be asked why, with the exception of *Seehund* and a solitary Japanese Type A, German and Japanese midget performance was disappointing. There were several reasons and the Russians must surely have recognised them. In addition, to the need for simplicity and reliability the most important lessons learned — positive and negative — can be brought up to date and summarised:

burst radio transmissions to and from the craft but, presumably, airborne platforms could also exercise control; and given a long-range underwater or satellite link so could submarines.

SPUR is the sort of vehicle that the Soviets probably have in mind, primarily for under-ice ASW operations but also for wider uses against NATO submarines. The US Navy has, more modestly, suggested small mobile sensor platforms (SMSPs) deployed from torpedo tubes to assist in detecting and assessing Soviet submarines in the Arctic.

The hybrid semi-nuclear propulsion described in Chapter 1.3 would be very well suited to an autonomous midget and the Russians are much more likely to send out a

1. Kamikaze tactics worked with aircraft because the pilots attacked at exhilarating speed in hot blood after a fairly short flight time. But prolonged, cold-blooded submerged operations, requiring meticulous navigation and the ultimate precise positioning of weapons, did not — and will not — succeed when certain death lies ahead. Hence the desirability of robotic vehicles for one-way trips. This is no reflection on a crewman's courage: it is

simply a fact of life. Indeed, although a midget submariner cannot afford to be a coward, extreme care to avoid counter-attack and overcome obstacles will be more richly rewarded than blind bravery.

2. Thorough, realistic training, lasting months rather than weeks, was — and is — mandatory: the Germans and Japanese failed, by and large, to provide it. This has to be borne in mind when intelligence indicates that a particular navy (eg, Iran) has acquired midgets of one kind or another — and attacking other submarines requires very long practise indeed.

3. Midget submarines, chariots and basic human torpedoes can be built quickly, cheaply and secretly — witness Iran's production line.

4. Practically any submarine or merchant vessel can be adapted to carry military submersibles without that necessarily being obvious.

5. No anti-submarine or anti-torpedo defenses have ever defeated an assault by determined and properly trained midget operators: they have been a hindrance and sometimes they have trapped a craft, but a proportion of the attackers have got through. Submarine bases today, however imposing they may look, are not invulnerable judging by history.

6. A very special kind of man is required to crew a midget; he is not likely to be the type who will excel in a normal peace-time career. This accords with current Russian philosophy both in regard to midget operators and *Spetsnaz* combat swimmers.

7. One man, by himself, loses heart: there must be at least two in a crew and, for lengthy operations, four is probably the minimum. Apart from training craft and genuine commercial or research vehicles, Soviet midgets probably have four men in the permanent crew. *Spetsnaz* personnel can be female but whether the sort of woman employed does much for morale is open to debate.

8. Covert attack units must be allowed to develop their own team spirit in their own unconventional way: that is what distinguished Italian wartime *Maiali* men. Considerable risks are implicit during peacetime exercises — they were a prime reason for disbanding the British X-craft in the late 1950s — but they must be accepted if crews are to be ready for war. The Soviet Navy is not unduly worried about risks, least of all in a highly secret midget organisation; and *Spetsnaz* units do indeed create a strong team spirit amongst themselves.

Most of these lessons relate to human factors and are no less important now than ever they were. In the midget field, exceptionally, the Russians should have few personnel problems.

Irrespective of what value the West assigns to midgets for its own offensive, ASW or surveillance purposes, something will have to be done, urgently, to counter the renewed threat from very small intruders. Harbor defense is, in most navies, a forgotten and neglected art but exceedingly valuable submarine assets need protection.

Regrettably — for it will not be popular — defenders may have to resort to clumsy, old-fashioned net-protection for port entrances. But there is one trick that nobody seems to have remembered. Conservationists will hate it but, if an intruder is suspected, oil pumped onto the harbor surface will blind a small periscope; and no midget submariner can do his job properly — even with navigation aids and sonar — if he cannot see where he is going. It sounds laughable against a background of complex ASW systems but, as a last-ditch measure, it will work. Midgets are uncomplicated craft: the best defense against them may, equally, be simple.

It is without doubt that the midgets are on the march again and they are a potential menace, long proven, which it would be unwise for ordinary submariners to despise, let alone disregard.

END NOTES
1. A rather similar conjectural Requirement paper was included in *Submarine Warfare Today and Tomorrow* by Captain John Moore and the author (Michael Joseph (UK), Adler & Adler 1986/7) but more recent information from various sources has enabled this to be amended in sundry respects.
2. Maritalia s.p.a. (Italy) have recently devised two much more promising types of midgets than the conjectural Soviet designs sketched here. These new craft are propelled by a simple and safe closed-cycle diesel system (with battery back-up), which allows very long endurance fully submerged and high speeds when necessary. Unfortunately, the craft are outside the scope of the book; but they could very well play a most important part in future submarine warfare — especially against enemy ships and submarines in harbor but very possibly under the ice in harbor approaches also.
3. Remotely operated vehicles.

1.11

SELF-DEFENSE

Soviet attention to surviveability is, as we have seen, marked throughout the newer submarine designs: we now need to examine the concept more closely. The methods used for self-defense and self-protection are much more extensive than in the West where ASW submarines, hitherto enjoying the advantage of being quieter, may now find themselves disadvantaged in a mêlée. Surface and airborne forces will also, of course, find it difficult to detect and sink the more recent Soviet boats and practically all ASW units are liable to counter-attack.

In other words, the outcome of any ASW engagement, especially submarine-versus-submarine, is even more speculative than it was a few years ago.

Western navies have concentrated on reducing emitted noise — successfully — but have largely neglected the physical protection thought advisable by the Russians. Reliance is mainly placed upon keeping quiet, detecting the enemy first and, if necessary, taking tactical evasion. In particular, double-hulls, despite their advantages not only for surviveability but also for stowage of certain equipment and weapons, have been rejected on the grounds that they add drag while the necessary limber holes increase noise. It can only be hoped that this trust in non-*matériel* protection will be justified in battle.

Nor have Western submarine services given overmuch thought to counter-measures and decoys against submarine attack. In fact, although new secret measures have been proposed and some systems are in service, it appears that a feeling of superiority over the Russian fleet has inhibited, in the past, all but some rather perfunctory gestures towards defense. However, there are indications that strenuous efforts are now being made to devise new methods because no longer can a NATO ASW submarine count on conducting a deliberate, carefully executed approach in its own chosen time. Snap shots at very close range are more likely when up against very stealthy enemy boats.

Standard sensors and weapon systems can obviously be used defensively if required although an exceedingly quick reaction time is implied and that is not necessarily associated with long-range weapons like wire-guided torpedoes. Moreover, it is said that too little attention has been given to quiet discharge procedures: the simple act of opening torpedo tube bow shutters and bow caps can be noisy and swim-out discharge — which is quieter than air or ram ejection — is not the method normally employed, not least because poisonous gases from the torpedo-engine exhaust are liable to escape back into the submarine.

Submarine self-defense and counter-measures are, rightly, classified so it will be best to look at probable Soviet capabilities in these respects using deduction based upon commonsense in light of the opposition which Soviet submariners know they are contesting.

Double hulls

There is nothing new about the idea of double hulls affording protection against torpedo attack: it was first mooted more than 100 years ago for battleships.

Most navies have used — and still do use — a type of double hull for diesel-electric boats in the shape of saddle tanks although these are disappearing in modern SSKs. The large lightly built streamlined blisters running along either side of the hull comprise main ballast tanks, which provide an adequate reserve of buoyancy on the surface, and fuel tanks. Extra fuel can also be stored in one or more of the ballast tanks themselves and sometimes high-pressure air bottles are stowed externally — a common practise in Soviet boats of all kinds.

Nuclear plants do not require internal stowage for fuel (although oil is, of course, carried for standby diesels) and a major requirement for saddle tanks ceased to exist with the introduction of nuclear power. Western navies therefore felt able to adopt single-hull designs for SSNs and SSBNs with internal strengthening frames: on these boats the pressure hull forms the outer surface for most of the length while the ballast tanks are right forward and right aft, shaped to continue the hull form and round it off.

Single hulls minimize the outside dimensions for a given pressure hull volume: hence the wetted area, which causes drag, is as small as possible while hydrodynamic flow noise is limited. On the other hand, reserve buoyancy comes down from 25 to 30 per cent to nine or ten per cent of surface displacement: nor, of course, is there any stand-off distance between the pressure hull and ASW weapon impact. Moreover, believing that 'our' submarines were much less vulnerable to attack, by reason of quieting, than 'their' boats the number of watertight compartments was reduced from the customary six to three in many cases. The consequence is that flooding, from whatever cause, is potentially disastrous in most Western nuclear submarines.

Soviet designers have taken a quite different stance. They have determined that their boats must survive, maybe only on the surface or at a depth above which internal bulkheads hold, if one or possibly more compartments and their adjacent ballast tanks are flooded. They believe that double hulls are decidedly not inferior in terms of speed or fighting efficiency provided that propulsion systems are sufficiently powerful — which they are, especially when 'slippery' techniques are applied to the hull; and that quieting methods are not unduly inhibited — which they are not because the separation between the hulls substantially diminishes noise before it reaches the sea.

Moreover, the Russians, albeit at considerable cost to habitability, have succeeded in reducing the size of pressure hulls (and have thereby kept the outer hull within reasonable limits) by miniaturizing engineering components; introducing automation to cut down crew numbers; using high-strength steel, titanium, composite materials (eg, GRP — Glass Reinforced Plastic) and Aluminum for pressure hulls, outer hulls and superstructures; and by employing external rather than internal framing in the main with,

probably, some deep internal frames at bulkhead points. The boats are still big but they are physically well protected.

One way and another, Russian submarines are theoretically able to accept a great deal of punishment while Western boats are not.

However, speedy and effective damage control is another matter. It is no good having bulkhead doors if nobody shuts them in time; and shock, even with a double hull and other protection, is liable to fracture pipes and systems which must immediately be isolated. The appalling record of Soviet submarine casualties strongly suggests that damage control, notwithstanding exceptionally strong construction, is less than efficient.

The shock factor

There are, in fact, ways of reducing shock and it can be assumed that the Russians, who are known to have explored a couple of methods at least since the mid-1970s, are now applying them.

Both methods are concerned with damping shock waves by obliging them to pass through a non-solid medium before striking critical areas.

One obvious answer, for a double-hulled boat, is to fill the space between the two hulls with honeycomb material rather than water. This can only be done adjacent to crucial areas because a large amount of ballast water will always be required to maintain the necessary reserve of buoyancy; but quite large expanses of pressure hull could certainly be protected from shock waves which would be attenuated in the honeycomb.

The Soviet 'Oscar' SSGN has a faired, low sail (without sailplanes) indicating good hydrodynamic stability at high speeds. Missing anechoic tiles (fixatives are notoriously unreliable) suggest a tile-thickness of four inches and the tiles may act as a compliant coating as well as reducing active sonar reflections by about 50 per cent: it appears from magnified examination of the photograph that there are connections which might be for fluid transfer on the hull below the tiling. Piping visible on the casing could be associated with these for making the boat 'slippery'.

DOUBLE AND SINGLE HULLS

Details of a Soviet double-hull are unavoidably conjectural but photographs, commonsense and intelligence reports suggest that the concept of survivability would be met by the structure illustrated below.

Most frames are external but there are probably deep internal frames, combined with pressure-resistant bulkheads, at intervals. With a very high reserve of buoyancy derived from large main ballast tanks, one compartment can be flooded without the boat being sunk. In fact, if the flooded volume is fairly small the boat may be able to maintain control submerged — but that will depend upon the type and degree of damage sustained.

Although there may be a thin outer casing around at least part of the pressure hull, Western SSNs are really single-hull boats without any useful stand-off distance between weapon impact and the pressure hull — as shown by this schematic drawing of a British 'Swiftsure'

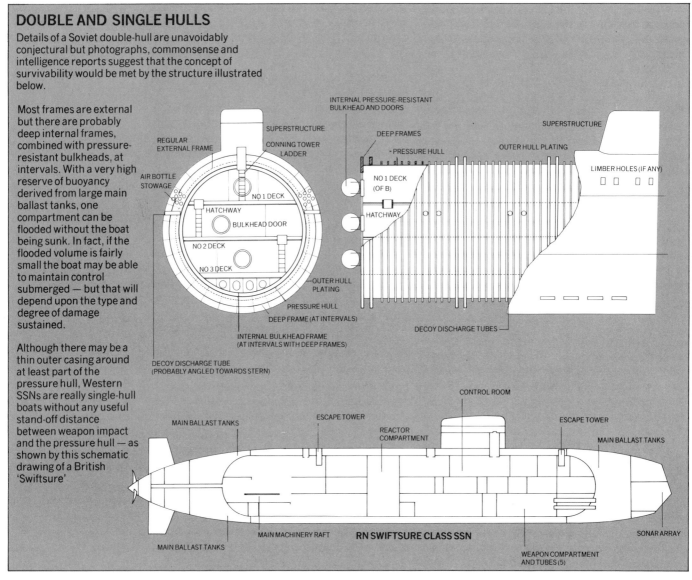

RN SWIFTSURE CLASS SSN

An alternative method is more ingenious and could be more flexible. Experiments have demonstrated that a very thin layer of gaseous bubbles passed upwards around the outer hull and superstructure can not only increase a submarine's speed markedly — bubbles are one way of making a submarine slippery — but they can also reduce shock passing through the hull by 50 per cent while at the same time contributing to the anechoic and noise reduction properties already provided by thick tiles. In other words the outer coating can be polyfunctional.

This concept can be further progressed by utilizing gas-liquid media, rather than a honeycomb or bubbles by themselves, between the outer and inner hulls. The addition of gas bubbles to a liquid in a moderate amount (say 20 to 30 per cent by volume) produces practically no change in the density of the medium (sea water in this case) but significantly increases its compressibility. The effect is that a shock wave resulting from an explosion in the two-phase medium will be significantly lessened before it reaches the pressure hull. Experiments have clearly shown that shock wave extinction, with an explosion occurring directly in the two-phase medium, is more pronounced than when a wave arrives at a bubble screen after passage through a layer of water.

The creation of a porous medium, consisting of gas bubbles suspended in water, should not be unduly difficult and, presumably, protection of this kind could be afforded over the whole length of the submarine including the main ballast tanks. A single hull, on the other hand, could only be given a thin bubble screen which would certainly be advantageous against non-contact ASW weapons besides the other benefits conferred, but less so than a two-phase medium. It may be that Soviet submariners are employing both methods, with polyfunctional outer protection and a porous medium between the hulls.

Meanwhile, Soviet platform noise is reduced, as in the West, by resilient mountings, machinery rafting, structural damping, anti-vibration balancing, idealized hull forms and sound-absorbent coverings. System redundancy is commonplace; vital components are doubtless pressure-proof; a very large high-pressure air capacity is maintained; and there is probably an ample number of powerful damage-control pumps. It is possible that pressure-hull patching techniques are — or will be — available while automatic fire extinguishers and deep-submergence emergency ballast blowing systems are virtual certainties.

ASW countermeasures and defensive tactics

Simply because Russian submariners knew their boats were, until recently, comparatively noisy they must have explored countermeasures to the full. It can therefore confidently be expected that most boats carry both static and self-propelled decoys — very likely mounted externally in many cases — and that active hull-mounted jammers are installed for use against incoming weapons. Closed-loop degaussing systems must also be high on the list of Soviet priorities.

Soviet tactics and equipment have also been designed to take swift evasive action while retaliating in kind.

It can be supposed that, in all but the older boats, low frequency passive sonar will be capable of detecting noises — perhaps only transients — from an attacking submarine, if the latter is relatively close, shortly before its weapons are fired; and that the noise source will be evaluated correctly for what it is. This presumes that the Soviet boat is at fairly low speed such that its sonar is fully effective: at moderate or high speeds it would probably hear nothing of a carefully handled approaching enemy submarine, although it may hear torpedoes even if these are themselves becoming very quiet. It is certainly likely to detect the fish if they are switched to the active mode.

What means, then, has a Russian commanding officer at his disposal in the event of a sudden threat?

Firstly, he has speed and three dimensions at his disposal. Even in a 'Foxtrot', caught perhaps while snorkelling, he can alter away and build up to 17 knots while going deep. These tactics will not save him from the best smart weapons like the Mark 48 torpedo or Spearfish; but if, as believed, his two small stern torpedo tubes are now kept loaded with mobile decoys, these may give him a sporting chance if his reactions are very quick indeed — although, frankly, it would be rash to lay bets on his survival in the open sea. In coastal waters an SSK stands a fair chance of avoiding detection in the first place and, if snorkel periods are minimized and irregular, the newer diesel-electric boats could reasonably hope, with a bit of luck, to escape most kinds of ASW prosecution. However, if the SSK is patrolling or minelaying in an area adequately covered by specialized coastal ASW submarines it will be at risk. The new German U-boats will be a considerable deterrence to Russian submarine operations in the Baltic; but it would be impossible for NATO SSKs to afford sufficient protection all around the coasts of Britain and continental Europe — and there are far too few surface ASW vessels, maritime aircraft and helicopters to cover these poor ASW operating areas.

There is nothing to suggest, apparently, that any more than a few Soviet SSKs are capable of instant counter-attacks against prowling NATO ASW SSKs: they have no overwhelming need of such a capability, desirable though it may be. But SSNs in deep water can undoubtedly retaliate to an underwater threat at the drop of a furry Russian *shlyapa* (hat). There would be no time for the crew to go to full action stations and, as in British SSNs, it can be assumed that torpedoes would be fired 'on the watch'.

It can be expected, too, that, in dangerous zones, a couple of tubes are kept loaded with smart but unguided ASW weapons. A defensive salvo, probably intended for the 2–4000 m bracket, will therefore be instantly available and it should take no more than moments to generate a fire-control solution, using MF active sonar, for the homing fish which will be pre-angled to take up slightly divergent courses embracing the enemy's arc. It would make sense for these defensive torpedoes to be fast and noisy and they might well be set in the active mode:

Ram the chopper!

In 1957 the commanding officer of HMS *Springer*[1] found an answer to one helicopter by purposely ramming and wrecking the sonar ball which it was dunking off Northern Ireland. It was an effective but costly tactic: the helicopter itself was not pulled down but *Springer*'s Captain only narrowly avoided a court-martial. The incident provoked thought and in 1964 — it took a long time for the idea to sink in — the possibility of equipping boats with anti-helicopter, anti-small-ship missiles was explored. In 1970, (six more years later) HMS *Aeneas* became the first (and last to date) British guided-missile submarine (SSG) with a battery of army man-portable blowpipe missiles on the redundant periscopic radar mast. They could be fired from periscope depth and worked quite well, but submariners felt it was too much of a last-ditch defense. The project was dropped when *Aeneas* was de-commissioned in 1972 — at which time somebody painted 'SS Gillette' on her stern, a cynical forecast of the razor-blade fate that awaited her, together with the grandly named SLAM (submarine-launched anti-aircraft missile system).

noise in this case is advantageous because, when used purely for defense, it is very desirable for the torpedoes to force the ASW opponent into a violent defensive maneuver himself. Hopefully, from the Soviet point of view, this will result in the wire of the enemy guided torpedo being cut while the Russian captain speeds out of danger, releasing a couple of decoys for good measure while triggering jammers. It would, incidentally, make sense for Soviet towed array sonars to embody a decoy system which can be initiated at will.

Together with decoys, 'Shoot and Scoot' is the obvious tactic. Thereafter the game of cat-and-mouse will be resumed while the Russian captain may well call up his friends, noting that another submarine is likely to be in the vicinity, to help deal with the situation. The original attacker might then find himself suddenly outnumbered — especially if he has set his sights on a group of transitters.

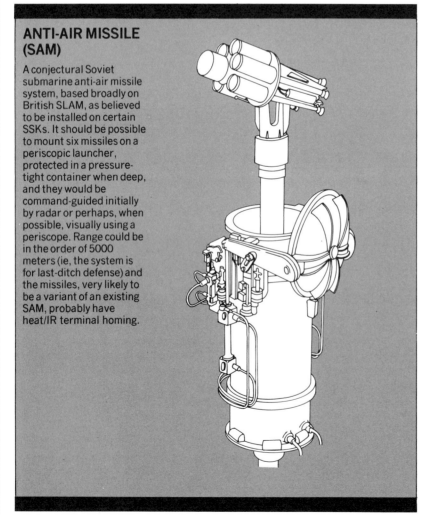

ANTI-AIR MISSILE (SAM)

A conjectural Soviet submarine anti-air missile system, based broadly on British SLAM, as believed to be installed on certain SSKs. It should be possible to mount six missiles on a periscopic launcher, protected in a pressure-tight container when deep, and they would be command-guided initially by radar or perhaps, when possible, visually using a periscope. Range could be in the order of 5000 meters (ie, the system is for last-ditch defense) and the missiles, very likely to be a variant of an existing SAM, probably have heat/IR terminal homing.

Anti-air missiles

Anti-aircraft guns were removed from submarines soon after the last war when it became unusual for them to operate on the surface. No active defenses then remained against ASW aircraft and helicopters. If a submarine was nailed from the air it could only try to evade and break contact. This is still difficult in unhealthy waters where no layer exists or when sonobuoys and a helicopter's dunking sonar can operate deep. It is particularly unpleasant to be ringed by a team of airborne ASW units in these circumstances: a submarine captain never knows where the next ping will come from, or where passive buoys have been laid, so there is no obvious avenue of escape.

SUBAIR tactics have featured in USN ASW affairs since the 1950s, albeit usually without much success or popularity. The Soviet Navy, with its predeliction for coordinated operations, has probably pursued the SUBAIR concept more enthusiastically and Western boats may well have to contend with a submarine-directed airborne threat when they would prefer their whole attention to be concentrated on underwater engagements. Incidentally, submarine-launched robotic drones are predicted as a possibility for the future.

One defensive solution is the promised American self-initiated anti-aircraft missile (SIAM) which is a fire-and-forget weapon; but the Russians have developed a mast-mounted system more reminiscent of the discarded British SLAM.

As seen on 'Tango' SSKs in 1985 and envisaged on 'Kilos', the SAM idea for submarines could clearly be developed further. In any form, it will have a major tactical impact on the way in which ASW aircraft and helicopters go about their business, because they carry no form of defense against IR or heat-seeking missiles; and the provision of screening would be costly in terms both of space and money. Chernavin and his men realize all this full well: a SAM system — even if it is more of a bluff than a reality as some NATO observers suspect — is another kind of deterrence which is worth exploiting at no great expense.

In short, Soviet submariners are well equipped, physically and tactically, for self-defense: but there are liable to be surprises of several kinds in a submarine-versus-submarine confrontation.

END NOTE
1. The author.

1.12

POWERFUL FORCES, PRACTICAL PROBLEMS

The Soviet submarine force is the largest and most powerful that the world has ever seen. At least, that is how it appears to observers on the surface. However, as implied more than once already, things are not always what they seem when we explore deeply into the murky world of underwater warfare.

Modern Russian hardware — hulls, propulsion, weapon systems — is, by and large, excellent: some of it is better than the West can offer in opposition. But, just how well does the software (which is mainly to do with men) match up? It is necessary to establish some kind of basis for comparison.

The Royal Navy, which has the management experience of a couple of hundred years or more behind it, believes that even in today's computerized society man is still the greatest single factor. British officers are rather shy of actually saying so and they do not often talk about leadership and morale in so many words. Nelsonian expressions like 'England expects every man this day to do his duty' would hardly be acceptable nowadays, especially in submarines, but the expectation is solid and justified nonetheless. (Interestingly, it was an American, Caspar Weinberger, former US Defense Secretary and created an Honorary Knight Grand Cross of the Order of the British Empire in 1988, who used these terms most recently when referring to British exploits in the Falklands confrontation: success was due, he said, to 'a supreme confidence in the justice of his cause and the willingness of every Englishman to do his duty'.)

The United States Navy discusses the need for leadership much more in open forum, which could imply an awareness that something is lacking although, when it has come to the test, American sailors have invariably proved superb. But in submarines,

the late Admiral Hyman G Rickover lost tactical ground for the USN by focussing attention on the nuclear kettle and its skilled minders aft, rather than on management amidships and torpedomen at the sharp end. The quality of USN personnel, in engineering terms, has always been very high indeed but there is a case for saying that fighting capabilities took second place over a long period during the Rickover reign.

Things have clearly changed for the better but one problem in the USN remains — the habit of overstating fitness reports which is no kindness either to the man or to the service. The effects have been felt far beyond deserved or undeserved promotions. A serious result has been that the cold-blooded, highly critical post-attack autopsies to which British command teams are traditionally and often embarrassingly, subjected have generally been avoided. Avoidance has led to over-confidence and lessons not being learned: it is certain that, before the last war, the weaknesses of America's submarine arm were not appreciated, let alone tackled. The truth of this was plain enough during the first year or two of war. British submariners were certainly not paragons and their tools were not the best; but, torpedo for torpedo throughout the war, they scored proportionately more goals than their American counterparts. The precise figures are debatable but the British success rate was probably about 50 per cent better and the attacks were frequently made in more difficult circum-

Soviet sailors training on board an elderly SSK — probably a 'Whiskey' — in the 1950s. The scenes are very similar to Western diesel-electric boats of the period where the cleaning problem was just as acute!

going to happen soon, the weapons to be used are bound to be prepared with special attention and no wartime stresses are present. Moreover, it is only human nature for everybody, from the firm who supplies the weapons down to the man who presses the firing button, to portray the result optimistically rather than objectively.

The Soviet Navy must have the equivalent of AUTEC for both the Northern and the Pacific fleets and there are probably limited ranges in the Black Sea and Baltic. But it is inconceivable, under the Soviet system, that unfavorable conclusions are widely published — save, perhaps, instructive Requiems for departed submarine comrades hewing a bleak existence in the salt mines. If the US Navy was formerly reluctant to adopt objective peacetime analysis essential to wartime success the Soviet Navy, in which visible failure is disastrous for all concerned, surely cooks the books to a turn.

The problem for small navies

Frankly, it is difficult to imagine how most of the smaller navies can perfect the art of submarine-versus-submarine warfare without comprehensive technical and tactical evaluation facilities — and those involve a great deal of money. Unfortunately, successful sonar approaches from deep against surface ships do not imply equal success against fleeting submerged targets and it is a costly business to lay on realistic ASW exercises.

Having said that, smaller submarine arms might set their sights a little lower and aim only at the most probable and threatening targets, inshore for example, rather than attempt to cover all eventualities. The German and Dutch navies are notably realistic and efficient; the Scandinavians have always been good submariners; the French, although not historically very good at torpedo attacks, could well delight in the logic and mathematics required in an ASW scenario; and the Japanese are adept at the kind of technology needed although their wartime submarine record is not impressive — primarily because the Imperial Naval Staff failed to grasp the principles of submarine operations.

The Canadian and Australian submariners are well equipped, well manned and well trained and they might well win the day through dogged determination. Nevertheless, it will be a long haul for the planned fleet of ten or twelve Canadian SSNs to achieve full effectiveness, especially under the ice;

stances. The key was — and still is — exacting analysis.

It is hard enough to analyse, comprehensively, a simple torpedo attack against a surface ship: the fact that the captain estimates target course and speed correctly is not enough in the usual peacetime case where torpedo fire is only simulated. It is even more difficult to work out from a simulated attack what would have happened in war when the practise target is another submarine. Even when, exceptionally, one or more expensive practise torpedoes are discharged, smart weapons (which carry their own recorders for exercise shots) are not always given a fair chance because they have to be offset for depth unless a padded target is available — and there are not many of those. Submarines themselves also have to be assigned safety depth strata. A three-dimensional range like AUTEC allows the best tactical assessment of an engagement but some artificialities are inevitably introduced, however much the participants endeavor to avoid them: the crews are on their toes, knowing that something is and the new Australian Kockums (Swedish) Type 471 SSKs will be slow to deploy while hardly being a match for opposing SSNs.

Meanwhile, the Chinese People's Liberation Army (Navy) — to give the force its full title — is third in the numerical batting order for submarines. Many of the 81 hulls[1] are in reserve status and most of the equipment is long outdated; but the quality of the personnel is exceptionally high by any standards and, given substantial help by the West to modernize the fleet, the Chinese should have a formidable submarine service well capable of ASW operations by the turn of the century if — quite a big if — that is what the PLA (Navy) wants and decides to afford with all its attendant infrastructure.

For the rest, noting that 42 nations now have submarines of one kind or another, they will be hard put to acquire an ASW capability of any real significance. So, to return to the largest navy — the foremost cause of ASW concern — how might Russian submariners fare in war against their own kind? We have seen what systems they have at their disposal but wartime operations have clearly indicated that systems are only as good as the men that serve them — and the Soviet Navy is beset by personnel problems.

Seventy-five per cent of Soviet ratings are conscripts who serve for three years. They undergo five months basic training and then, if drafted to the submarine service, they go to a submarine training establishment, the largest of which is in Leningrad, before joining their boats where they form, on a cycle system, one third of the crew.

Each conscript serves for two years in submarines so, at any one time, less than half the crew has any meaningful experience. This may not be true of the latest boats which could well be manned predominantly by officers and senior ratings — mostly Chiefs with hardly any Indians. In the fast little 'Alfas', for example, there are no more than three or four junior ratings in the complement and those are employed on menial duties such as cleaning and cooking. Automation and computerization are commonplace but there is reason to think that they lead to very stereotyped drills which can also, incidentally, result from co-ordinated operations.

In the majority of Russian submarines the rapid turnover of conscripts presents formidable training difficulties and an individual is normally groomed for one specific duty only. There is no flexibility amongst the crew and, anyway, it is Communist dictate that the

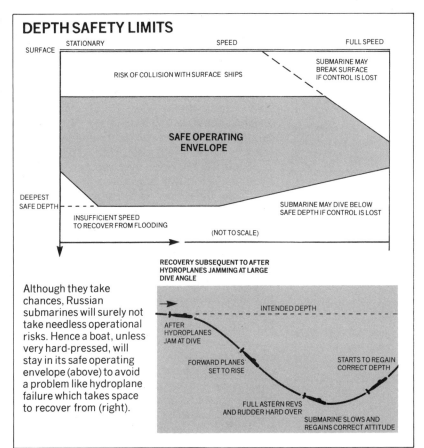

DEPTH SAFETY LIMITS

Although they take chances, Russian submarines will surely not take needless operational risks. Hence a boat, unless very hard-pressed, will stay in its safe operating envelope (above) to avoid a problem like hydroplane failure which takes space to recover from (right).

left hand must not know what the right hand is doing.

Nobody has vouchsafed, so far, a detailed internal description of a Soviet SSN but the older boats, like the 'Romeos' for example, have what Western submariners would consider the most appalling control room layout: it is designed so that no one man in one position can see everything that is going on — and that is evidently deliberate. The chart/plot is in a tiny compartment of its own and so is the Sonar Office; the torpedo control calculator faces aft at the after end of the control room; and the hydroplane control (one man, two buttons) is situated forward where the operator cannot easily be overseen. Thus, only the Captain or *Zampolit* (Political Officer) can know, by wandering around, what is happening. And if, as is often the case, a senior staff officer is on board the Captain may well be obstructed in his view.

Like as not, that was the cause of the notorious 'Whiskey on the rocks' incident at Karlskrona in October 1981: it could well be that the unfortunate Captain, encumbered by the Division Commander as well as the *Zampolit* during a very tricky navigational passage at periscope depth, was unable to get to the chart table in its tiny hutch while his political superiors were poring worriedly over it at a crucial moment.

The personnel problem is compounded by the wide variety of languages within the USSR: there are at least 90 different ethnic groups speaking 120 languages. Nor are the groups all inclined to be comrades in the friendly sense. Slavs comprise 63 per cent of all Soviet conscripts and 24 per cent are Muslims: the latter increased their share of the ranks by six per cent between 1977 and 1987. The remaining 13 per cent of the conscripts come from other minorities and 15 per cent of the total cannot speak Russian which is the official armed forces language. It has been said that a man coming from Moscow or the RSFSR (the ruling Republic, admitted or not) has about as much in common with a citizen from the borderlands as a New Yorker has with a native of central America.

A submarine commanding officer, or rather his *Zampolit*, has a major racial conflict on his hands — and the Muslims are said to be increasingly assertive. Tensions can be considerably greater than anything arising from black and white relationships in the United States Navy or, come to that, the sort of sociable altercations relished in British boats between deeply rooted Celtic elements of the United Kingdom. One wonders, by the way, whether strict Muslims in any navy are permitted to pray towards Mecca at the appointed times. USS *Tautog* (SS-199), with two Javanese Mohammedan agents embarked, provided them with the relative bearing of Mecca and space for prayer mats thrice daily in 1944 — so there is a precedent for the proper procedures to be followed.

The *Zampolit*, backed up by a Deputy Political Officer in the larger boats, is kept fairly busy. Besides administering a daily dose of Communist dogma to the crew, lecturing and conducting discussion groups for an hour or more to each and every section, he is responsible for welfare and morale. It is not easy to hold the interest of weary conscripts during lengthy ideological sessions; and diatribes against American imperialism soon become repetitive. In fact, there are credible reports to the effect that cynicism exists amongst Soviet leaders, at all levels, about Marxist-Leninist theory; and even a *Zampolit* gets bored himself. It is also said that conscripts sitting at the back of the class in the crew's mess-room are prone to take a

nap or write a letter home while the *Zampolit* is droning on.

One hard-line Political Officer, Captain Third Class Sablin in the destroyer *Storozhevoy*, became infuriated with what he regarded as ideological laxity in the wardroom and decided to demonstrate the laziness of other officers by taking the ship out of Riga harbor while most of them were ashore. Presumably he felt that this would teach them to pay more attention to affairs on board and prove that he, the *Zampolit*, was really in control. The short mutineering voyage naturally caused a furore in Moscow when the ship was reported to be steaming, unauthorized, towards a Swedish island on 8 November, 1975. Ships and aircraft were despatched to chase the erring vessel which was speedily returned to its rightful port. The hierarchy was not interested in Sablin's motives: like many another good Communist who has strayed from the straight and narrow, he was shot.

No other Political Officer has apparently been tempted to take such a dramatic action to overcome ideological indifference; but, in a submarine, the *Zampolit* undoubtedly has great influence. He used to have his own code for radio messages and he probably still does: the Captain knows that he is constantly watched and reported on, so he himself has to watch his every step.

Control at sea

Administration, operations and tactics must conform absolutely with the Rule Book: there is no room for individuality and it must be very difficult for a captain to adapt to an unexpected situation. Furthermore, submarines at sea are rigidly controlled from shore: in fact they have to be when such large numbers are involved.

Fear is the basis of the discipline throughout the armed forces and it permeates the whole of Soviet society. Much leadership is fear-inspired and the leaders are ever wary of a rising from below. Fear militates against change and the consequence is more inflexibility. Yet Western commanding officers would say that success is dependent upon changing tactics unhesitatingly to meet situations which can never be predicted with confidence in the ASW world.

If morale is indeed a crucial factor, as the West believes, we noted earlier that confidence in weapon systems and the command's ability to use them is also important. Soviet submariners should have no lack of confi-

HABITABILITY

Wartime 'life below' is contrasted with modern habitability in these pictures. Comfort mattered less in WWII because, except for the Captain or officer at the periscope, relatively little prolonged concentration was needed by the crew. Today, everyone on watch has to be fully alert which implies a need for reasonable comfort, a constant temperature and carefully planned displays and controls.

Below: The torpedo room, which also served as a bunk area for some of the crew, in a USN Fleet boat in 1943. It is impossible nowadays for crewmen to share space with the latest weapons: the weapons, not the crew, cannot stand the strain!

Left: The Seamen's Mess, HMS *Tribune* in 1941: conditions were relieved by the daily issue of one eighth of a pint of rum.
Below: The icy kiosk in the Soviet *K-21* in 1942 during the Arctic winter. It is hard to think that the Captain (Lunin) operated the telegraph, but perhaps anything more interesting that that and the klaxon was censored.

Above: The dining hall in USS *Ohio* (SSBN 726), barely distinguishable from a surface ship.
Far left: The galley in a British Bomber (*Resolution*).
Left: The wardroom, HMS *Trafalgar* (SSN).

dence because strenuous efforts are made, from top to bottom, to make sure that everything appears to be thoroughly satisfactory. Oddly enough patriotism — the feeling that a crew is safeguarding their country's interests — is not a conscious part of morale in any navy's submarine service, notwithstanding the honorary Sir Caspar's kind remark. A *Zampolit* tries to imbue some kind of patriotic fervor but it is very doubtful whether his attempts have any real impact. A submariner, anywhere, is much more concerned about life day by day — and continuing survival in war — than about the rights or wrongs of politics.

Mundane matters like living conditions and food are therefore uppermost in the average submariner's mind. As a matter of historical interest, comfort in submarines did not contribute much, if anything, to efficiency during the last war. However, the long American Pacific patrols would scarcely have been possible if the wartime Fleet boats had been as squalid as the smaller British submarines which were generally out for shorter periods.

The picture has changed today. Modern sensors and machines demand intense concentration by the operators who need comfortable, warm, clean and quiet surroundings. Cleanliness is a basic essential: long experience has shown that a dirty boat invariably has failings in other respects. There was a time when Russian officers turned to with the crew, as the Chinese still do, to clean ship but this practise has not been continued. Attention to detail is not a Russian trait and cleanliness in submarines today is probably superficial. When the small British 'U-class' submarines on loan to the USSR were returned after the war they were in a dreadful state; and it was discovered that the meagre messes allocated to senior rates and sailors had been converted into cabins for the officers. Officers are decidedly more equal than the rest in Communist society: rare sightings of officers' accommodation and that of junior ratings in modern Soviet ships suggest that class differentation continues with a great divide between the upper and lower levels.

Habitability in American submarines, by contrast, is excellent for all; and in British boats it is reasonable if not nearly so good as it might be. It is still common to 'hot bunk' in the latter with a man turning in to the warm pit just vacated by his relieving watchkeeper. Hot bunking and overcrowding are accepted in the Royal Navy but much could be done to improve conditions by miniaturizing equipment and reducing crew numbers by automation. The new British Type 2400 SSK has only 44 officers and men and there is no reason why SSN crew numbers, typically between 115 and 145 at present, should not be cut quite drastically if similar methods are applied.

An additional trouble is that there are almost always passengers to accommodate in peacetime — trainees, observers and scientists — so that *ad hoc* bunking has to be created. The situation is doubtless the same in Soviet boats.

Food in Western submarines is good and the cost in British SSNs equates to meals in a three star hotel. Submariners in SSKs are not quite so well fed and, apart from the new boats, they are not nearly so comfortable: nevertheless, they are incomparably better off than their wartime predecessors. Food in Russian boats is said to be not bad although it comes nowhere near Western standards except, perhaps, in the wardrooms. Fish and red (not black) caviar used to figure prominently in Soviet submarines during the war when food was severely rationed ashore; and Russian submariners are still better fed than the civilian population.

Alcohol is a problem throughout the USSR and the Soviet Navy is not exempt: it is used to fuel standard torpedoes, whose tanks are reliably reported to be tapped by Russian sailors for light refreshment. The USN deliberately contaminated the alcohol in Mark 14 torpedoes but the Soviet Navy has evidently not taken the same precaution — or else the sailors are past caring about the after effects. French submariners enjoy a generous supply of wine and wardroom officers are not averse to Scotch; beer is available in British boats (although, nominally, it is rationed) but the officers very seldom drink at sea; Russian conscripts are forbidden legitimate alcohol but officers and senior ratings probably still enjoy a daily ration of vodka or wine; and the US Navy, of course, is dry although a submarine usually carries a medicine chest containing a plentiful supply of supposedly medicinal whisky. Generally speaking, it is safe to say that alcohol and submarining do not mix.

Quietness implies, amongst other things, suitable deck coverings; the atmosphere must be fresh; humidity must be kept low so that damp does not affect electrical and electronic equipment; there must be ample water for personal cleanliness; and cleaning throughout the boat must be as easy as possible so as not to detract from the crew's operational functions. Decor has to be chosen with care (the Russians favor huge landscape paintings incorporating the birch trees which are so dear to them) and background colors must be restful; bedding needs to resist dirt; and uniforms, usually sketchy at sea, must be easy to clean or wash. Personal hygiene and health are vital to efficiency nowadays; scant attention was paid to these factors in the past although, somehow, men did their jobs and did them well. Rats and cockroaches used to be a scourge but, hopefully, these have been eliminated by pesticides.

Fighting efficiency today depends quite heavily upon good habitability. But traditional Captain's Rounds must include the inspection of more than just cleanliness and good order. The word hygiene can be applied to anti-magnetic measures (ie, magnetic hygiene), sound and shock insulation, quietening and nuclear integrity. The Captain can no longer glance approvingly at a sparkling, well ordered compartment and nod: he must delve into matters to which formerly he paid scant attention. If failures to inspect thoroughly are sometimes evident in Western boats, it is sure that they are a good deal more common in Soviet submarines. It is not in the nature of a Russian to be thorough and it is very much the practise to paper over the cracks which appear everywhere in the Soviet facade.

There are, however, a couple of nagging thoughts about the much improved appearance of submarines internally. Piping and circuitry are tidily hidden by a sort of inner shell and minor damage — a small leak or weep for instance — might not be noticed until it grows to dangerous proportions. Similarly, the clumsy old knife switches for electrical equipment, the solid valves and handles for air, hydraulic, water and fuel systems as well as main vent operating levers have given way to push-button controls which are space-saving and neater. But more elderly submariners may wonder whether these new devices would stand up so well under shock or whether they would be so quickly repairable as the old-fashioned 'handraulic' fittings. Practically everything is shock-mounted and shock trials are routinely carried out; but submariners with experience of wartime counter-attacks, although impressed by all that they see in the modern boat, sometimes raise an eyebrow when they

think of damage control. And computerized gadgets — including weapons themselves — imply a certain fragility at variance with the robust construction deemed necessary during the last war. As we have seen, however, the Russians have taken steps to lessen the effects of shock.

Poor maintenance in Russian submarines was noted earlier; and it is not easy to carry out external work — securing the casing against rattles for example — in sub-zero temperatures. It could also be that, despite first-rate designs, quality control during construction is variable. It may have progressed in recent years but some remarkably primitive construction was apparent in the section of the 'Golf'-class SSB recovered by the *Glomar Explorer* in 1973 some five years after the boat was lost, due to an internal explosion, in mid-Pacific. Wide variations in the

Above: A Soviet 'Golf II' SSB (three SS-N-5 sail-mounted missile tubes) similar to the boat which went down with the entire crew of 88 after an internal explosion 1000 miles NW of Hawaii in 1968.

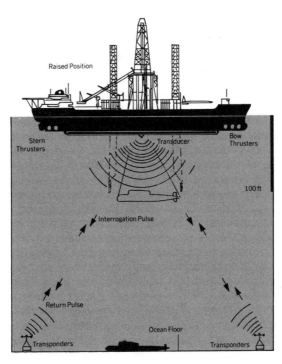

Left: Schematic drawing of the 618 ft *Glomar Explorer* which was said to have recovered at least a part of the sunken 'Golf', one crucial section breaking off irretrievably when the submarine had been lifted from 16 600 to 8000 ft. There is little doubt that the operation was feasible but disinformation from the CIA was such that very few people know what was actually brought up. Some grisly details about the corpses recovered, and then reverently laid to rest, were published (*Glomar Explorer* apparently had a refrigerated morgue) but these simply added to wildly conflicting accounts.

thickness of the inner and outer hulls were found; welds were uneven; and there was dangerous pitting — by no means all of it due to the normal corrosion expected after lying on the seabed for so long. Most surprisingly, four-by-two wooden beams were used for internal structural support, contrasting starkly with the sophisticated weaponry on board.

Turning to operations, the Russians would be very rash if they did not accept the restrictions relating to speed and depth which are normally imposed in Western submarines. A submarine near to its maximum operating depth or close to the surface is in danger from depth-control failures; and the effect of these obviously increases with speed; consequently, an SSN keeps within a safe operating envelope, which becomes narrower when it goes faster, to avoid the possibility of breaking surface and colliding with surface ships or plunging below collapse depth. The envelope is quite restrictive and it is unthinkable that an 'Alfa', say, will sprint along at 45 knots at its maximum depth of around 1000 m. Hence, high speed is not always useable at will. At the same time, low speed at great depths implies the danger of not being able to recover from the effects of small leaks or hull penetrations; and, Murphy's Law being what it is, these are quite likely to be associated with a failure of primary propulsion. Russian preoccupation with damage limitation and control is fully justified.

Speed/depth limitations are not unduly inhibiting but they have to be considered when a Soviet attack submarine needs rapidly to close a distant datum, often determined by a third party observation, before the information becomes too stale for localization by active sonar.

There is also another kind of limitation, usually forgotten, which is partly due to the nature of operations and partly to the quality of commanding officers. History, subsequently reinforced by war gaming, shows that only a proportion of the submarines available can be expected to engage the enemy and, of those, a relatively small number will conclude successful attacks. Attack opportunities against naval units have never been frequent; and in submarine-versus-submarine warfare the chances will be still more rare because submarines are becoming less detectable. Moreover, and most importantly, history insists that the commanding officers (and their teams) who are good at the game will be few — particularly in the Soviet fleet.

In round figures, during World War II, 25 per cent of US Navy submarine captains sank 75 per cent of the Japanese shipping which went down to torpedoes. On the German side 2.2 per cent sank 31 per cent — which is not really a fair statistic because U-boats early in the war had a heyday which latecomers did not; but there is no doubt that a few achieved the most while, on all sides, an astonishing number had no results worth recording. In the Royal Navy 8.6 per cent of the commanding officers sank 30 per cent; but in the Soviet Navy extremely few captains were successful at all. It is impossible to arrive at exact figures for the latter because of gross distortion by Soviet propaganda, but the relationship was in the order of 2 per cent sinking 90 per cent of the remarkably few targets engaged.

A statistician could drive a coach and horse through these raw unqualified percentages; but they are highly indicative and many of the conditioning factors — Rule Book rigidity, the fear of acknowledging failure and not learning from mistakes, poor training and maintenance prominent among them — are present today in the Russian underwater fleet. Nor does inflexible control encourage aggressive tactics.

In short, Soviet weapon systems are not likely to be employed to full advantage, impressive though they appear, save for quite a small proportion of the boats on patrol. Bearing in mind that the number of submarines at sea at any one time is far less than the number listed in the Order of Battle the threat, although substantial, is not quite so great as some observers would have us believe.

Finally, the Soviet submarine admirals have another major difficulty. How, and politically when, can they deploy large numbers of submarines through guarded choke points leading to the Atlantic and Pacific oceans?

To put it another way, power has its problems: Soviet attack submarines are very strong on hardware and NATO submarine services will have to take energetic measures to regain a lead. But Soviet software — men and maintenance in particular — could well prove weak in war.

END NOTE
1. Despite the numbers listed in naval catalogues such as *Jane's*, this is the correct number, checked in the People's Republic by the author, in 1987.

PART II

ACTION AND FACTION

With the facts established, as best they can be in a deeply secretive arena, we can stage some conceivable underwater scenarios. Needless to say, set a little in the future, they are wholly speculative; and it must be emphasised in the usual way that the players, as well as the events, are entirely imaginary and are not intended to portray any persons living or dead: any resemblance is purely coincidental.

Nevertheless, nowhere does history have the habit of repeating itself so frequently as underwater. Submariners who search their memories will recall practically every incident in one form or another. For instance, there are few of us who have not at some time mistaken the noise of a fishing vessel for a snorkelling submarine; and several of us — author included — have become involved, so to speak, in the consequences. All we are doing in the following chapters is to update such incidents in an illustrative context; so it is hoped that the events described — mainly from the Soviet point of view — will be much more akin to faction than pure speculation.

2.1

SOVIET SSK TACTICS

I t can be assumed that Soviet diesel-electric ASW submarines (SSKs, or PLs to use the Russian acronym) have a fairly short-range active sonar capability in the medium and high frequency ranges; but they do not have the long-range low frequency active equipment installed on SSNs because there is neither power nor space for it. On the other hand, the modern boats ('Tangos', 'Kilos' and their predicted successors) should be virtually silent, except when snorkelling of course, and their low frequency passive sonar arrays ought to give them the edge over most enemy SSNs unless the latter are operating in their quietest modes.

Collision in the Norwegian Sea

We will imagine (without much difficulty) that tension between the Soviet Union and the United States has mounted sharply due to what each side considers to be reneging by the other over the latest Strategic Arms Limitation Treaty in the European and Atlantic areas of interest. Britain and France are nominally staying on the touchlines and there is no immediate threat of hostilities — but it is realised in Moscow and Washington that a false move by anyone, including the onlookers, could easily strike a spark. This is not, at the moment, liable to occur in the Pacific: it is in the West, from the Kremlin's outlook, that danger threatens.

SSBNs and PLARBs are on station in their usual numbers; but four 'Typhoons', held in reserve for the moment, have been brought to the third degree of readiness (missiles at 12 hours notice) in their nuclear-proof bunkers burrowed out of solid rock at Zapadnaya Litsa, inshore of the Ribachiy Peninsula and barely 50 km from the Norwegian border. British and Norwegian Long Range Maritime Patrol (LRMP) aircraft are covering the Greenland–Iceland–UK gap, although there is nothing unusual about that, and Soviet Bear F ASW aircraft are busy further North.

Apart from the boats which happen to be already in the outfield, the main Northern Fleet attack submarine force is in harbor, waiting to be deployed. At Severomorsk, Kola

HQ, Admiral Bigatov,[1] the new C-in-C Northern Fleet and a submariner by trade, wants his boats to break through enemy submarine barriers before they are fully activated and before minefields are laid; but on the other hand he is anxious not to send them so early that they have to be recalled again for rest and reprovisioning before the first bang.

The Defense Council has secretly been whisked, by Metro running beneath Leningrad Prospekt from the Kremlin, to Khodinka, the so-called Moscow Central Airfield which is idle as a rule, and thence by luxury jet transport from the First Task Force of the Civil Air Fleet (a misnomer if ever there was one) to Kurumoch. This is another empty but fully operational airfield conveniently close to the honeycombed Supreme Command Post 300 m below the granite monolith of Zhiguli, some 600 km South-East of Moscow.

The five members of the Defense Council, the most powerful men in the Soviet Union headed by the General Secretary, are now sitting in more or less permanent session. They are secure in their massive fortress against any kind of weapon, just as Stalin was when he led the State Committee for Defense here in 1941, although the Metro-like tunnels were not then nearly so deep; and nor did they run for tens of kilometers between command posts, communication centers, stores and living quarters as they do today.

The C-in-C at Kola is also well dug in and protected (probably better than his British opposite number and Flag Officer Submarines — COMSUBEASTLANT — at Northwood) so that the principle command organisation of the Soviet Union and its navy is now living a troglodyte existence — like the submariners at sea. There is some significance in this: the top cadres expect their submariners to be the survivors in a nuclear war just as they expect to survive themselves. The relationship is obvious and psychologically important.

However, the Defense Council has no wish whatever to see tension escalate to nuclear warfare — or to conventional war either for that matter. The Red Army member, Minister of Defense Marshal Modin representing all the armed forces, is painfully aware that his troops are by no means ready to take on the West and the KGB representative is always snidely hinting at the fact. But Modin, with confidence in his naval Deputy, is sure of his submarines — and the great thing is that they will not provoke escalation if they are handled and deployed with care.

C-in-C Northern Fleet is therefore ordered to reinforce the Barents Sea and Arctic bastions, and hold the bulk of his off-station PLARBs, cruise-missile and torpedo-attack SSNs therein, while establishing a submarine barrier, primarily with SSKs, across the Northern stretch of the Norwegian Sea.

A great many other moves are being made, of course, but we are concerned at the moment with the Russian SSKs and for illustration we will select a 'Kilo' for a start — the *Academy of Sciences* to give the boat a name.

Academy of Sciences is commanded by a political favorite, Captain Second Rank Arseniy V Kolyshkin whose father is in the Politburo. He was permitted to choose his own *Starpom* (Assistant Captain — Executive Officer) and he too is a present-day aristocrat, arrogant and fundamentally lazy but a good Party man who obtained exceptionally good marks on the Staff Course and will eventually succeed Kolyshkin in command: he gets on very well with the *Zampolit*, a creepy individual who joined the boat with strong recommendations from Political Administration although he knows next to nothing about submarines.

On the face of it, *Academy of Sciences* is clean and bright: she has usually been chosen by the Squadron Commander at Murmansk for display to VIPs when they visited the base and they always went away impressed. Of course, they walked only through the main compartments and never peered below the main deck or behind machinery. Neither does Kolyshkin bother himself about matters which are, in his opinion, beneath a captain's notice. The *Starpom* takes his cue from the Captain: if the boss is happy, he is happy and, although a *Zampolit* is never observed rejoicing, the Political Officer is content as well.

The human factor

Fortunately for the Captain, *Academy of Sciences* has an excellent Chief Engineer Officer. He has been with the boat since she was laid down at Krasnoye Sormovo Shipyard No 112, inland at Gor'kiy, 320 km East of Moscow (a pleasant place for the Chief's family during the long fitting-out period) before being towed down the Volga to the Black Sea and thence making her own long way round to the Kola inlet. The Chief is a worried man. His captain believes that everything is fine but it is not: the mechanical and electrical ratings, with a couple of exceptions, are a poor lot and the Shipyard workers skimped wherever they could. As for the weapons system — well, that is the Torpedo Officer's problem: although Chief is responsible for maintenance, nobody has kept him up to the mark; and he is thankful for that because he has much else on his hands. The Chief hopes, profoundly, that this expedition will not lead to a meeting with one of those accursed *Amerikanskiy* boats or an Englishman or a *Frantsuskiy*. The *Zampolit*, no friend of the wholly practical engineering section, constantly denounces the Imperialists as useless but the Chief has private doubts about that.

The *Academy* is assigned a square patrol area, thirty miles on a side, bordered by the Lofoten Islands — a prime position, according to Intelligence, for intercepting NATO SSNs *en route* to the Barents Sea ahead of carrier or amphibious task groups. Adjoining squares are occupied by other SSKs and the *Academy* can communicate with immediate neighbors on secure long-range underwater telephone. The buoyant wire VLF antenna is U/S due to bad insulation and a massive ground (the radio technician failed to screw the external hull gland tight before sailing on a very cold night) and the communication buoy has never worked: so Kolyshkin must come shallow every four hours to receive the routine broadcast on the loop antenna. This is a nuisance, especially with a gale blowing, and battery power will be wasted keeping depth in the rough sea. It is impossible to keep beam to sea, which is best for depth-keeping: signals are too weak for rapid teletype reception unless the boat is bow or stern to the shore transmitter.

Between these excursions to periscope depth (which can be omitted for 12 hours if absolutely necessary because broadcast messages are repeated three times) Kolyshkin will obey tactical instructions to the letter and steer East–West courses at minimal speed (two knots) on the main motors at 70 m. Snorkel-charge periods are restricted by doctrine to no more than 20 minutes at a time twice a day during hours of darkness. But the wire antenna malfunction quickly puts paid to doctrine. During the first three days the battery gets lower and lower — unaccountably so, even taking into account the five or six knots necessary to avoid broaching at periscope depth.

Unknown to Kolyshkin there are a number of sick cells in the battery which ought to be cut out and treated. But the Chief dare not admit to them: he merely says that the low voltage and diminishing battery density (which is down to 1180 at dawn on the fourth day, 60 points below what it should be) is due to over-use of power by the Officer of the Watch and a heavy hotel load. This is a tricky one for Chief because he himself is the principal trimming officer and if he complains about the OOW too much he will find himself watch on, stop on; but the Captain is not technically minded and contents himself with switching off a few lights and blaming everyone in sight.

The result is that the Academy, willy-nilly, has to snorkel continously for three hours in daylight and, sure enough, after an hour the OOW at the periscope (which is partially fogged and badly needs dessicating) sights a smoke float close aboard — obviously dropped by an aircraft on a visual datum to mark a sonobuoy pattern.

He presses the action alarm and orders a ten down angle to 300 m, unwisely ordering 150 revolutions immediately rather than increasing speed slowly as the boat goes deep to avoid cavitation.

Kolyshkin leaps out of his tiny cabin and takes charge, reducing the revolutions, but he knows full well that enemy sonobuoys have heard him: in NATO terms he is now a PROB-SUB.

Nothing further happens: war has not been declared; but the opposition now knows where he is. He reflects gloomily on his situation, logs the OOW, contrives a suitable story for the Zampolit and retires to brood alone in his cabin.

A couple of hours later, still deep and now silent, sonar reports a contact on the LF bow array bearing 210°. (There is no towed array because it was dropped while trying to clip it on from the tender when leaving the Kola.) The contact is classified a possible snorkelling submarine but conditions are bad and there is a lot of sea noise.

Kolyshkin is desperate to vindicate himself. What better than to make a practise attack? That should demonstrate zeal and satisfy the Zampolit. He orders the crew to battle stations but, naturally, he does not bring torpedo tubes to the action state. Chief heaves a sigh of relief at that.

The tactics are simple. Kolyshkin alters course to point the target and continuous, albeit inaccurate, sonar bearings soon start to develop a meaningful curve on the Time Bearing Plot in the Control Room while the computer digests the information coming in. After a few minutes the Starpom declares that the target is definitely moving right. Kolyshkin alters course 90° to starboard and increases speed to ten knots for a second leg. The fairly accurate MF/HF passive sonar now gains contact. The maneuver, providing

The published Soviet view, probably now outdated, on how the Norwegian Sea and Greenland-Iceland-UK gaps are guarded by NATO ASW units. The 'barrier' formed by SSNs (numbered patrol areas) has been realistically renamed the 'sieve' by some Western observers. It would clearly need a massive concentration of force to seal the mesh completely — and counter-attacks must be expected.

ASW BARRIERS

GREENLAND

CAPTOR MINES

550 NM

700 NM

900 NM

KOLA

MURMANSK

BODO

1   2   3

4

ICELAND

5

KEFLAVIK

6

FAROES

NORWAY

1000 NM   650 NM   8

SHETLANDS

ORKNEYS

KINLOSS

ST MAWGAN

⊙ SOSUS Sensors

• Surface ASW patrols

☐ SSN patrol areas

⏛ Long-range ASW patrols

that the enemy does not himself change course or speed, should give the plot and computer all the information necessary for target motion analysis: course, speed and range will then be known within reasonable limits. The computer does its job: target course is North, speed 12 knots, range 8000 m.

The *Academy* is too deep for torpedo fire so, with commendable realism, Kolyshkin comes up to 50 m and maneuvers to close for a bow shot with minimum initial angle for his (simulated) fish.

A thoughtless move

All is going well according to the book. Splendid. But Kolyshkin neglects to use commonsense. Why would an enemy submarine be snorkelling in these waters? Intelligence only indicated SSNs: the Americans have no diesel-electric boats and it is hardly possible that either the British or the French would blithely send an SSK rumbling North as far as this at top speed, especially after the ASW aircraft incident.

Sonar still only rates the target as a possible submarine. The revolutions-per-knot don't make sense either for a 12-knot target and there is a lot of clattering on bearing — but Kolyshkin presses on regardless.

The senior sonar operator is now agitated. The contact is extremely loud and there is something odd about it. Kolyshkin ignores him: the computer must be right. In fact the computer is hopelessly wrong — Kolyshkin's fault for trusting inaccurate LF bearings and not repeating the first leg for the benefit of MF/HF sonar.

The target is suddenly audible in the Control Room on the underwater telephone — a disturbing noise which means it is practically on top of the *Academy*. Kolyshkin debates feverishly what to do, rushing first to the computer, then to the plot, then into the sonar office. There is nothing in the Tactical Instructions to guide him — simply because the Rule Book did not foresee a submarine mistaking a very slow (and hence close) trawler for a relatively distant high speed snorkelling submarine.

Kolyshkin dithers distractedly for too long, watched sardonically by the *Zampolit* who has a notebook in his podgy paw. The crash, when it comes, is surprisingly violent: trawl wires are immensely strong and they snatch at the sail like giant steel fingers.

We will leave the luckless *Academy of Sciences* in this predicament. She will get out of it. Chief is on the trim: some energetic

backing and filling will release the trawler's grip eventually. But what then? With the submarine's battery nearly flat, the sail and masts damaged, Norwegian fishermen telling the world what has happened, a fascinated LRMP aircraft overhead, some genuine NATO transitters on their way and the *Zampolit* calling a Party Meeting, Kolyshkin is bound to feel that he is no longer odds-on in the promotion stakes. Even his father won't be able to help him out when the boat limps back to Murmansk where a grim reception committee will be waiting. The *Zampolit* will doubtless be first ashore.

Will the Fleet learn from all this? Probably not. C-in-C cannot afford to jeopardise his own position by washing dirty linen in public; so that will be done behind closed doors before a carefully laundered version is offered to the Defense Council. The officers concerned will simply disappear in the usual way; and the crew, including the Radio Technician who really started the disastrous chain of events, will be transferred to some kind of labor camp where no tales are told.

An unlikely story? Not at all. Submariners practically everywhere will recall failures and mistakes which could very easily follow one another in such a way guided, in this instance, by a Slavic version of Murphy and his inexorable, universal law.

Bridge and sail of a Soviet 'Kilo' SSK with one periscope, radio mast and navigational D/F antenna raised. Soviet bridges are better protected than on Western boats, and there is a lower viewing platform with scuttles because a submarine may have to make a long passage from base on the surface, in Arctic weather, before it can dive. (*Naval Forces*)

SSK versus SSN in the Barents Sea

Meanwhile the Defense Council has been left sitting around the table at Zhiguli. Let us imagine next that it decides to declare the Barents Sea an Exclusion Zone. After all, it is what the British did (without much success) around the Falkland Islands in 1982, so there is an international precedent for banning intruders by physical force. Moreover, in a statement to the United Nations, their Ambassador mentions the approaches to what they regard as their own waters but does not define exactly what these are, nor where the boundaries lie. There is, he claims, justification in that the United States has, from time to time, made somewhat bellicose remarks about mining certain international sea areas, notably the Greenland–Iceland passage, in such and such an eventuality.

What happens now? Do NATO submarines obediently stay away? That is extremely improbable with crisis looming. Submarines can take care of themselves, says the Pentagon, and the British COMSUBEASTLANT, controlling NATO boats in his own wide area, agrees.

So we arrive at a situation where war has not been declared but where opposing forces are virtually bound to come head on against each other. The Soviet Rules of Engagement are assessed at Northwood as free-for-all anywhere North of the Arctic Circle — which is to say about halfway up Norway. NATO submarines are instructed accordingly and the French, at this juncture, decide to join in. COMSUBEASTLANT's Operations Officer suffers a migraine spasm, but he has a Contingency Plan in the safe and the French Liaison Officer at Northwood is duly welcomed into the fold.

Things are going to get nasty, no doubt about that. Nobody is going to back down but there is a fair chance that any fighting will be strictly underwater, at least for the time being.

Returning to the Russian SSK barrier we will, this time, follow the fortunes of Captain Third Rank Seregin in 'Tango' *Yaroslavsky Komsomolets*, 100 n miles northward of the slot once occupied by the *Academy of Sciences*.

Seregin is a Pomar. He considers raw cod the greatest delicacy; and he delights in chewing it straight out of the deep-freeze — particularly if a senior officer is on board.

Not many senior officers ride *Yaroslavsky Komsomolets*.

The crew comprises nine nationalities (the *Starpom* is a Lakh) and they hold their Captain in great affection and regard: he came up the hard way from conscript through *Michman* and there is not the slightest hope of him rising further. He knows his job, his men and his boat intimately. In turn, the men know all about him and are perfectly aware that his control-room tantrums at two o'clock in the morning are just part of the act to get them all moving. They call him *Dyadya*, (Uncle) amongst themselves and cover his tracks when he staggers back on board, with the spirits running out of him and reeking of cheap perfume, after a night in the Officer's Club at the Polyarniy base where the lady officers are party-minded with a small 'p'.

Dyadya is getting on in years and the alcohol in his blood-stream is there to stay — he keeps it topped up at sea — but he has never been incapable on patrol. True, he is a little slow off the mark for the first 48 hours after a spell in port; and his *Starpom* generally has to guide the boat out of harbor by quietly giving orders down the voice-pipe (which the Coxswain obeys) while Seregin bellows strange commands on the intercom (which the Coxswain acknowledges and does *not* obey).[2] But when submerged in the 'Old Lady' (as the submarine is known, with reason) *Dyadya* is in his element. He goes through the boat at least once a day and no nook or cranny is too small to investigate. He can operate every machine on board and his elderly but practised ears often pick up a contact before the sonar operator.

The *Zampolit*, Gusarov, is a true comrade — crony would be a better word — to the Captain. He, too, has no hope of advancement up the political ladder and his superiors have long since given up trying to enthuse him with Marxist-Leninist dogma. So far as they are concerned, Gusarov is beyond redemption and best left to himself. His talks to the crew are perfunctory, politically speaking, but he has an inexhaustible fund of crude tales which he embellishes with words drawn from various vulgar dialects well understood on board. He frequently takes a turn at the periscope or at the controls to give watchkeepers a break.

There are, of course, the normal conscript training problems; but Seregin has his own way of dealing with these. A keen football supporter, he divides the crew into two teams — the Dynamos and the Reservists.

The Dynamos (about half the ship's company) have been on board for six months or longer and have passed *Dyada*'s personal examination. This discounts the voluminous theoretical textbooks but requires every man, individually, to dive and surface the boat, to operate the pumps and associated valves, and to work all the fire-fighting and damage control equipment — the basics in fact. They pick up specialised knowledge by watch-keeping alongside experienced partners until they are competent to carry on by themselves, calling for help, if and when they need it, without feeling ashamed. More detailed esoteric training goes by the board except for the handful of men who are clever and keen enough to seek advancement.

The schooling effort is still considerable; but Seregin has cut the number of normal watchkeepers to the bone in order to leave officers and *Michmaniy* free to train the rest — on the understanding that when the intercom orders 'Dynamos close up' the first eleven takes over at the rush whether or not they are due on watch.

The Navigator is appointed Training Officer and, to give him time for this, the Captain, *Starpom* and a senior *Michman* undertake most of the navigation at sea. There were some raised eyebrows when the navigator — Muhamed Vadyaev — joined because of his Muslim background; but *Dyada* and Gusarov took him to the Officer's Club where he broke most of the Islamic rules in short order and thereafter became quite relaxed about religion.

In short, neither the 'Old Lady' nor her people have any false pretentions; and *Dyadya* welds them into a first-class fighting unit. They are about to demonstrate their mettle.

The patrol orders are simple by Soviet standards, covering no more than a dozen sheets of pulpy foolscap. Sifted, by Seregin, they amount to one thing: sink any enemy submarine which comes your way but don't bother to come back if you start a full-scale war by mistake — that is, if you allow yourself to be identified. Seregin and Gusarov chuckle over the instructions and abstract a fresh bottle of vodka from the wardroom refrigerator.

It is an hour before daybreak. The battery charge has just been broken and the boat has settled back to the most tactically convenient depth at 80 m, in an intermediate layer which the Sound Velocity Meter has revealed between 60 and 460 m. Transitting

SSNs will therefore almost certainly be in the same layer as *Yaroslavsky*.

Four of the six 533 mm bow tubes are loaded with standard ASW torpedoes and the other two with anti-surface weapons. Two of the stern tubes are also loaded with anti-surface fish — not a satisfactory arrangement tactically but ships are low priority targets — while the other two carry self-propelled decoys. There were not enough SS-N-15 ASW missiles at base to go round so none are embarked; but Seregin is not too sad about that; the probability of being permitted to fire them with their nuclear warheads is negligible. Nor does he much regret the lack of the towed array sonar fitted only on the later boats: he feels he would not understand how to use it and, anyway, the 'Old Lady's' relatively low speed (16 knots at best) would make it difficult to get within striking range of a distant SSN. The LF bow array, however, is in good shape and ought to pick up transitters who betray themselves in his patrol area — and that is just what happens, suddenly and without warning.

The sonar operator sings out 'Transient Red nine zero'. The Dynamos race to their stations. Seregin brings the four ASW bow tubes to the action state and interrogates sonar.

The recorded play-back of the transient noise sounds very like masts being raised and bow caps opening — not far away. Seregin checks the noise monitors — his boat is propelling on the center shaft driven by the creep motor — and he is confident that no noise is being emitted. The enemy submarine obviously heard him snorkelling and is stealthily searching the location. Very faint machinery noise and blade-rate is now registering — classified French 'Rubis'-class SSN. Seregin rubs his hands and nods approvingly.

'Hush, hush', he whispers repeating the old Russian proverb, 'little mice must keep quiet when a cat is on the rooftop'.

He guesses that the enemy has come up to shallow depth in order to check visually and with ESM that there is nothing on the surface to confuse his picture — wise in the circumstances (nobody can afford to shoot a non-combatant) but he has, to a small but critical degree, sacrificed stealth.

All contact is lost five minutes later. The Frenchman has gone deep again.

'Wait for it', says Seregin to himself, 'he'll go active next'. Then to the Weapons Control Officer:

'Standby Numbers One and Two tubes.

Overleaf:
Two French L 5 ASW torpedoes are decoyed and miss 'Tango' *Yaroslavsky Komsomolets* — which retaliates successfully.

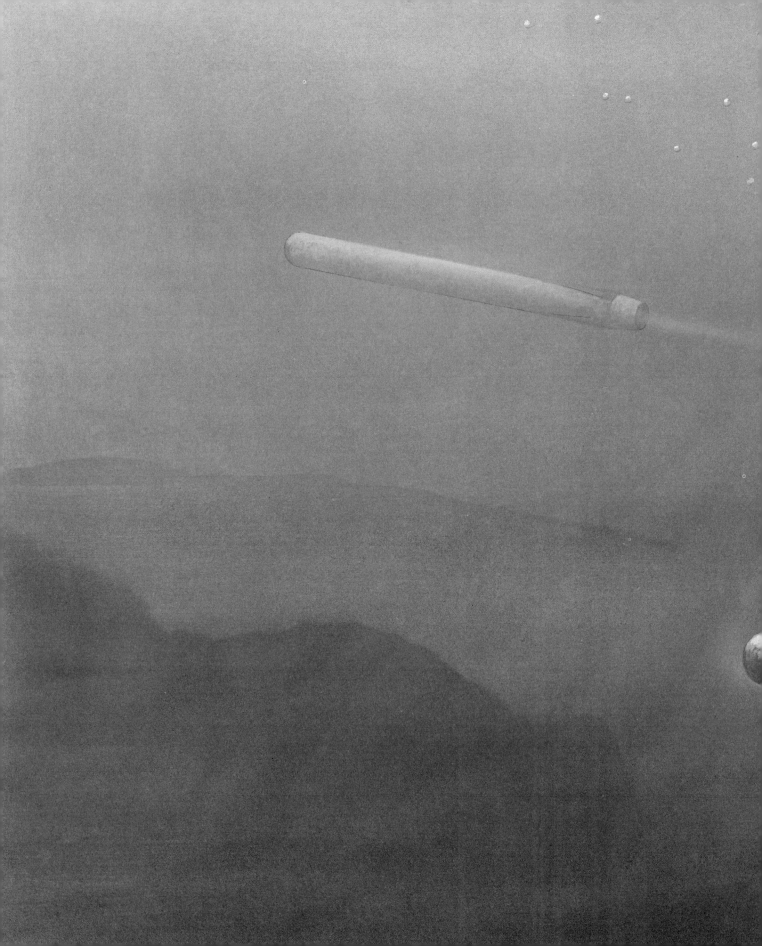

French 'Rubis'-class SSN, the smallest of its kind in the world at 2385/2670 tons and 72.1 m (236.5 ft) long. Commissioned between 1983 and 1987, there are currently four of the type at sea with two more planned. The complement of 9 officers, 35 petty officers and 22 junior ratings is also comparatively small. There are four bow tubes for 18 torpedoes and adapted Exocet anti-ship missiles or a larger quantity of mines. Top speed is believed to be 25 knots and, until recent quieting improvements were made, the boats were said to be rather noisy. (*Naval Forces*).

Do not open bow caps until ordered. Damage Control State One.'

To the *Zampolit*: 'Pass the word forward and aft — tell them what's going on. Oh, and say I will personally cut and mince anyone who makes the slightest noise: then I'll fire him through the garbage ejector.'

The men smile. *Dyadya* is on top form.

The moment comes. A prolonged wave of sound strikes the pressure hull, clearly audible inside, followed 20 seconds later by another.

'Active sonar transmissions Red four zero,' reports the sonar *Michman* laconically, 'true bearing two eight zero. In contact. Definite French sonar designation DUUA-2B. No other noise on bearing.'

Seregin orders Number One, Two, Nine and Ten caps to be opened as soon as he hears the second burst: with any luck the rippling

transmission will help to mask the unavoidable clang and hydraulic whistling while the heavy metallic parts swing aside.

Almost simultaneously sonar sings out: 'Torpedo, Torpedo, Torpedo.'

The Frenchman has put one, maybe two, self-guided active fish in the water. Seregin orders a fifteen down angle, increases to maximum quiet speed on all shafts and discharges two mobile decoys from the stern tubes.

At this point the French captain, presumably because he knows he has already given the game away by going active, decides to alter course away and increase speed a little in case his target has the counterfire weapons he has been told about by intelligence. It is a false move. Seregin checks his dive, levels the boat and looses off two wire-guided homers, at ten second intervals, set to the passive mode. He is taking a calculated risk, but the decoys are said to be pretty effective and GRU espionage has enabled them to be accurately tuned to enemy frequencies.

The decoys do indeed perform as intended and the French free-running L5 fish chase them fruitlessly. Meanwhile, Seregin's two weapons are steered silently towards their target which sonar is holding firmly.

At minute seven after firing, the second torpedo signals back down the wire that it has acquired the noise source itself. The Weapons Control Officer presses the button for release and, quite shortly afterwards, the crew of the *Yaroslavsky Komsomolets* hear what they have been waiting for. The explosion is dull but unmistakeable. A bright flash illuminates the visual sonar display and then, slowly, fades.

An elderly, rugged SSK has put paid to a sophisticated SSN. Of course, it could easily have been the other way around. Seregin has no illusions. Next time, who knows? He was lucky — but, then, he always has been. Modestly, he declines congratulations in the wardroom over a glass or three with Gusarov and the *Starpom*.

'Let's drink to the Dynamos' he growls, 'it was a team effort. Of course he is right. Fortunately for his enemy, there are few of his colleagues who share the same view.

END NOTES
1. The names of people in this chapter are all fictitious, but place names are real.
2. This has actually happened on more than one occasion in a certain anonymous non-Soviet submarine.

2.2

SOVIET SSN TACTICS

We will assume that the situation is the same as that outlined in the last chapter but that nobody, on any side, is yet aware that a French SSN has bitten the dust or that a Soviet SSK is on its way home in disgrace. Nevertheless, Soviet and NATO HQs, to say nothing of the Soviet Defense Council, are hourly expecting reports of submarine-versus-submarine transactions because they are clearly inevitable. Let us now imagine how some SSNs are conducting themselves in this curious but credible undeclared war.

Protecting the Barents Sea

The Red Banner 'Sierra' *Dekabrist* is one of a line of SSNs guarding the Western approaches to the Barents Sea: the center of her patrol area is 20 n miles off the North Cape. Sonar conditions are good and the *Batitermograf* shows only a slight, steady negative gradient down to the bottom at around 300 m. There is not much room for high-speed maneuvering and there is no layer for anyone to hide beneath. The sea is glassy calm and there is dense fog.

Captain First Rank Antonovich Ivanov, newly promoted *in situ*, might reflect that there is quite likely to be a radar duct at the surface, leading to over-the-horizon (OTH) ranges, but he has other things on his mind. The brand new laser-ring SINS, a laboratory breadboard model based on intelligence gathered in America by the GRU, is playing up; and the standard gyro — which the *Shtorman* (Navigator) has paid little attention to because he has become accustomed to relying entirely on standard SINS — seems to be wandering a little. Nor has the *Shtorman* had much practise in bottom-contour navigation; and the chances of celestial fixes through the periscope are zero in the existing visibility. On the communication side, the towed VLF/LF reception buoy winch makes an appalling noise when the cable is wound in or out — Ivanov curses the base maintainer — and all frequencies, including UHF SATCOMS are crowded out.

For the rest of the 'Sierra', Ivanov's officers have not reported any major defects but he knows perfectly well that this proves nothing. True, because *Dekabrist* is a new boat, his crew are 60 per cent hand-picked and pretty reliable — in normal peacetime circumstances — but the old stagers, which he is thankful to have on board, are not innocent of certain subterfuges. As the saying goes, they have eaten bread out of every sort of stove. For example, the Assistant Chief Machinist wears a permanently glazed expression (which the torpedoman who has his own socket-spanner to fit the torpedo fuel chambers could explain if grilled KGB-fashion); and nothing apparently will ever stop the senior Chief Petty Officers from stuffing their tools and personal belongings behind pipes and machinery, just as they used to in the rackety boats of yore. Nor are the *Michmaniy* enthusiastic about fulfilling the preventive maintenance schedules drawn up in such detail by the Technical Staff ashore: putting things right when they go wrong is quite enough. Besides, a new-fangled boat like the *Dekabrist*, with all its gadgetry, ought to be able to look after itself. Didn't the instructors at the Advanced Mechanical Course say that the computers dealt with their own faults? Well, then. If ever there was a true Soviet Trade Union it can be found in the Senior Ratings Mess of the *Dekabrist*: its members work strictly to rule. They are currently muttering amongst themselves and to the Deputy Political Officer (who lives with them in this boat) about the great inconvenience of putting to sea in a hurry. Several of them, it seems, had unfinished business in the Warrant & Chief Petty Officer's Club next

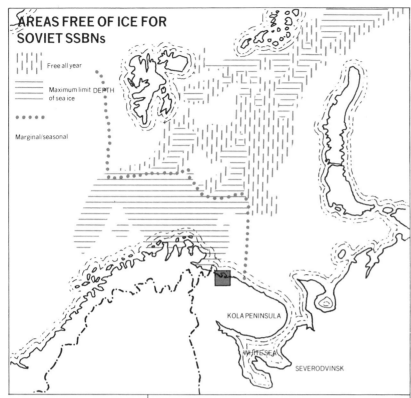

AREAS FREE OF ICE FOR SOVIET SSBNs

| | | | Free all year

Maximum limit DEPTH of sea ice

• • • • • Marginal/seasonal

KOLA PENINSULA

WHITE SEA

SEVERODVINSK

The Kola peninsula is thick with submarine bases, ports, anchorages, command posts and bunkers all of which are well protected geographically as well as by fortifications. A question arises: could a group of determined midget submarines, including robots perhaps, penetrate the undoubtedly strong defenses — at least to some of the more crucial points?

RYBACHIY

• PECHENGA

ZAPADNAYA LITSA BAY

POLYARNY

SEVEROMORSK

NAVAL AVIATION BASE

MURMANSK

exactly where everybody else will be — that, he knows, would be inadmissible. As a matter of fact, C-in-C Northern Fleet and his Submarine Deputy are also given the least possible amount of information about activities outside their direct areas of command while the submarine Brigade and Division Commanders know next to nothing of the big picture. Delegation of authority is minimal and there will come a time — not quite yet — when the Main Staff is hopelessly overburdened. At the end of the line, in the *Dekabrist*, the Captain makes all, repeat all, the decisions — which is fine were it not for the fact that he is expected to chair a meeting, if time allows, of key personnel and Party members (assembled by the *Zampolit*) before taking any major steps, tactical or otherwise.

The objective is clear

The thrust of the orders to the *Dekabrist* is similar to the rest: enemy submarines are the only permissable targets until (codeword) 'Freefire' is broadcast; and nuclear weapons are not to be employed unless specifically ordered. Authentication is then to be checked by the Captain personally, agreed in writing by the Political Officer, and acknowledged to HQ by two-word coded messages assigned for the purpose. (However, no acknowledgement is required for the commands to PLARBs to fire ballistic missiles or to PLARKs to launch land-attack cruise missiles which will be given in much the same way. Authentication at each HQ is initiated by C-in-C himself who in turn personally decrypts, checked by the Chief Political Officer, Top Secret codeword messages of this kind from the Defense Council.)

Dekabrist has now been nearly a week on patrol with no incidents of note. The boat is at 80 m with the towed array streamed and the communications buoy deployed. Speed is five knots on North–South ten-mile legs. The principle sonar window being examined is at the bottom end of the frequency spectrum where bandwidth analysis is, according to intelligence, most likely to yield results.

The conscript sonar operator, who can hear all kinds of noise on his broad bandwidth audio receiver, quite reasonably asks the Sonar Supervisor, sitting behind him, why they are interested in this particular range of low frequencies when there is so much else to hear. The Supervisor is temporarily stunned by an ignorant young *matros* asking a question at all; but he has just enjoyed a good

door to the comparatively sedate Officer's Club just down the road from the Barracks.

Ivanov's patrol orders (he obediently refrained from breaking the seal until clear of harbor) are complicated by reason of very numerous friendly units in the general area. That is, anyway, obvious from the frenzied communication networks. He is told just enough to guess that mutual interference is a real possibility, but not enough to tell him lunch (heavy apple dumplings to conclude) and is feeling kindly for a change.

'What you can hear, my little pigeon, is fishes. They do not concern us. The crackles and pops are shrimps making love (actually he uses a shorter expression) and it is *nyekulturniy*, not cultured, to listen to them. How would you like it if you and your girlfriend...?'

He follows with a lengthy, lurid description of what he, the Supervisor, and his lady-love would, like as not, be doing if they weren't stuck in this God-forsaken tube waiting for Hell-bound capitalist underwater boats. Well into his stride, he suddenly notices a line beginning to mark on the waterfall display at 60 Hz, seizes the intercom with one hand and a lead-bound volume from the shelf above with the other:

'Contact. Narrow-band. Discrete frequency. Nothing audio.'

Ivanov leans into the Sonar Office to have a look for himself. The series of little inverted 'Vs' on the waterfall display are unmistakeably building up into a fairly solid line. There is something there; and the Supervisor, thumbing through the tome on his lap (weighted in case it has to be ditched in the event of trouble) suggests a possible American 'Sturgeon'-class SSN. The young *matros*, a bright lad, figures it out for himself. A steady 60 Hz (cycles per second) signal means that some bit of machinery is whizzing around at 3600 revolutions per minute. That's the sort of speed you might expect from a pump — at least, that's what they told him at Leningrad. It all begins to make sense. Could it be a nuclear plant main circulator? The Captain thinks it could: it's worth investigating.

But where is the signal coming from? The source is obviously very distant (none of the hull-mounted sonars are picking it up) and it could come from either side of the towed array. Ivanov must maneuver so as to resolve the ambiguity. He knows, from bitter experience, that there will be hour after hour of patient work before he can analyse target motion meaningfully even when the initial bearing is determined to within a few degrees. After each turn the towed array must be allowed to stream out straight; other bandwidths must be analysed for the smallest clues to identity and movement; and the hoped-for Doppler shift must be carefully measured with due regard to the input of own movement. There will be plenty of time to hold a meeting in the wardroom and discuss the plan of campaign.

Ivanov wryly remembers the attacks on surface ships he practised during his final Command Course. They were over in minutes and there was never much doubt about the target or what it was doing. Now he must piece together tiny, intermittent scraps of information, like the great English detective *Sherlok Gomes* — one of the few foreign characters allowed in the small library on board.

Intermittent is certainly the word in this case. Bearing ambiguity was easy enough to resolve because commonsense told him that the enemy was coming from the South-West; and an intelligence message confirms that a 'Sturgeon'-type SSN is likely because a fixed seabed array (which Ivanov has private reservations about) evidently had a sniff of one earlier. He is surprised that it is not one of the newer boats in the van. Could it be that the 'Sturgeon' is cannon-fodder? Surely not, but maybe it is taking the easy navigational route to the Barents while the 'Los Angeles' and 'Seawolf' types are headed for the Arctic via side doors in the ice-bound Straits.

Eventually, the combat team start piecing together the jig-saw puzzle. The computer and plots, together with a measurement of blade-rate now apparent, suggest that the target is making 12 knots (Doppler is a great assistance in assessing speed) on a mean course of 050°. The range at noon is about 15 nautical miles and Ivanov prepares to attack. Fortuitously, there will be no need to close the target's track at speed: *Dekabrist* can play the game like an old-fashioned submarine, a mobile mine, and lie in wait with only one of the two reactor plants in operation — and that cooled by natural circulation. The eight knots available at low power will be quite enough unless the enemy makes a radical alteration of course away; and, anyway, the other plant and the main circulating pumps can be brought into operation in less than three minutes if necessary.

However, Ivanov feels uncomfortable on two counts. Firstly, he is not as sure of his position as he would like to be — and if he is a few miles out there is some danger, albeit slight, of long-range weapons hitting a friendly neighbor. Secondly, the sonar plot is showing a vast amount of surface activity to the East, some of it very clearly audible on MF, and Ivanov has a nasty feeling that an ASW group may be on its way out of the Barents. If so, he has not been warned — that is not entirely surprising because of the radio traffic density — but he would dearly like to know if he is about to be overrun by surface forces.

The *Zampolit* agrees that an excursion to periscope depth would be advisable and Ivanov briefs the radar and ESM operators. He is loath to use radar but his appreciation of the situation is that the enemy boat is deep and will therefore not be able to intercept transmissions. If Ivanov brings *Dekabrist* shallow enough — to 20 m with the masts exposed — the Navigator ought to get a reliable fix on North Cape with a few sweeps on the back-to-back antennae. Meanwhile, ESM will record surface radars in the vicinity and help to establish what friendly forces are doing.

The snag is that this will require reeling in the communications buoy and making noise — but if the enemy hears it, as he almost certainly will, Ivanov hopes that his picture, too, will be confused by the surface ships beyond.

Ivanov is over-optimistic. The American boat, whose captain knows full well he is in a danger zone, reduces speed to a quiet seven knots and broadens his zig-zag, partly to clear his sonar baffles and partly to complicate a listening enemy's TMA problem. He also decides to come up to have an electronic 'look' in order to clarify the situation.

Tension increases

As luck would have it, both boats — now only some ten miles apart — arrive at ESM/radar depth simultaneously. The American boat's outdated WLR-4 EW equipment is not integrated and it takes painfully long minutes to relate ESM, sonar and intelligence data. The periscope is, of course, useless in the fog but an emitter bearing about 060° is identified (with a high level of confidence) by frequency, pulse width, pulse interval and scan period (three recorded emissions only) as the type of Soviet submarine 'Snoop series' radar fitted in 'Sierra' and 'Mike' SSNs. Radar ducting is undoubtedly being experienced but, nevertheless, the emitter must be quite close. ESM ties in nicely with the strange creaking noises reported by sonar a short while ago.

The American Captain goes deep, orders the crew to Battle Stations for a Mark 48 attack, and brings two of his four tubes to immediate readiness.

The *Dekabrist* goes to 40 m — no need to stream the communications buoy again because the nearby VLF transmitter comes in strongly on the loop at this depth — and continues his cautious approach, opening

Numbers Three and Four bow caps (for wire-guided weapons) and Five and Six bow caps for the standard self-defense salvo in the event of counter-attack. The hydraulic pumps are working overtime to recharge the reservoirs; and this is where the recalcitrant senior Chief Petty Officers are to blame for subsequent events. One of them has wedged his tool box between the forward pump and the hull where it won't be robbed by junior ratings — but where it effectively shorts the sound insulation.

The hydraulic pump noise registers distinctly on the console of the American boat's BQQ-5 hull-mounted sonar, and blade-rate from a six-bladed propeller is now also analysed with faint cavitation on broad band showing as a harmonic on narrow band. The Soviet submarine is evidently not using any esoteric form of propulsion and, probably, one of the blades on her screw is chipped. Ivanov knows about this: he ran across some floating timber on his way out of harbor and the self-noise monitor aft has indicated occasional cavitation as well as singing. He endeavors to avoid the critical revolutions and depths at which this occurs but necessarily has to pass through them sometimes — as he does now on his way down. Still, there is no indication whatever that the enemy has counter-detected him: the transients *Dekabrist* might have heard when the American made his tubes ready have been masked by self-noise arising from the up-and-down maneuvers and by a loose bolt in the casing forward which is making things difficult for the bow fire-control sonar. Again, Ivanov curses the maintainers at Polyarniy.

The Russian boat fires a little before the American which hears the incoming fish and endeavors to evade — but there is no layer, no adequate depth for drastic maneuvers and, wriggle though the Captain does, the weapons latch on. There is no shaking them off. But his own (non-ADCAP) Mark 48s, also in the passive mode, are well on their way: one of them acquires the target and goes in to attack. At almost the same time one of the Russian weapons strikes home, rupturing the single hull in the engine-room section and sending the American boat to the bottom. There is absolutely nothing the crew can do to stem the huge inrush of water. Mercifully, it is all over very quickly: the rapid rise of pressure alone renders the men unconscious.

The *Dekabrist* is equally threatened — and that damnable loose bolt made it impossible to detect the Mark 48. The explosion, amidships against the outer sheathing, shakes the 'Sierra' mightily — but, distanced by more than two meters from the titanium pressure hull and softened by porous material in between, it does not result in flooding. True, the fire-control computer goes off the board, joined by the dubious SINS, and reload weapons in their racks are severely jolted; but the damage control pumps cope adequately with sundry hull-gland leaks. Main propulsion — despite an automatic shutdown (or 'scram') which is quickly reversed by battle override procedures — is unaffected. Sonar retains a limited capability: when the mess has been cleared up, it appears that substantial parts of the array are still functioning; and electronic units are repaired by replacement.

The real problem is that the crew is in a state of shock — stand fast the Old Comrades who recommend, through the Deputy Political Officer, that the submarine carries on. They have no wish to return to the Kola unnecessarily: prospects would be bleak on arrival. They would much rather stay on patrol and become heroic defenders of the Motherland than risk an indeterminate spell as unheroic workers in a labor camp. The Party meeting convened in the Control Room, which Ivanov dare not quit until everything is sorted out, ratifies the recommendation. Let us hope, thinks Ivanov to himself, that no other enemy boat is detected: but impaired sonar performance should take care of that unwanted possibility.

Unfortunately, *Dekabrist* is now more noisy than she was. Really, she is in no shape for an ASW patrol. Ivanov decides to stay as quiet as he can in the circumstances: a word with the Sonar Supervisor ensures that any contacts will be judiciously disregarded — or, at least, that they will only be whispered to the Captain personally — on the overt grounds of maintaining morale in case the *Zampolit* becomes suspicious.

On ASW patrol off the Kola

Some way astern of the ill-starred American SSN (which was lost by the fortunes of war and not through any fault of its people — although if Congress had appropriated more money for modernisation they would have been better placed) a British 'Trafalgar'-class SSN — HMS *Tantivy* — is bound for ASW operations off the Kola. Coincidentally, the commanding officer has the same first name as Ivanov — Tony; but he is a markedly less solemn individual, notorious for irreverence. He has learned the book inside out; but six years in command, first in an SSK, then in the old SSN *Warspite* and now in the virtually brand new *Tantivy* allow him to bend tactical and administrative rules without any qualms of conscience. He is known, throughout the Submarine Service, as Tony the Yoni (a Kama Sutra reference to his principal recreational interest ashore) or, on board, simply as 'The Yoni'. A little notice in his cabin constantly reminds him of what he claims to be the family motto: 'Live long, be wise — decentralize'. Flexibility is his watchword.

Tantivy is streaming her Type 2046 towed array and broadly zig-zagging to give it a fair chance of picking up contacts ahead. At 12 knots she is practically silent: noise hygiene is The Yoni's other hobby and woe betide any member of the crew who jeopardises it. The maintenance staff at Faslane are terrified of *Tantivy* (as the Captain himself is called, by ancient custom, on formal occasions) and they have done their work meticulously. No one is safe from The Yoni's prying eyes: he is for ever strolling through the submarine peering into this or that and questioning the men on watch. His knowledge of nuclear theory is not as detailed as his American contemporaries but it is quite enough for practical purposes: he concentrates his mind almost wholly on tactics against the opposition while letting his technical officers worry about their part of the ship. In fact, he has rounded North Cape more than once in recent years and brought back a lot of invaluable intelligence, besides reinforcing his own opinion that Russian submariners are emphatically not ten feet tall.

Tantivy's sonar has some strange markings on the historical waterfall. The Yoni has not seen anything quite like them before — except when he fired a live warhead at an obsolete frigate during conclusive trials of Tigerfish. Some kind of action seems to have been taking place in the area which he is now stealthily approaching. His Operation Order tells him exactly who is where on the NATO side, and he receives a continual stream of intelligence from Northwood although the bursts of noise ahead have no obvious relationship to the messages so far. The five tubes forward are loaded with Tigerfish Mod 2 torpedoes and there are 20 reloads in the racks. He does not have to worry about a mix of weapons: none of the

Overleaf:

HMS *Tantivy* (SSN) versus *Dekabrist* ('Sierra' SSN). Following earlier damage by the US 'Sturgeon' the Soviet 'Sierra's' pod propulsion is U/S. She is propelling on her single shaft with only one of the two reactors on line although neither was seriously affected by the first explosion. However, *Tantivy*'s Tigerfish, programmed to home in passively for the kill by leading the principal (propeller) noise source in the direction of target movement, is fatal.

The Tigerfish attack, after initial wire-guidance, is autonomous: the on-board analog computer took command from the moment that the controller in *Tantivy* accepted that the torpedo had itself acquired the target. The submarine could have reassumed command if necessary, but if the Tigerfish failed at the first pass it would automatically have commenced re-attack maneuvers.

scarce new Spearfish weapons were allocated to *Tantivy* and Sub-Harpoon was deemed undesirable for this patrol which is to be devoted exclusively to submerged targets. If the orders change Tigerfish will cater pretty well for most, if not all, surface targets. Nevertheless, he often hankers for a few good old straight-running Mark 8's with their big warheads. He dismisses the idea as silly — there are none left in the service anyway — but the thought persists.

Amongst the items destroyed on the *Dekabrist* by the explosion were the self-noise monitors: apart from indications on the partial sonar suit remaining, that noise is being transmitted to the water — mostly from the outer hull in all probability — Ivanov does not realise how detectable he is. The Yoni, on the other hand, soon gets to know: his sonar operator reports an extraordinary medley of tones up and down the scale. The initial, typically unawed, classification is a vintage motor car in the process of falling to bits. Analysis is hardly necessary. A careful 'look' on Searcher ESM establishes that there are no nearby surface radars although Warner indicates a Bear ASW aircraft radar approaching danger level — whereupon The Yoni lowers all masts and slips down to 100 m.

Soviet submarine cornered

Surface radars would certainly be operating in this fog if ships were in the vicinity; and maximum ESM range on those would be outside the sonar contact's fairly close position which the plotters have roughly calculated. So Tony the Yoni reckons, rightly, that he has nailed a Soviet submarine.

Tantivy's tactics are child's play. So long as the boat is stealthy, it is just a matter of maneuvering to refine the fire-control solution and firing when within weapon range. When The Yoni is sure that he is in a good position he orders Numbers One and Two bow caps to be opened slowly and silently by a crafty method recently devised. He then contents himself with telling the Weapons Control Officer to get on with it and stands back.

A single Tigerfish is launched towards the target which might have been specially made for optimum passive acquisition: no point in despatching a second fish yet. The *Dekabrist* hears nothing until the last — and this time fatal — bang. The Russian SSN cannot stand the second shock. The hull is not completely ruptured but a split develops aft (where the torpedo struck and where the hull

separation is least) and several large important hull fittings are fractured.

Ivanov desperately orders Full Ahead — alas, on the battery with both reactors well and truly scrammed, that won't amount to more than four knots — and blows main ballast while his *Starpom* checks that watertight doors and bulkhead openings are shut. The Chief Engineer blasts high-pressure air into the stern compartment where the leaks are worst — too bad about the men inside. For a short while it looks as though these measures will succeed; but the depth and pitch indicators in the Control Room soon start to show the truth. The *Dekabrist* is doomed.

However, the forward bulkheads will resist water pressure on the bottom where the boat thuds down at 230 m; by the Grace of Marx she has settled on a relatively shallow patch. The surviving crewmen cannot breathe indefinitely without the usual air-production plant but foot-pedalled carbon dioxide scrubbers and emergency oxygen bottles will enable them to last for several days in what journalists would relish describing as a living tomb. What are their chances, if any?

Perhaps we have speculated enough already. It might be kinder to imagine no further; but it is relevant that *Dekabrist*'s predicament is not beyond hope — or, rather, all would not be lost in normal times. The Northern Fleet 'India'-class rescue submarine could be on the spot, with her two deep submergence rescue vessels (DSRVs) in less than 48 hours (if not already busy with military midgets) in response to the automatic distress message continuously broadcast by the pair of emergency buoys which Ivanov can release. In fact, whether the Captain orders their release or not, it is odds on that one of the Old Comrades will turn the little handles (probably only secured by seals) to let them float to the surface.

What then? NATO will unquestionably intercept the buoy's transmissions as well as Soviet receiving stations. Will the distress call bring everybody to their senses and result in a combined Search and Rescue operation?

That is almost as conceivable as the other scenarios we have been conjecturing. And, incidentally, if the errors and omissions, the functions and the malfunctions, the good and bad performances seem a little far-fetched, submariners themselves might agree them to be pretty much par for the course.

BLACKMAIL

Besides the possibility of terrorists planting a mini-atom bomb beneath the Empire State Building, there are means of nuclear blackmail which are all too easily conceivable in the not very distant future. None have anything to do with the supposed villain of the piece — the Soviet Union — which some would say has become the least likely of all the major powers to brandish nuclear weapons seriously, let alone recklessly.

The possibilities, all concerned with the same theme, involve relatively small powers who acquire — or have acquired — a modest nuclear arsenal. There is no need to say who these might be but there are several of them.

Supposing that country X threatens nearby country Y with nuclear attack that if such and such is not done or agreed, it can carry out its threat with missiles, bombs or (less likely) with guns.

It is seaborne cruise missiles which concern us primarily in the submarine context and they can be deployed with two quite different purposes in mind.

Firstly, noting that it is quite simple and inexpensive to adapt ordinary submarines for launching cruise missiles, they can be used for straightforward shore bombardment. The Chinese Navy had little difficulty in equipping some of its 'Romeos' with cruise and other navies could follow suit. Granted, the 'Romeos' have to surface in order to fire but that is no great hardship in areas where ASW protection is weak or non-existent. Tomahawk-type weapons, of course, are launched from submerged but they are far from readily available while standard surface-to-surface missiles embarked in cannisters are quite easily obtained.

Secondly, cruise missiles can be mounted for deterrence. That is how major powers could most easily keep minor powers in check — and realists might agree that this is a predictably needful task for the future. Realists may also concur in the avoidance of ballistic missiles for limited war (because they are too liable to trigger global response by virtue of their detectability) while placing cruise missiles in submarines where they are con-

cealed until the moment arrives.

However, although nuclear missiles seem to be the only effective means of deterrence (because everybody understands their devastating effect) chemical or biological/bacteriological warheads could certainly be used for attack. Gas has too often been employed in the past to deny the possibility — indeed probability — and a number of countries are known to have researched germ warfare. Again, submarine-launched cruise missiles (SLCMs) are excellent vehicles for carrying unconventional warheads; and, as pointed out in Chapter 1.8, they can be exchanged for conventional warheads as and when circumstances dictate.

All in all, quite apart from anti-ship attacks, SLCMs can be expected to figure more and more prominently in submarine warfare. And it is extremely difficult to mount a guard against them save with ASW submarines. Submarines are the only units possessing the necessary endurance for long-term search and surveillance and which are not apt to precipitate hasty action — use them or lose them — by prospective perpetrators.

Israel faces a nuclear threat

For the sake of illustration we will imagine that Israel's outstandingly good intelligence organization learns that a hostile Muslim state has plans to blackmail her with newly acquired nuclear SLCMs: the missiles are supplied by a major power but the warheads are manufactured locally with expertise derived from another source. The diesel-electric submarine missile-carrier is by no means modern or particularly quiet: the navy

Overleaf:
An SSK converted to SSG (no particular type or nationality in the imaginary sequence) surfaces to launch cruise missiles against Tel Aviv.

Radar is used for guidance to ensure that the 'birds' assume their initial course at low level towards a geographical feature before their self-navigation system takes over.

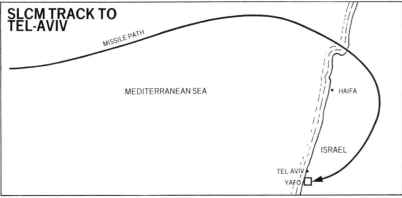

SLCM TRACK TO
TEL-AVIV

MISSILE PATH

MEDITERRANEAN SEA

• HAIFA

ISRAEL

TEL-AVIV
YAFO

Top: A submarine-launched (conventional HE) Tomahawk cruise missile about to detonate over its assigned target during tests from off the US West Coast. Precision is the principal attribute of an SLCM like Tomahawk or the Soviet SS-N-21.

Above: A missile envisaged in the scenario illustrated on the preceding pages would head for a distinctive landmark — say Haifa Bay — where terrain-matching will commence to steer it, by means of the on-board navigational system, southerly towards the Israeli capital. This sort of route has the advantage of surprise because defenders would look primarily to seawards for the threat.

concerned (as is probable in any conceivable case) has not interested itself in submarine-versus-submarine warfare which requires much more sophisticated and silent boats than middling grade anti-ship warfare.

What can Israel do, unilaterally, to defend herself against a nuclear onslaught from the sea? Given that the range of cruise missiles is measured in hundreds of kilometers it will be impossible, on the face of it, to keep an eye on all possible launch positions without active assistance from a friend, say the United States, who might afford satellite and/or ASW aircraft coverage. But the problem might not be quite as great as it appears.

Assuming that the missiles are not of a very advanced type and lack 'low observable' (stealth) characteristics the enemy will prefer to fire them from not too far away. Then they have to pick up a significant landmark to commence their computerized terrain-matching course inland to selected targets — or indeed to detonate over the

capital Tel Aviv which actually borders the sea. Any mistake in their self-navigation would be disastrous for neighbouring countries so the attacker must make things as easy as possible for the birds to fly correctly to their destination. That requires very detailed mapping inputs for the computers: it is, in fact, the seeking of navigational information beforehand which may alert Israeli intelligence in the first place.

It might, therefore, be feasible to delineate a high probability launching zone which will, incidentally, be clear of normal shipping routes in all probability and well away from areas regularly patrolled by any navy's ASW forces. The latter considerations alone should help to narrow the field.

It is reported that Israeli SSKs will soon be carrying American Mk NT37-E dual-purpose homing torpedoes — well tried and tested weapons — and their Plessey sonar is believed to be able to detect, passively, all but quiet targets. If two SSKs (out of three) are operationally available they should be able to patrol a total area of about 13 000 sq km (nearly 4000 sq nautical miles) which is a sizeable chunk of sea. It is impossible to estimate detection probability on an intermittently snorkelling submarine but it ought to be high enough to make the search worthwhile — especially if a friend assists with other intelligence.

What does the Israeli Commander do if he does uncover a submarine? Very seldom can sonar classification be trusted to the point of positive identity outside the most advanced analysis systems, and then only in quite limited circumstances: so how does he know if he is tracking a hostile missile-launcher? Exactly the same difficulty faces any kind of ASW unit, of course; but an SSK stands a fair chance of being able to latch on to a contact which, if it is a missile boat, will be disinclined to move far from its chosen position. But when can the SSK attack? Another good question. It will be obvious when the missile boat surfaces preparatory to firing — although that implies visual observation through the periscope assisted, at night, by infra-red viewing or image intensification.

Is an operation of this sort practicable? The answer (regrettably like so many other answers) is anybody's guess. We took Israel merely as an example, encouraged by the efficiency and flexibility of her submariners although they cannot have had all that much practise in submarine-versus-submarine tac-

primary task but smaller countries. In some cases conventional warheads might do the trick without going nuclear at all. However, it has to be repeated that cruise missiles need maps, which take a lot of effort to compile, in order to find their way: they cannot be loosed at random if they are to strike targets with an acceptable degree of accuracy.

Whatever the difficulties, if a submerged launcher is to be nailed, the job is probably best done by another submarine. Maybe, if successful in his search before hostilities commence, the hunter-killer should then content himself with keeping overt tabs on the opponent (calling up other forces to help if they are available) while making sure — by active sonar or underwater telephone — that the enemy knows he is being observed. It has also been suggested that the hunter-killer might 'bell the cat' by firing a stick-on tell-tale device — difficult but not impossible, apparently.

Which leads us back to the most enigmatic question of all: can SSBNs be discovered in their hiding places and, if so, at what stage can they be attacked?

tics. In fact she might well answer blackmail with a nuclear threat of her own, rather than trying to find an enemy launcher. But the principle is pretty much the same anywhere.

At the other end of the scale, stealthy USN and Soviet SSGNs (or missile-equipped SSNs) would be exceedingly difficult to find because, with very long range missiles, they have such a wide choice of patrol zones. The same would be true of British and French submarines if they adopted a system like Tomahawk to deter not the USSR as their

The submarines of all navies, perhaps most especially those belonging to relatively small nations, may well have to guard against the threat of SLCMs. Cruise missiles, as well as being an excellent deterrent at a lower level than SLBMs (and much less likely to provoke an international nuclear exchange), are also a means of potential blackmail — which cynics might say is much the same thing as deterrence.

Some of the boats which might be involved in helping to defeat an SLCM threat are illustrated here. **Top:** One of the first-rate Japanese SSKs which will be succeeded by the new 'Improved Yuushio'-class from 1991.

Far left: The outstandingly efficient Australian Squadron at sea with only one of the six 'Oxley's' missing from the picture. Equipped with Mk 48 Mod 8 torpedoes, Sub Harpoon, Type 2007 long-range passive sonar, Micropuffs and American Singer Librascope fire-control they have a formidable weapon system; but the ageing 'O' boats are to be replaced by Swedish-designed Kockums SSKs, which not everyone agrees to be the best answer for the RAN. Perhaps Australia was not aware of what Italy has to offer in the shape of very fast air-independent propulsion system for SSKs which thereby become, in effect, 'Green Nukes' capable, in one design, of 30 knots for 3000 miles fully submerged. **Left:** Norway is in the front-line of NATO defenses and her bases are eyed acquisitively by the USSR. Her 11 small 370/435-ton 'Kobben'-class (*Kobben* pictured) are well armed with 8 American NT 37C and Swedish Type 61 dual-purpose torpedoes (all in tubes, no reloads). Six of a new 'Ula'-class, larger at 940/1300 tons, are starting to commission.

2.4

SUBMARINE PIRATES

If major powers confront one another, minor powers can be expected to seize the opportunity of settling old scores and furthering their local interests. Outright piracy is bound to be tempting in such circumstances and submarines are ideal for that. Indeed, many authors, from the time that submarines were first conceived, have described their actions as piratical even during formal warfare.

Doubtless trouble-makers have read the history books and will use their imagination — as we must ourselves to devise nefarious underwater schemes for implementing when the world's attention is distracted elsewhere. Submarines will probably not be the only tools which they employ but they are likely, by their stealthy nature, to figure importantly. So we will imagine a scenario well removed from the main areas of high tension envisaged already.

Supposing that merchant ships start to vanish in the Mediterranean amidst a flurry of distress messages which tell only of heavy explosions, it will be some time before international authorities (as well as Lloyds London insurance brokers who have taken a battering in recent years) decide what villains are responsible. Are saboteurs or mines or torpedoes doing the damage?

Intelligence organisations, which are remarkably well forewarned about sabotage nowadays, conclude that sabotage is unlikely and mines along the fairly deep-water routes are, on the whole, improbable — which leaves submarine attack as the most probable cause in our scenario.

Events in the Spanish Civil War and the subsequent Nyon Patrol are recalled by a few officers who paid attention to historical lessons during their Staff Courses. It is sure that neither Spain nor Italy are to blame this time but there are several Mediterranean countries with a submarine arm. Could it be Algeria?

No: her two 'Romeos', on long loan from the USSR, are solely for ASW training purposes and, anyway, Algeria is not inclined to look for trouble at sea. Nor is Israel with her three IKL/Vickers Type '540s': she has enough trouble on her hands already although her very efficient boats are prepared to act swiftly for defense. Greece? No: she is admittedly a rather difficult member of the Atlantic Alliance but she stakes a lot on the trade which has resulted from joining the European Common Market. Turkey? Definitely not: leaving aside the ongoing quarrel with Greece she has no wish to jeopardize strong Western contacts. Syria? Possibly, but her three ex-Soviet 'Romeos' are not thought to be in very good shape for offensive operations.[1]

Albania? Conceivably — she is a somewhat unpredictable State — but her pair of operational 'Whiskeys' are very long in the tooth and they have had no spares from the USSR since the split in 1961. Could Russian submarines themselves be responsible for the sinkings?

No to that on two counts: firstly, Hammer-and-Sickle merchantmen seem to be endangered as much as the rest; and secondly, the Kremlin prefers to get other people to do the dirty work in circumstances like this. No other country outside the Mediterranean is sufficiently keen on creating mayhem on these crucial trade routes, to risk coming a long way and transiting the Gibraltar Straits which are liable to ASW blockade.

The finger therefore points, in our imagination, at the remaining State which, for a purpose which does not have to be logical by Western ways of thinking, might resolve to embark on a Mediterranean anti-shipping campaign — Libya. (Colonel Gadaffi's mining exploits in the Gulf of Suez and the Red Sea between July and September 1984 were not rational but they were warmly applauded by Khomeni from Iran.)

Libya seeks to plunder

We will therefore suppose that, for reasons best known to himself, Gadaffi has despatched a brace of 'Foxtrots', *Al Khyber* and *Al Hunain*[2] to do their worst. The first is patrolling 50 miles south of Cape Spartivento, the southernmost point of Sardinia, and the second is 30 miles North of Cape Bon in the Sicilian Channel. Each boat carries 14 free-running Soviet anti-ship torpedoes (5000 yards at 45 knots with no homing): six are loaded in the bow tubes. The four stern tubes, with four reloads, are for rudimentary 406 mm anti-escort homing weapons with an alternative but very limited ASW capability.

The initial merchant targets have been easy meat — no zig-zags, constant speed and every ship long enough to make at least one hit certain from a mile with salvo fire. There will be medals all round (no one will be left out) on return to harbor and maybe a few Iranian decorations will be thrown in.

The NATO Alliance, preoccupied in the North, could do without these depredations in the Med. The USSR, on the other hand, is delighted even though, inadvertently, some Russian ships must suffer: KGB livers-in at Tripoli have done splendidly to ensure that the Colonel has taken such a precipitous course of action. Somebody in the West will have to do something about it — and that means less forces available for challenging the situation developing above the Arctic circle. And all without cost to the Motherland — apart from the usual modest outgoings on KGB salaries and 'expenses'.

The 'somebody', elected unanimously by the United Nations to cope, is, naturally, France. The prospect of glory, international gratitude even, is on offer — and it is an offer which the French President cannot refuse. But some hasty consultations with the Chief of the Naval Staff and members of *Conseil Supérieur de la Marine* suggest it would be as well to enlist the help of Italy: the Mediterranean is a big place and French naval resources are stretched in preparation for what looks like a coming crisis.

The two naval staffs get together and decide primarily on submarine ASW to winkle out the Libyan SSKs (intelligence has by now confirmed the source of the trouble) because stealth will be needed when the Libyan boats are so close to their own home port and, although other units will be deployed in a supporting role, surface ships could be at some risk: no losses can be afforded — especially the big prestigious air-

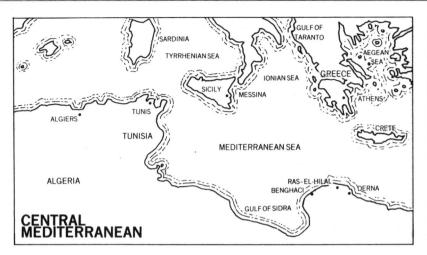

CENTRAL MEDITERRANEAN

craft carriers. However, the elderly LPH[3] *Jeanne d'Arc*, with eight operational but unintegrated and unaccustomed ASW Lynx helicopters urgently embarked, will be sailed around from Brest (where she is normally based for training duties) *à toute vitesse* to the critical arena.

The Italian Navy, noting that an all too detectable surface force could simply result in the Libyan boats sneaking back to base before they are caught, is deploying (besides submarines) an ASW task group centered on the light carrier *Vittorio Veneto* with nine AB 212 helicopters on board: this group will stand back while the French SSN *Casabianca*[4] from Toulon will be ready to move to center stage quickly when directed.

The French go to work

The exceptionally small 2670-ton *Casabianca* has recently been converted under the 'Amethyste' program (AMelioration Tactique HYdrodynamique Silence Transmission Ecoute) to a high standard of ASW efficiency: in her original anti-surface role she was rather noisy for submarine-versus-submarine operations but all her machinery is now quietened. She has DSUV-22 low frequency passive sonar, DUUA-2B active sonar (8kHz) and DUUX-5 passive-ranging equipment. Her usual complement of SM-39 'Exocet'-type anti-surface missiles has been reduced to three (all in the racks) for this patrol: two of the four tubes are loaded with 35-knot L5 passive/active homers (range 7000 m) and two with 25-knot E15 passive homers (range 12 000 m). The E15s have a good acquisition capability and, with a 300 kg warhead, carry twice the explosive power of the L5s, but they can only be employed against shallow, noisy targets.

The central Mediterranean is just as crucial strategically as it ever was and merchant shipping is vulnerable to submarine attack, especially in the fairly narrow Straits where routes are predictable.

The main Libyan submarine base is at Ras el-Hilal, east of the Gulf of Sirte, but this is not the only harbor from which Libyan submarines could sortie if the kind of events imagined in the scenario actually took place.

A French Maritime Reconnaissance 'Atlantic' aircraft patrol is continuously maintained over the area.

Two Italian submarines, the relatively new 1662-ton Improved 'Sauros' *Salvatore Pelosi* and *Guiliano Prini* with excellent integrated sonar systems and Type A 184 wire-guided torpedoes, are sailed to a long-stop patrol zone some 20 miles from the Libyan Ras el-Hilal submarine base, just far enough offshore to avoid the danger of defensive mines which Libyan boats are believed to have laid along the 100 meter line.

Casabianca has free rein throughout the Sicilian Channel and as far West as the longitude of Cape Spartivento. All NATO submarines and military aircraft in the Mediterranean have been diverted to keep well clear: Claude Favrolet, the SSN's *Commandant*, has no-holds-barred orders to shoot any submerged boats which he discovers. The two Italian submarines have similar orders but, to avoid mutual interference, are not to approach within 15 miles of *Casabianca*'s southern boundary.

The 'Atlantic' aircraft on task is not permitted to attack any contact unless under the direct control of *Casabianca* and nor are any other forces if they enter the SSN's clearly defined patrol area.

The two Libyan SSKs are, frankly, enjoying themselves. The crews have been trained in the USSR (where replacements are given instruction on a continuing basis) but they have only been taught to attack simple surface targets — which is all that their fire-control systems are capable of anyway. It took a very long time for the boats to reach a

satisfactory standard but, after a dozen years, the proof is in the pudding: they are achieving hits. In fact, they are having it all their own way: apart from having to point the bows towards Mecca at appointed times the captains are unrestricted. Ship recognition is not their strong point and one of the merchantmen that goes down is a Soviet vessel. But no matter: sinking a non-Muslim ship (none belonging to a True Believer is likely to pass by) is a matter for praising Allah, whoever it belongs to.

In short, the Libyan captains are entirely confident and well pleased with themselves. They are ignorant of submarine-versus-submarine warfare (which is a closely guarded secret at Leningrad) but they are prepared to face surface ASW forces if they appear over the horizon. They have had no experience of ASW fixed-wing opponents because the Libyan Armed Forces do not include them. The two squadrons of Mi-14 'Haze' and 'Super Frelon' helicopters do exercise occasionally with submarines but their mutual ability in realistic circumstances is an unknown quantity. Stop Light broad band ESM is installed on its own mast in all 'Foxtrots', principally as a 'Warner': danger levels are understood in principle but total lack of practise against Maritime Patrol/Reconnaissance aircraft is bound to mean that officers-of-the-watch stop snorkelling rather arbitrarily when radar emissions are detected, even if correctly recognised by the Stop Light operator.

All forces are now, for the sake of our story, in position. *Al Khyber* has moved clear of the latest flaming datum and is at periscope depth in a calm sea awaiting the next victim. Periscope drill is immaculate in a Russian parade-ground sort of way. The Officer-of-the-Watch, standing rigidly to attention when not applying himself to the eye-pieces, orders the periscope to be raised for precisely one minute at a time: all round sweep in low power (× 1½ magnification) then half-a-revolution in high power (× 6 magnification). No other masts are raised and the 'Foxtrot' is propelling at three knots on the center shaft.

Nothing, apart from a collection of small fishing boats, has been sighted for some time and sonar has no significant contacts. But half way through a spicey dish of mutton and rice, the Captain is called to the control room. There is a wisp of smoke on the horizon to the West. Masts eventually appear and the boat is brought round to an intercept track based

The Italian 1476/1662-ton *Salvatore Pelosi* completing in 1986. The two SSKs of this 'Improved Sauro' type have six tubes for Type 184 dual-purpose wire-guided torpedoes (6 reloads), and have a good ASW capability with the integrated acoustic Type IPD 705 system comprising a linear passive array, passive HF, passive ranging and active sonar in the bow dome. Maximum depth is 300 m with a safety factor of 2. Top speed is 20 knots submerged.

on the Captain's estimate of target course by angle-on-the-bow which is very broad. Speed is increased to six knots between 'looks', ducking down to 33 m in a doctrinal gesture to avoid cavitation. In fact, cavitation is not entirely avoided, the casing rattles at this speed and the starboard screw is singing lightly: all this is audible on own sonar but the operator is fully intent on trying to pick up the target through the welter of self-noise so he says nothing about it apart from a continual grumble to himself. The Captain can see no ASW vessels and there are no active sonars registering on the sonar intercept set — so he is not concerned with anything except getting within range for the next shot.

Al Khyber starts to get clumsy

His lack of concern will prove *Al Khyber's* undoing. *Casabianca*, approaching from the West above the layer at ten knots, hears him loud and clear at an approximate range of 26 km (judged initially by intelligence information and the French automatic Sound Ray Tracer). From now on it should be easy for the SSN; but to be quite sure he is not tracking a non-combatant (despite definite classification on DSUV 22) Favrolet slows down to four knots, comes silently to periscope depth and calls up the 'Atlantic' on UHF.

The aircraft is keeping a plot of every surface contact over the entire area embracing 22 000 square km — no problem. He now homes on the beacon provided by the SSN's UHF and overflies the submarine which vectors the 'Atlantic' accurately out towards the contact: radar is switched off until close to the estimated position. The pilot confirms that there is no surface shipping along the vector line, but the radar operator reports a small disappearing blip and the co-pilot believes he saw a slight swirl as he passed over the spot. A classical pattern of passive sonobuoys is dropped and, a couple of minutes later, the TSM 8200 acoustic system is processing faint signals from buoys four and five. Favrolet, duly informed, tells the aircraft that he is going to attack: to be on the safe side he reminds the pilot that airborne weapons are 'tight' and are not, repeat not, to be released.

Meanwhile, *Al Khyber* merely notes the unwelcome presence of an ASW aircraft and disgustedly accepts that he must not use the periscope as he would wish. A sonar fire-control solution will probably not be good enough (the system lacks an adequate computer) and he will have to show the 'scope

again before long. For the time being he will continue to close the track at moderate speed: the Torpedo Officer at the calculator announces that, at this rate, the attack will last another 45 minutes (the boat was way off track to start with) but that is all to the good: the aircraft may, hopefully, get bored and go away before the submarine is due to fire. There is, of course, no indication in the SSK either that sonobuoys are in the water or that an avenging SSN is silently approaching.

Favrolet has only one real difficulty — time. It is obvious what the *perfide pederaste* is up to. The merchantman is on *Casabianca's* plot and the distance between it and its would-be attacker is shortening too rapidly for comfort. The mental mathematics involved are what Favrolet enjoys most: he is, like most of his contemporaries, a latter-day Hornblower in this respect: he delights in beating the computer to a solution. Will it be best to get within 7000 m for the fast L5 torpedoes — or should he shoot the slower E15s at a longer range? A pleasant little problem: he conjures it for a moment and decides on a salvo of two L5s programmed for direct active and/or passive attack from 5000 m. The plots, computer and sonar indicators all match: as soon as the range is right he shoots. Torpedo running time, allowing for the lead angle and swerve in after acquisition, will be five minutes — quick enough.

Two explosions follow one another at 20-second intervals. One would have been quite sufficient. Favrolet, a spasmodically good Catholic, dedicates a brief prayer of thanks to the boys at ECAN, St Tropez where the weapons were manufactured. In the *Al Khyber* there is no opportunity for prayers of any kind.

Some hours later, after darkness has fallen, the *Al Hunain* starts to snorkel. The main battery, now on its third commission, has held up fairly well but it needs about four hours recharging every night. There is no standard doctrine for doing this — opportunities are taken as they come. The OOW, acting on ESM warnings, presses the 'Stop Snorkel' alarms 11 times in the first couple of hours: on each occasion, the Captain tumbles out of his bunk but the snorkel and ESM masts are always down by the time he arrives on the scene. He is tired and disgruntled. He accuses all and sundry of not knowing their business and resolves to stay in the control room where he can decide if and when to stop snorkelling himself. He has only a sketchy idea of when incoming radar signals signify

Overleaf:
The Libyan *Al Khyber* in this factional confrontation falls victim to L5 torpedoes from the French SSN *Casabianca*.

possible contact but he is going to make sure of topping up the box before daylight.

In consequence, the 'Atlantic', already alerted by intermittent contacts and craftily using sector-scan procedures, soon has a reliable plot of the submarine's movements. Sonobuoys are dropped as a matter of routine although they are hardly necessary. Enemy reports are flashed back to HQ and thence to all forces in the area.

The Staff appreciation ashore is that *Casabianca* will not reach the reported position quickly enough at quiet speed and that surface forces must be brought to bear. *Jeanne d'Arc* has been busting her 30-year-old boilers at 26 knots and, still keeping outside the SSN patrol area, is now 100 miles due North of Cape Bon eager for action. She makes a noise like the wrath of God: when *Al Hunain* finally has to stop snorkelling half-an-hour before sunrise, with the battery nowhere near charged, her sonar tracks the helicopter carrier easily — but without identifying *Jeanne d'Arc* as an ASW vessel. Obligingly, the French ship alters course to the South and slows to 15 knots: the SSK's sonar bearings steady and *Al Hunain's* Captain, weary but keen, prepares for a visual attack.

Soon, helicopters appear ahead of the carrier. Their movements seem aimless: clearly they are not — the Libyans know that — but the truth is that the small squadron is not cohesive. Helicopter control is a trifle haphazard: it could hardly be otherwise after such a rapid deployment with no chance of working up — but the politicians would not understand that, thinks the *Jeanne d'Arc's Commandant* grimly.

The Libyan Captain is not deterred. His target is zigging but Russian schooling taught him how to deal with that. He ignores the choppers, trusting in God — and God sees him through. Two torpedoes from a well spread salvo of six strike the *Jeanne d'Arc* forward and amidships. The ship does not sink but operations have to be halted.

The *Al Hunain* now has only two torpedoes remaining — his earlier attacks on merchant ships were profligate — so the Captain decides to call it a day and return to base. The 'Atlantic' (a relief aircraft) is circling the crippled LPH and the SSK is allowed to slip away, homewards, to the South. A few hours ago the Libyan boat was heading for trouble — but the tables have been turned as they so often are in submarine warfare.

Of course, the Libyans do not know when or where ASW retribution will be attempted. It seems wise to make best use of the existing confusion and use high speed to get away. That will flatten the battery, but it is less than 600 n miles to base and it should be safe to snorkel for the final leg.

But it is not safe — not safe at all. Once again, the Libyans are blind to the submarine threat. They have what might be called the *Belgrano* mentality — if you are on your way home nobody is going to attack you.

To cut the story short, the *Al Hunain*, blithely snorkelling at ten knots and no more than a couple of hours from Ras Hilal, home and glory, is kippered by the *Guiliano Prini*. The Italian Captain can't believe his luck. He even glimpses the distinctive 'Foxtrot' snorkel head sticking high out of the flat calm water. He has had to approach very close to ensure that he was not shooting a non-belligerent target and, for a while, he thought the snorkel, with a brown smudge of exhaust behind it, was the sail of a surfaced submarine. It is a mistake that has been made elsewhere (oh, yes it has) and it caused, for a short while, a gross over-estimation of range. This in turn led to a wordy Latin altercation with the sonar plotter: fortunately, the latter won the debate but tactics had to be rapidly revised. The fish did not, in the event, have far to run — in fact there was little need to guide them through the wire for a quartering shot — and the resulting explosion shook the Italian boat considerably.

Farewell two Libyan 'Foxtrots'. So perish all pirates: their fate serves them right in our imaginary scenario. Anyway, there is a moral in this tale. Undersea pirates who have no anti-submarine ability themselves would do well to think twice before setting their sights on vulnerable victims, if ASW submarines are around.

END NOTES

1. In fact, in April 1988, after the type was set for this chapter, it was reported that the Soviet Union was transferring three 'Kilo'-class SSKs to Syria. This puts a very different complexion on the latter's capability although it will probably be quite a while before the crews are properly trained, and the boats are fully operational.
2. These are the real names of the two 'Foxtrot' SSKs most recently acquired from the USSR in April 1982 and February 1983 respectively.
3. LPH — Landing Platform Helicopter or Amphibious Assault Ship: but in this instance the *Jeanne d'Arc* (ex-*La Résolue*) will be employed as an ASW carrier.
4. Real name of the third 'Rubis'-class SSN (S 603) first commissioned on 12 November, 1986; but the Captain is fictitious.

2.5

SPIES AND TRACKERS

Nothing is ever said officially about surveillance operations (to use one of several euphemistic expressions) mounted by submarines everywhere; and we have no intention of trying to pry into Western intelligence gathering. It is enough to guess that it continues. Nor will we attempt to calculate where Western SSBNs lie hidden or what routes they take to their patrol areas.

There is no harm, however, in speculating about what Russian submarines are up to. They are often reported out of area in various places where ordinary exercises would hardly lead them: it is fair to establish, if we can, their real purpose. This chapter, like most of the others, will therefore be written primarily with the assumed Soviet point of view in mind.

It has already been shown that smart weapons and electronic countermeasures are no use unless enemy characteristics are known in great detail. For example, a rising mine will not attack the right target unless it is suitably programmed, and a Soviet ship cannot jam a NATO radar unless the jammer is turned to the relevant frequency: in fact much more information than just the frequency is usually required, especially when counter-counter-measures are involved. Similarly, a Soviet submarine decoy or jammer must respond or transmit on the exact frequency of active homing torpedoes. All this is plain commonsense and not secret.

Obtaining data for subsequent use, both tactically and in the design of systems, is a truly massive task: and it is not surprising that the USSR has such a huge intelligence organization. There is nothing wrong about gathering intelligence in the open sea, whatever Western propaganda has to say. It is essential for everybody although it is true that smaller navies could not possibly afford the range of tools required to do a comprehensive job: nor could most of them reach the very high operational standard required. It is difficult enough for the major powers to keep up with developments by the opposition — and they are certainly not willing to transfer their intelligence collections. It is largely this

problem which raises the question of just how effective some of the world's forty-plus submarine services would be in war.

For example, at least two first-class British firms are willing, and permitted by the UK Government, to sell ESM equipment to the People's Republic of China. Fine — Chinese submarines are very much in need of it. But sophisticated tactical ESM (as distinct from a simple warning system) needs an extensive library on board — usually computerized nowadays — and that is definitely not for sale. So a transfer of, say, RACAL's excellent 'Porpoise' system — which is probably the best and simplest on offer — will be like selling a book-case without the books. There is no way of getting around that: the Chinese, and any others who purchase ESM overseas, will have to compile their own library. That will take quite a long time, with specially equipped first-line submarines, and continuous effort will be necessitated to update and amend the pages.

As a matter of fact, the Chinese PLA (Navy) is well capable of all this and so is the Canadian Navy which is in a rather similar position with regard to its projected SSN fleet. But what about the Egyptians, or the Libyans, or the Brazilians? Supposing that these, and many like them, can acquire electronic and underwater intelligence about their immediate neighbors, by one means or another, they will scarcely be able to do so with regard to potentially hostile nations further away. Sheer espionage — stealing documents or whatever — is not, by the way, the solution in this case. And ELINT is only a part of the story. What is to be done about intelligence for sonar analysis and training which by itself covers a vast and expanding

Right: The Chinese navy — known as the PLA(N) in the People's Republic — currently lacks the sort of sophisticated ESM and Sonar analysis/recording facilities needed for modern intelligence gathering and subsequent tactical usage; but it is believed that kits will soon be acquired, probably from the UK. Meanwhile, boats like this home-built 'Romeo' are exceptionally well manned: the crews are well capable of advanced intelligence operations given the necessary equipment and quieting, although the latter will require substantial work on existing SSKs. Little is known of SSN capabilities except that they, too, are almost certainly looking for better (Western) ESM and Sonar.
Far right: An American 'Los Angeles' SSN looking uncommonly glamorous on the surface, but exceedingly stealthy submerged and doubtless well equipped for intelligence gathering.

field? The trouble is that there is another chicken and egg situation here: on the one hand you must have data to be operationally effective, and on the other hand, you must be operationally effective to collect the data. The substantial Indian submarine force, now augmented by an ex-Soviet ('Charlie 1') SSGN, and probably with more nuclear boats to follow, comes to mind. Is it really conceivable that, as a particular instance, an Indian boat, however well crewed, could embark on an ASW patrol with any confidence? Is it worthwhile installing sophisticated ESM and Sonar equipments at all if there is no way of compiling the libraries to support them?

Questions like this must have been raised within navies that have only a limited intelligence-gathering capability. Or is it the fact that the majority of national submarine arms are principally acquired in the hope of making maritime intervention in their area prohibitively expensive? In the Indian Ocean this reasoning seems very likely. But that is by the by: the point is that modern warfare depends very heavily indeed on accurate, detailed intelligence of a kind which may well not be appreciated by the politicians who ultimately control a nation's armed forces. And nowhere does intelligence play a more crucial part than in submarine-versus-submarine tactics: the Soviet Defense Council

and Politburo members (noting that three-quarters of the latter have engineering degrees and are able to understand such matters) appear to be appraised of this even if certain governments elsewhere are not.

So, to return to Soviet intelligence operations, it is predictable that specially equipped submarines will continue to patrol on foreign doorsteps and take a covert part in Western exercises.

It follows, from what has been discussed so far, that the boats sent far afield will be amongst the very best although not necessarily the most modern. 'Victor IIIs' are the obvious choice — proven, quiet, capable and fairly roomy SSNs while being a lot smaller than the 'Mikes' and 'Sierras'. Their commanding officers will, of course, be selected for political as well as tactical reliability; but doubtless the *Starpoms*, and perhaps a couple of additional aspiring officers, will be given every opportunity of gaining realistic experiences for future command. The *Zampolits*, too, will be hand-picked.

Inshore intelligence operations are a different matter altogether. Leaving aside midget craft for the moment, it would be logical to employ small and, if the worst ever came to the worst, expendable boats for trespassing into national waters — an expectation fulfilled by the 'Whiskey on the Rocks' incident at Karlskrona. It was this boat which broke the eleventh and twelfth commandments — thou shalt not be caught out and thou shalt not be identified.

On station off the US East coast

Resorting once again to imagination, we will visualize the 'Victor III' *Ivan Rogov* (which actually happens to be the name of a notorious wartime Commissar, late Chief of the Navy's Central Political Department, known by Russian submariners as Ivan the Terrible) commanded by Captain First Rank Nikolai Lunin, son of 'The Terrible's' contemporary, the Captain of *K-21*, who was an (undeserving) Hero of the Soviet Union.

Lunin is a linguist. He was Assistant Naval Attaché in London until the British Security Service demanded his removal on the grounds of activities incompatible with diplomatic status: in other words he was accused, correctly, of being a spy. His intelligence team all speak English fluently: although very little comes over the airways *en clair* as it used to, there is still an occasional bit of indicative chatter.

The *Rogov* is watching, listening and

recording some way off Long Island where the GRU expects the USN Submarine Development Squadron — SUBDEVRON 12 — from New London, Connecticut, to conduct preliminary trials of advanced sonar and communications with a couple of SSNs. Naturally, Lunin's task is to find out all he can. The smallest snippets of information, which are all that Lunin can reasonably expect, will be studied by specialists on return to the Kola. Carefully assembled with other fragments from here and there — articles and even advertisements in journals like the *United States Naval Institute Proceedings* or *Jane's Defence Weekly* — a very helpful picture will eventually appear.

Submarines intent on an evaluation or post-building/post-overhaul tests can be expected to let slip something of interest from time to time: scientific personnel are sometimes prone to make an unguarded remark — on a TBS (talk-between-ships) voice circuit, perhaps — which is insignificant by itself but adds up on analysis.

Lunin's job is to follow the American

A Soviet 'Victor' bows-on — a bit close for a photograph even by intelligence-gathering standards.

boats to their assigned area (where, like as not, a Soviet surface AGI intelligence collector will be hanging around) and then get close enough for his various sensors to hear what is going on while staying far enough away to avoid detection — a nice balance of judgement. At the same time, he ought to be able to obtain some standard noise recordings of the two boats on broad and narrow bands. He will have to note target aspect because low frequency analysis requires the basic frequencies unaffected by Doppler; so it will be best if he can station himself more or less abeam for this purpose.

Distances will be judged by the passive underwater ranging set based on early American PUFFS with three hydrophonic baffled arrays mounted on each side of the submarine. Whether 'PUFFSKY' or the bow array is employed, tracking will be automatic when Lunin orders a target to be held. The clip-on towed array was streamed when leaving harbor and is in good order. It might prove an encumbrance if *Rogov* tangles with one of the American boats but it has quick-release gear operated from inside the submarine. Incidentally, *Rogov* has transitted nearly 5000 miles to reach her destination at no more than moderate speed, with a 15-knot speed of advance, to avoid the loss of Cluster Guard anechoic tiles and outer hull plates which have a habit of dropping off during high-speed dashes: she is quiet.

The transit, by a somewhat circuitous series of safe lanes, was uneventful; but Lunin is now faced with a strenuous week or more. For much of the time he will have to be in the attack center himself, taking a short nap if and when he can. The *Starpom*, sound though he is, cannot be entrusted to handle the boat at such close quarters: any mistake will be attributed to the Captain personally. The crew will have to conform to snooping routine: no kind of noise is permissable — no maintenance, no films — and everyone off watch will be encouraged to stay in his bunk. All potentially noisy machinery is switched off when in the area including reactor pumps (both reactors will be kept critical on natural circulation); and electric drive — avoiding main reduction gearing — will be employed when in the ultra quiet state. There will be quite a long delay in coming to full power if the *Rogov* has to scoot, but that is acceptable.

Like *Dyadya* in a former scenario, Lunin has a first eleven who will be closed up whenever things are tricky: they won't get much sleep either.

Unfortunately for all concerned, merchant ships and occasional warships are continually passing by. They hold up the trials but impatient messages, passed between the two American SSNs in consequence, offer a few more clues to Lunin's intelligence team. The 5000-ton AGI SSV 465 (*Sudno Svyazy*, communications vessel) formerly the *Primorye*, is, as predicted, just over the horizon blandly pretending to mind its own business.

Rogov is, of course, stored for war: she is in a prime position if skirmishing spreads beyond waters close to the USSR. Until then it is business as usual.

One day, apparently as a precaution, two Navy ASW helicopters dunk and ping their way through the area; but they are not unduly suspicious of anything other than the AGI and their hearts are not really in the search. Anyway, one of the SSNs curtly informs them that they are fouling up the tests. The *Rogov's* Cluster Guard is sufficient to prevent them gaining solid contact and they classify some very faint echoes which appear as shoals of fish. Before departing they zoom over SSV 465 and take photographs to justify their mission. The Russian Captain waves politely.

It does not matter, for our purposes, what intelligence Lunin collects: suffice to say that he is in the sort of situation where something valuable will be gathered. If he gets into trouble he might consider taking shelter beneath SSV 465 — a friendly mobile haven which can, if it wants to, make a lot of physical and electronic noise to put pursuers off the scent.

Meanwhile, what could be happening in the non-Soviet SSBN world? Obviously, with crisis looming, all available Boomers, Bombers or whatever (French Frappers?) have either been sailed or soon will be. We will assume that at least one Russian SSN is permanently disposed off each and every SSBN base except, perhaps, in the shallowish waters adjacent to the mouth of the Yangtse river where a pair of SSKs is stationed to keep an eye on movements. The Kremlin has made every conciliatory effort (rather coolly received) to ensure that Beijing remains neutral and the Defense Council discounts any military action by the Chinese in support of Western interests. The Russian border guards strung along the long frontier between the two great countries are instructed to withdraw rather than shoot, if provoked: there has been too much squabbling lately and the USSR cannot afford to be distracted from affairs elsewhere.

The Soviet dilemma

Anti-SSBN operations seriously deplete the main Soviet submarine attack forces in the Northern and Far Eastern fleets. Both C-in-Cs are inclined to think the SSNs involved could be better employed — none has achieved anything to date — but the Defense Council insists. In fact, it has ordered the operations to be stepped up wherever the chances of trailing SSBNs are best. So the 'Victor III' West of Scotland, attempting to find and follow American Boomers from Holy Loch and the British HMS *Vanguard*, expected to commence her second deterrent patrol from Faslane shortly, will soon be joined by a comrade SSN. (Clandestine *Spetsnaz* units and/or midget submarines may, in the event, do some dirty work in harbor before SSBNs sail, but that is another story told in Chapter 2.6). The 'Victor III' patrol zone at the edge of the continental shelf off Brest (the French SSBN base) will also be reinforced. 'Tango' SSKs are prowling further inshore at the Clyde approaches and around Ushant while a flock of 'Foxtrots', carrying 24 ground mines apiece as well as torpedoes, await orders to lay their eggs.

The British and French are both believed to be adept at sanitizing exit lanes and all SSBNs have frequently rehearsed delousing procedures — to the embarrassment, it is whispered, of certain Soviet SSNs. But a fair proportion of the usual support forces will be engaged on other business at this juncture. Surface ASW units, to say nothing of minehunters, are in woefully short supply and by no means all are equipped with the latest systems. The Soviet Navy has been laughing to itself for years as cut after cut has been imposed in the West and on the reluctantly respected Royal Navy in particular.

There were even articles in the English Press not long ago saying that fuel for ships was to be rationed — presumably to help pay for *Vanguard* and her sisters. The Russian admirals shake their heads: surely it can't be true. They also reckon that SSN 'minders' to clear the way for SSBNs will be grudged — but if they are used in that way there will be fewer advancing on the Motherland. All to the good.

On reflection, the Soviet Submarine Staff decides that the Defense Council's demand to nail some SSBNs, especially the so-called independent deterrers, is more practical than it first appeared. Not that the British or French boats are expected to launch missiles in any circumstances (you can never tell with the Americans) but the loss of a Western SSBN, whoever it belongs to, might have a very salutory effect on Western intransigence as the Politburo sees it.

The Capitalists have been heard to express the same view about clobbering a PLARB — and nobody seems to think that escalation to nuclear war would result. A sinking, on either side, would probably not be realized ashore for quite a while in the normal course; but the word could quickly be spread around by the attacker's government if immediacy was important.

Aggressive action against American Boomers out of Bangor, Charleston and Kings Bay, Georgia is a different kettle of caviar. There are too many of the beasts; and the mighty United States Navy should easily be able to support and defend them in areas where they might be vulnerable. Of course, any opportunity of catching an 'Ohio' must be seized. The Soviet Staff is inclined to heed a pre-Revolutionary proverb — 'if they beat you, run away; if they give you, take'.

Shifting to the Western viewpoint, an unclassified report from Norway about the 'wasp-waisted Yankee' converted in 1986/87 to carry between 20 and 40 SS-N-21 cruise missiles amidships, fired vertically, is an unwelcome reminder that ballistic missiles do not constitute the only threat to territories. (It had previously been thought that the rebuilt 'Yankees', 10 m longer, would carry no more than a dozen SS-NX-24s launched from torpedo tubes.) A large number of other Russian types, SSGNs and SSNs, can be deployed with land-attack cruise missiles; and a lesser number of American SSNs can also switch their role to shore bombardment with Tomahawks. The unavoidable inference is that Russian and American missile carriers are so numerous that there is no way of entirely safeguarding a country against them.

Arms reduction talks continue at the time of writing (April 1988) but the gloomy prognosis is that a plentiful supply of nuclear underwater weaponry will remain for a long while yet. The question is whether Western ASW submariners could dent the Soviet arsenal sufficiently to change the outcome of a confrontation. The answer to this, presumably, is that they would have a very good try and they are putting in a lot of practise now: we will set them in supposed scenarios later on. No other units can do the job in the Barents Sea or Arctic (from where the most powerful threats of a nuclear strike originate) and nor, usually, can aircraft or surface ships trail Soviet submarines in the open ocean as efficiently as SSNs.

A Soviet 'Victor III' SSN, the type which has most often been involved in intelligence operations in many areas, almost invariably with a very senior commanding officer and *zampolit*. Incidentally, the 'coke-bottle' shape of the outer hull indicates good laminar flow; and a difference in the color of paint on the outer surfaces has been noted, by Western intelligence observations, which suggests a polymer stain concerned with boundary layer flow conditions.

2.6

MIDGET MARAUDERS

There are so many conceivable scenarios involving midget submarines that it is impossible to set the mind to work on all of them. There are, however, some areas of particular concern: while the principal cast is getting itself ready for Grand Opera elsewhere, we will imagine selected players acting out mini-Operettas against some differing backdrops.

Koporskiy Zaliv bay, in the Baltic Sea

Opening onto the Gulf of Finland, on its South shore some 80 km short of Leningrad where it ends, there is a bowl-shaped bay called Koporskiy Zaliv. A stubby finger of land points to seaward from the bottom of the bowl, creating a spacious, sheltered cove between it and the Western side of the bay. Immediately inland of the cove lies a brackish lake, Ozero Kopanskoe. The cove itself is not named on the charts: we will christen it Vodichka — Little Water.[1]

The region is sparsely populated and can only be reached by a single road or by sea. The nearest railhead is Ust'Luga, 40 km to the West. It is now that conjecture must take over.

Vodichka can easily be screened and kept secret: it is reasonable to think that midget submarines operate from there with a tender to support them — perhaps one of the old ex-German 'Wilhelm Bauer' class, say the 5500-ton *Kuban*. We will suppose that another depot ship — maybe the 6900-ton 'Don'-class *Dmitry Golkin* — serves six 'Whiskey V's which are permanently attached to the midget Squadron. Both support vessels provide accommodation for the crews in harbor and are capable of major repairs in their workshops.

Basic training for combat swimmers, charioteers, canoemen and the like is conducted in the lake which is 12 km long by 3 km wide at its broadest point close to the cove: it could not be more convenient.

The main barracks and facilities at Leningrad are less then two hours away — half-an-hour by helicopter — yet they are sufficiently removed for no unauthorized personnel at the giant naval base to know what is going on at Vodichka.

There are two covered slipways leading up the beach from the water: midgets are hauled up these on trollies for maintenance every six months. A craft is parted (by unbolting) at the engine-room and forward bulkheads for ease of access.

The Squadron Commander (who is also Captain of *Kuban*) is a tough, stocky suburban Muscovite: he accepts no excuses for anything not working properly and is in no way inclined to treat the permanent operational midget crews as special. However, he is a little cautious in his dealings with *Spetsnaz* troops whom he regards as supernumaries: they are not directly under his command and some of the more bizarre characters are apt to whisper complaints up the line to the Head of Department Three at HQ. The women are the worst in his opinion, fancying themselves as Prima Donnas. He admits, grudgingly, that they are superbly fit and there are Gold and Silver Olympic medallists amongst them. But at what a price they won their awards — all muscle, and stuffed with chemicals like as not. He wouldn't have one to share his bunk at any price — although a couple of fairly feminine officer candidates recently offered their services on a voluntary basis.

As it happens a fresh contingent of *Spetsnaz* personnel arrives at the jetty while the Squadron Commander is musing. He observes them through his binoculars. They are a dangerous looking lot — two or three young blonde Aryan boys, pale and thin-lipped; they could well have been Nazis of the nastiest type 50 years ago. They would murder their grandmother for a kopek, he thinks. He is right: their speciality is *mokroe dela*, 'wet jobs', meaning assassinations. A popular children's song from the old days floats through his head and he hums the catchy little tune. The words are typically Russian in their macaber humor: 'I have gone down the drain. I have slaughtered my father and mother, ripped up auntie and devitalized Uncle Vanya . . . .'

Yet these ruthless elites are pampered. They live soft ashore. The coach which brought them has lace curtains on the windows and lace covers on the seats. He spits over the side disgustedly. Back to business. Operation *Tanets*, 'The Dance', is due to commence tomorrow: he must make sure that the two midget crews and their *Spetsnaz* swimmers fully understand their orders.

Preparing for Operation *Tanets*

Piskar (Minnow) and *Rebyonok* (Sprat) have been nicknamed by their captains. Strictly speaking they are Job No.48 and Job No.57 respectively — nomenclatures which give no clue to their identity. (Similar precautions have been taken in the past by other navies; and it is fair to guess that a Job Number, or something like it, would be assigned. For instance, Britain's first submarine was constructed at Barrow in a wooden building labelled Yacht Shed, the boat itself being known before launch in 1901 as Pontoon Number One; and the prototype British X-craft was initially referred to as Job 82).

Piskar (like *Rebyonok*) is a general-purpose craft — one of a hundred or more 15 m steel cylinders, assembled in sections that have rolled obesely off the production line onto waiting railway trucks at Sudomekh Shipyard and thence been taken, covered by tarpaulins, to points near their destinations. *Piskar* herself completed the journey by low-loader road transport from Ust'Luga before being craned into the water by slings attached to permanent eyebolts welded to the hull. When topped up with diesel fuel, and with the battery charged from the tender's electrical supplies, she was immediately ready for service. It would not have mattered to the four-man crew which craft of this type they were appointed to: all are identical in every last respect save for the name — and that is not officially recognised.

Junior Lieutenant (Ensign) Gregoriy Valentinovich Molotov commands *Piskar* proudly. He is unmarried, of course, and dedicated to the Service. He joined the Communist Party, in effect, when he enrolled in the Kiev Young Octobrists organisation at the age of six. During his last two years at school he participated in compulsory pre-military training for the prescribed 140 hours. In the short period between leaving school and being accepted into the Naval Academy specializing in Submarine Warfare at Leningrad, he joined the Naval Club where, as a future submariner and diver, he was taught basic principles in a training submarine and learned (according to the textbook) 'to read drawings and schematics, draw sketches and measure underwater structures; and carry out rigging, assembly, repair and construction work while submerged'.[2] At that time, he had not even heard of midget submarines but he was being prepared for them, both practically and psychologically.

Command of *Piskar* came quickly after a quite brief familiarisation course — but gruelling months of exercises followed before he and his men were pronounced fit for active operations. The concluding sea-going inspection, with the Squadron Commander himself on board (a tight fit) was, by all accounts, far more rigorous than equivalent affairs in standard boats.

At last he and *Michman* (Warrant Officer) Stakhanovich, captain of *Rebyonok*, are ready. They have memorized their orders and handed them back: nothing classified can be taken on the operation despite the self-destruction charges installed below the deck plates in the bow and stern of every midget. As for the men, each carries a small bite-or-swallow-and-recycle cyanide capsule which will be held between teeth and cheek in the event of capture and interrogation.[3] The poison pills make Molotov feel a real Hero of the Soviet Union but Warrant Officer Stakhanovich has not the smallest intention of putting one anywhere near his mouth whatever happens: if he had the chance he would ram his up the Squadron's *Zampolit* who gave an inspiring lecture on the subject of patriotic suicide.

The Defense Council, intensifying submarine strategy from the remote underground bunker at Zhiguli, has ordained that NATO submarine bases are to be mined. Full-scale submarine minelayers will take care of the approaches later: for the moment, operations are to concentrate on the ports and harbors themselves. The mines will not activate automatically for seven days after being laid: if Operation *Tanets* goes according to plan (as it must or else) that will coincide with the date on which the Defense

Council intends to broaden its anti-submarine offensive. However, divers armed with acoustic 'torches' can visit the weapons to shorten or lengthen the setting on the delay mechanisms or deactivate them altogether if necessary. (This could be fanciful but it is hypothetically practicable. In fact it has been tentatively mooted that a midget or an ordinary submarine might have ways of activating or deactivating minefields without divers. Certainly mines can be controlled by agents from shore. One way or the other, it is certainly a very desirable capability.)

Kiel, 800 nautical miles from Vodichka, is the target for both the craft in our story. The Federal Republic's reputedly skilful U-boats, notably the Type 206s and the new 211s with their SUT and *Seeschlange* torpedoes and Krupp Atlas sonar, are going to be a menace to the elderly Soviet submarines, to say nothing of amphibious ships, in the Twice-Honored Red Banner Baltic Fleet unless they are eliminated at the outset.

At 0400 hours the next morning, well before first light, the midget crews shake hands individually with the Squadron Commander and step down the ladder to their craft lying alongside. It is really too early in the day to pipe the captains over the side but they are accorded the honor all the same. Molotov has had butterflies in his belly for the past 24 hours: he would have liked a few stiff drinks last night but the depot ship bars are prudently forbidden to all midget operators a day before sailing. Stakhanovich, older and knowing the ropes, keeps a private stock of firewater in his cabin safe: his head is now too heavy to worry about anything much.

The 'Whiskeys' have already moved out into the bay: the two midget COs shove off in the darkness and take their craft alongside their respective 'tugs'. All vessels are darkened except for shaded stern lights on the 'Whiskeys'. Connecting up the tow and screwing home the telephone plug in its (hopefully) watertight socket is therefore tricky. (British X-craft men would sympathise: they remember the procedure all too well.)

On board the midgets only the Captains remain up top, conning through the raised engine-induction mast which doubles (not very satisfactorily) as a voice-pipe to the helmsman below: hatches are shut.

Out in the open Baltic the two midgets, now being towed slowly, dive. A static trim submergence had been conducted in harbor, so they settle at 30 m with no difficulty. The

THE EASTERN BALTIC

BALTIC

GULF OF FINLAND

LENINGRAD

KOPORSKIY ZALIV

VODICHKA

LAKE KOPANSKOE

The only map which shows the conjectural (but very likely) location for a secret midget base, with its training lake inland, is Russian: the Eastern Baltic section, with Leningrad on the right and 'Vodichka' superimposed on the bay at center, is reproduced above.

'Whiskeys' themselves thereupon dive and start to snorkel at eight knots for the first part of the passage. They will stop snorkelling and proceed on main motors at five knots when they reach less friendly waters. Every six hours (following British custom) the midgets break surface, raise the induction mast and run their diesels for 20 minutes to refresh the air and batteries.

Both craft have the same mission so it will be sufficient, for our purposes, to follow the fortunes of *Piskar*.

Piskar prepares to do its work

Molotov surveys his crew. The Chief Petty Officer Engineer is on watch at the hydroplane and steering controls — a single column with an autopilot for depth and azimuth when not maneuvering — while the Warrant *Starpom* has a nap, curled up against the diesel aft. The fourth member of the crew, the Electrical *matros*, has plenty to do keeping switchboards and circuits dry, checking for grounds — a never-ending job because condensation rains down. Droplets splash the chart and Molotov has to roll it up in an oilskin packet before it becomes a soggy mess.

One of the two *Spetsnaz* corporals is

asleep on the wooden platform forward over the battery. Good luck to him if he lets his hand trail over the terminals, thinks the *matros*: anyway, gas from the dwarf cells will leave him with a splitting headache when he wakes up. The other *Spetsnaz* diver is technically female. The Engineer glances at her squatting heavily on the only available seat — the hand-pumped *Vaterkloset* in the diving lock between the battery compartment and control room: the dim lighting may be playing tricks but he could swear she sports a military moustache.

Four days pass drearily. Food is nauseating although boiled sweets (pear drops) and oranges are still just palatable. The 'head' stinks (the heads usually do in Russian ships for some reason) and on the second night a typical Baltic gale had blown up: the craft rocked and rolled abominably while 'guffing through' on the surface and vomit slopped into the bilges. Fortunately, the olfactory senses (in any submarine) become insensitive to human smells; but sights and sounds of people being ill or even performing their natural functions are less than invigorating; and, all the time, the cold, damp atmosphere, an almost tangible variety, chills the very marrow.

It would be better to have followed the Royal Navy's wartime custom and employed two crews: one was for passage while the operational team luxuriated in the towing submarine until 50 n miles or so from their objective, at which point the two crews changed over. But that would mean both boats surfacing and that is unthinkable in guarded waters nowadays.

Time has lost its meaning and the telephone line, as is its wont, went virtually U/S shortly after departure. Molotov has to guess what the barely audible crackles and grunts from the other end indicate. Fortunately he guesses correctly, just after midnight, that he is to slip the tow (by means of an internal handwheel forward) and go on by himself. Presumably *Rebyonok*, a few miles to the North, is also free. There is no means of knowing — it is unwise to transmit on underwater telephone needlessly.

Molotov waits until the craft has slowed right down before ordering the motor ahead at 60 revolutions — three knots — and coming cautiously to periscope depth. It is pitch dark: there is no shipping in sight (the periscope horizon is less than two miles) but the loom of an occulting light ahead confirms that he is on track. There are no messages for

Job No.48 on the broadcast: the lucky devils back at Vodichka have probably forgotten him. Suddenly he feels very, very lonely. The damnable butterflies return. He shakes himself. There is much to be done. His EP on the chart shows there are 22 n miles to run. The 'Whiskey' skipper is a good man — he took his sibling as far as he possibly could, skirting close to Fehmarn Island and into the Kiel Bight itself. Molotov thanks him silently from his soul before addressing the crew: 'Comrades, the time has come. Divers to dress in case you're needed. You shouldn't be on this trip but you never know. We'll go ahead at five knots to reach the outer harbor at dawn — then we'll see'.

The Engineer crosses himself and kisses a small leather wallet hitherto concealed somewhere on his oily person. It is odd that old customs never die: the wallet holds the faded replica of an icon; and opposite to it is a picture of the wife he buried — how long ago? — a victim of the plague that swept through the rat-ridden villages of Turkmenistan. He jerks himself back to duty. It seems a funny way to sink submarines — a flea-sized boat like this sneaking into a big defended naval port full of arms and armor. He'd rather be in a proper double-hull submarine and fire torpedoes from a safe distance. Still, those plain, ugly mines strapped either side are sure to do their work — more reliable than dainty electronic tin fish any day.

The *Starpom* relieves 'Chief' at the control column. He is responsible for trimming and will be working the pump himself besides the main motor, auxiliary electrics and engine. All he lacks is enough hands. The Engineer and Electrician, tool boxes and wooden damage-control plugs at the ready, go aft and keep out of the way until needed. The Captain himself navigates — no easy business when he starts to enter the narrowing channel leading to the submarine pens.

The two divers in their rubber suits hunch themselves together in the lock, sharing the WC seat between them. They have spoken scarcely a word from the start: it is not the *Spetsnaz* way to engage in idle chatter. It might be misinterpreted and reported. They both know the story of the girl who cracked: she was handed over to the KGB and incinerated live in the simple crematorium reserved for such occasions on the perimeter of Moscow's military airfield.[4]

There is quite a lot of shipping about, including minehunters and ASW corvettes. The latter are pinging continuously and sonar transmissions frequently resound around *Piskar*'s hull — around because the equipment is little use against a miniscule target and the operators have never had a chance of practising against a midget. The occasional faint echoes are disregarded. HF mine-hunting sonar might achieve results but that is not geared to anti-submarine sweeps. Molotov only has to dive under ships when they approach and keep periscope exposure to the minimum — two or three inches at the most, seconds at a time. Once, returning to periscope depth, he is alarmed to find almost the entire tiny lens filled with a pair of boots: by chance a harbor launch is drifting silently, broken down in mid-channel, and a seaman is hanging his legs over the side. A close call but still *Piscar* is not detected.[5] Nor do the German bottom-laid magnetic loops reveal her presence: the Electrical *matros* double-checked the craft's degaussing apparatus after slipping the tow.

'Nearly there. Cross-bearing *that*. Transit church spire and beacon coming up...four zero revolutions comrade *Starpom...now*.'

Molotov spins first the port-side mine release handwheel; and then, 70 seconds later by the stopwatch, the starboard. The interval will result in the mines being spaced 75 m apart, precisely where ordered — right on the track which U-boats must take to and from their berths. The mines are, of course, booby-trapped in case the Germans find them.[6]

The first side-cargo, looking like a slim main ballast saddle tank, drops smoothly away to the bottom, its extremities flooding

THE WET AND DRY CHAMBER

A wet-and-dry exit and re-entry chamber (the British X-craft arrangement is shown here) must be flooded and drained down without upsetting the midget submarine's trim. An internal tank — which could be a main ballast tank if fitted with a Kingston valve at
the bottom — is therefore used for the purpose. However, some modern Italian midgets have a hatch at the bottom of a compartment which functions much like a diving bell.

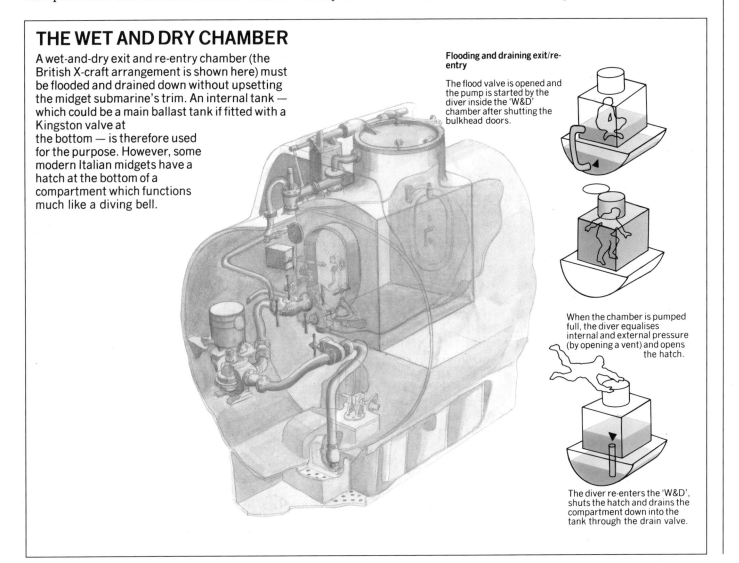

Flooding and draining exit/re-entry

The flood valve is opened and the pump is started by the diver inside the 'W&D' chamber after shutting the bulkhead doors.

When the chamber is pumped full, the diver equalises internal and external pressure (by opening a vent) and opens the hatch.

The diver re-enters the 'W&D', shuts the hatch and drains the compartment down into the tank through the drain valve.

automatically at the first quarter-turn of the release wheel to make it negatively buoyant. But the second — the Starboard sow, may the Devil take her — hangs up. Worse, the forward 'ballast tank' on the mine floods, but not the after one. Hence, *Piskar* loses trim, lists to starboard and pitches bow down.

The *Starpom* struggles with the trim using the single joystick control to direct water forward to aft via the pump and from the forward trim tank to the sea. The trim is delicate at the best of times: a bowl of potmess passed from the cooking apparatus in the engine room along to the *Spetsnaz* corporal in the battery compartment is enough to cause a slight (but manageable) bow-down angle when hovering or going very slowly.

The partially flooded charge makes quite dramatic action necessary. Trim is, in fact, regained quite quickly but Molotov must get rid of the side-cargo somehow.

The craft is stopped, brought gently down to the bottom and Corporal Anna Rastinov is briefed. She sits impassively on the throne in the 'Wet and Dry' lock and adjusts her breathing apparatus while the heavy bulkhead doors to the battery space and control room are shut and screwed tight. The pressure-hull hatch is directly above her. There is no room to do more than bend a little or reach upwards to work valves, vents and levers.

Getting outside the craft
Two taps on the control-room door tell the entombed Anna to flood up. She pushes the pump lever and water immediately starts to enter the lock from a special internal tank directly below it, thus not upsetting the trim. The water is cold — very cold — and her bare hands are soon numb. The water rises inexorably: any diver with a streak of imagination must have visions of slow drowning despite the breathing set. It reaches the top of the compartment quite quickly (although the process seems to take an age) while the air is automatically vented inboard into the control room. But the pump keeps on working at fairly high pressure. Consequently — and very suddenly — the pressure exerts itself on Anna: the human body is compressible but water is not. The result is known by divers, without affection, as The Squeeze. Apart from ear-drums and vulnerable organs (Anna is rather better off in that respect than a man would be) the Oxygen bag on her chest is flattened, leaving her lungs unsupplied. It is a horrible experience for the uninitiated; but

Anna knows the drill and opens the Oxygen valve wider. The bag expands again — more pressure on her body and more acute discomfort. No matter, she is breathing normally again.

Now she must open the vent in the upper hatch to equalise pressure before opening the hatch — another squeeze as she does so.[7] She climbs out of the hatch onto the casing and allows herself to sink slowly down the craft's Starboard side. The water is muddy and visibility poor but the snag is, fortunately, apparent. One of the side-cargo's retaining catches is free but it has not lifted. There is nothing she can do about flooding the after tank but if the mine drops clear it should stay on the bottom, albeit, perhaps, nose down.

Anna considers the situation calmly. Kicking her legs, she swims up to the thick glass viewing port set into the upper part of the hull amidships, and presses her mouth against it. The laminated glass acts like an underwater telephone transmitter: spitting out her mouthpiece for a few moments, she is able to tell Molotov what has happened and what she is going to do about it. He shouts a laconic OK and waits.

The job does not take long. Lying on top of the casing, Anna can just reach the recalcitrant catch. Seconds later the crew can hear scraping and a thud. The mine is free and not too far out of position. There will be an Order of Lenin, Third Class, for Corporal Rastinov on return.

Meanwhile *Rebyonok* has enjoyed complete success. Stakhanovich, having come up to command the hard way, is a more practical — and cynical — man than Molotov. He personally greased and worked the mine catches before departure, distrusting from long experience depot ship maintainers of any kind. He planted his mines a few hundred meters to seaward of *Piskar*'s at about the same time.

Para itti — it's time to go. The 'Whiskeys' will be waiting (with infra-red homing lamps) at the assigned rendezvous off the Polish coast to the West of the Gulf of Danzig. The Polish naval authorities have been invited to keep the area clear of shipping but without telling them why the 'Whiskeys' will be there. The Polish corvette *Hutnik* will police the RV, mutually identifying itself with the Russian submarines by IFF.

The RV is much further away from Kiel than the slipping position because all concerned will have to surface in order to reconnect the tows. So it looks like a long, long haul back for the midgets — a good four days under their own power implying an 'indiscretion rate' of 13 per cent — ie, the proportion of time spent charging the batteries on the surface or (a bit dicey unless the sea is very calm) snorkelling through the surface induction mast. The *Spetsnaz* corporals will take their turn on watch but conditions will be even more miserable than they were during the outward passage.

However, we can assume that *Piskar* and *Rebyonok* get home safely with a major strategic mission accomplished, undetected and unsuspected behind them.

The mission continues

Other midgets have been active in the Baltic while Job Numbers 48 and 57 were away. We will instance one — Job No.172 — a curious craft from a small group secured separately from the rest alongside the depot ship. Seen from above it vaguely resembles *Piskar* and *Rebyonok* but, although fatter, it carries no side cargoes. Besides the usual stubby periscope fairing — forward on this type with a transparent domed hatch abaft it — there are a number of brackets on the broad substantial casing which look like weapon-holders of some kind. The bottom half of a sister craft on the slipway (covered not just to protect workers from the weather but also, with camouflage netting, to prevent satellite observation) recalls a light tank or APV although the tracks seem rather more delicate: they, and the wheels round which they rotate, appear to be made of heavy plastic or rubber. There is an external torpedo/mine cradle on each side, two searchlights are recessed in the bows and, between them, a mechanical arm with a claw-like tool on the end, is folded back into a cutaway portion of the forward superstructure. The single propeller at the stern (shrouded as in all midgets) shows that the vessel is an amphibian.

Job No.172 has a grinning toad painted on either side of the casing forward: the toad is the Squadron Commander's grudging concession to the crew who pleaded with him to allow their rather unprepossessing craft an informal name. They suggested 'Ugly Little Octobrist' (the Captain, Lieutenant Pavlov, was accepted by none of the Young Communist Organisations in his youth and is still not a Party Member) but the Division *Zampolit* was deeply affronted by the proposal and formally forbade such an impious christening. The name, never to be used out-side the Amphibious Division, was thereupon shortened to 'Ugly' — *Dornoy* — hence the satisfied toad.

Not for *Dornoy* are the long, abominably uncomfortable transits suffered by the GP midgets. One evening a dirty medium-sized ferry waddles into the outer bay and anchors bow and stern. A whiteish motorboat is lowered and the *Starpom* (a GRU officer) scuttles across to see the midget Squadron Commander and Divcom. While he is absent the ferry unaccountably begins to sink as if instantly heavy laden. A watchful observer would notice three oddities. Firstly, she is definitely not taking on cargo; secondly, the bow doors and ramp are now underwater; and thirdly, the draught marks in her low buoyancy state are obviously incorrect — she is drawing much more water than they indicate.

The ferry is, of course, a midget transporter. Tomorrow morning the 'Ugly' amphibian will dive alongside the depot ship and make her way towards the ferry where Pavlov will find the submerged doors open and the ramp lowered, ready to receive him.

However, tonight he must read his orders and commit them to memory. Besides the regular chart of the area, he is given a very detailed expanded section showing a small but vital portion of Karlskrona harbor — the important Swedish naval base and communications center. This special chart, reproduced on shiny paper impregnated with chemicals, can be ignited by the simple expedient of folding it and rubbing any of the edges together. His navigation within the harbor will need to be precise to within 10 m: the chart and his two accurate gyro compasses are good enough for that.

The task is relatively straightforward and none of the mines, torpedoes or flame-throwers with which *Dornoy* can be equipped will be required although personal weapons (and the normal suicide pills) will be carried. All he has to do, explains the Divcom, is to sit his craft on to the harbor bottom close to a certain seabed telecom cable which is probably buried in the silt. Divers, with or without the aid of the craft's remotely operated mechanical arm, will do the rest.

'That's all?', thinks Pavlov ruefully, 'and the cable won't be visible?' He has practised the evolution frequently in the bay — but there, on home ground, it was easy to cheat. There can be no cheating in this operation. Questions race through his mind. Is the exact lay of the cable known? Yes: somebody has

Overleaf:
The *Dornoy's Osnaz* Lieutenant about to go to work, with electronic intercept equipment, on the seabed communication cable which the amphibious midget's mechanical arm has uncovered and raised in Karlskrona harbor.

been there before and the KGB Chief of Line PR (Political Intelligence) in Stockholm has confirmed, from sifted data supplied by the Illegals Support Officer, that the cable has not been shifted. (A similar report had come from the senior GRU man but it arrived later because the KGB and GRU were having another of their tiffs and the GRU is currently one down.)

'How deep might the cable be?' 'Half-a-metre at most.' 'What are the divers going to do with the cable?' 'That is no business of yours.' 'Who will the divers be?' 'Three Osnaz communications-intercept experts — a Lieutenant and two Sergeants.' 'Do I fit a claw or a digger or a grapple to the mechanical arm?' 'That is your problem: you will take alternative tools with you in the casing locker — the Sergeants know how to change them underwater. They have also had experience in a 'Type 150' series craft. The Lieutenant will do no physical work: he has...other duties. And by the way you are to land him afterwards together with certain equipment. You will be told where in due course.' 'Are there any anti-submarine nets?' 'Yes. The Sergeants know how to operate your net-cutting shears: they will check them out before sailing so open up the hydraulic supplies to them tonight.' 'Any mines?' 'None are activated so far as we know.' 'Magnetic and acoustic defenses?' 'All manned, all operating. So switch on your degaussing gear, keep quiet — and don't panic if you think the Swedes are smelling your backside.'

'They probably will at some stage — they're much more clever at the game than the other stupid Westerners — but nobody, repeat nobody, has ever been caught. So don't assume that noises overhead or depth charges alongside mean they've got you, that's one of their favorite tricks — running backwards and forwards making bangs to try and scare you into showing yourself or making a noise. Don't fall for it. And by the way, we still think that if you get into real trouble with the ASW boys you are better off underway than on the bottom.'

Pavlov remembers that the latter point has long been a contentious issue amongst midget submariners. It arises from German midget experience during the war when commanding officers reported that depth charges had been dropped so close that their explosions illuminated the inside of the craft through the plexiglass dome — yet there was no important damage. Why? German, and subsequently, Soviet shock investigations showed that a very small boat, although tossed about, was far less affected than a large one because (as Pavlov understands it) most of the shock waves, radiating outwards in an expanding circle, passed around a tiny target while they struck a larger submarine at fractionally different intervals along its length, thus causing differential — and often fatal — stresses or whip.

The analogy offered, for those who found the mathematical model difficult to understand, was the comparison of tossing a matchstick and a plank into an angry sea. The matchstick would simply ride the waves (because they were so very much larger than its own 'wavelength') while the plank was liable to be smashed to pieces — especially against the beach.

Final question: 'Comrade Commander, you told us that the Motherland was conducting a defensive anti-submarine campaign in the North. The Zampolit said that the only targets were submarines and that our own ASW submarines were winning the battle. How is this operation going to help the Rodina?'

The answer is carefully phrased in the form of another question (the Divcom has recently attended the naval Political Long Course in Moscow): 'Do you not think that NATO communication lines to Sweden, who calls herself neutral are important, noting that she has 16 very good little submarines of her own?'

Pavlov is no fool. He realises that there is something else at stake. Sweden is the gateway to Norway and if the Soviet Navy can acquire submarine bases in Southern Norway, it will be immeasurably easier to sortie out into the Atlantic: that is only commonsense.

The ferry stops engines for ten minutes off Karlskrona, hoisting the international 'Not Under Command' signal to indicate that she has a problem — which is, naturally, an artifice. This is quite long enough for Dornoy to slip out of the hold and start its short trip to the Swedish harbor on the main motor.

The internal arrangement, based broadly on the German wartime Seeteufel, is quite different from the GP midgets. The diesel generator is in the bows and the 'W & D' diving lock has plexiglass set into the outer hatch. A secondary, very short and strong, periscope is installed in the engine room, immediately forward of the fixed and faired induction mast and two underwater television cameras are associated with the searchlights in the bows for directing the mechanical arm. Divers are provided with short-range underwater telephone sets which can either transmit and receive through water, or be linked directly to the craft with light cables.

A substantial high-capacity bank of silver-zinc cells is situated in the after section together with the sound-insulated main motor which can be geared either to the propeller or to the traction mechanism. The Captain has a directional high-frequency sonar set mounted on the after casing: the very simple display, augmented by headphones, is adjacent to the main periscope. An HF radio transceiver, together with an automatic VLF receiver, is tucked away into a corner of the control room. Ample but space-demanding Carbon Dioxide scrubbers and Oxygen generators are installed for eight days total submergence — three times the endurance of a GP midget which is one reason why the Type 150 series is so fat.

Trimming is automatic (with instant manual override) and, apart from the Captain, the three-man permanent crew have little to do as a rule.

Comfort is not associated with the Type 150 but there is space for the three Osnaz personnel to relax and dress in their diving suits on decking above the battery. The WC in this type is horribly public, set at a tilted angle amidships like that in a German wartime Seehund: only a contortionist can use it satisfactorily. (This drawback explains why the Osnaz team is all male.)

Pavlov navigates his craft to the cable at the recommended position without difficulty, despite a plethora of patrol craft, and gently bottoms. The two Osnaz Sergeants climb out to survey the bottom and conclude that some digging will be necessary: fortunately, the shovel gear is already attached to the arm but the craft has to adjust its position by engaging the caterpillars. This makes noise — and so does the digger when it starts work.

The Swedes smell a rat

One Swedish acoustic listening post hears strange sounds, matches them with those recorded previously and alerts Naval HQ. Although the organisation is first-class after numerous rehearsals, it takes a little time to fetch two patrol boats to the spot and longer still to clear surface traffic out of the way. Meanwhile the cable is uncovered and the Osnaz Lieutenant, carrying pressure-proof electronic equipment and a long coil of cable, joins the other two comrades. Pavlov has a

shrewd notion that provisional arrangements are being made either to intercept communications or to pump messages into the circuit: he is right in both respects.

In due course, after he is landed well away from the scene of the crime, the Lieutenant will be arranging for other Osnaz divers (who have been living as Illegals near Karlskrona for the past year) to swim out and connect up the circuitry.

There is barely time to make the preparations before the patrol boats arrive. Their first move is to plaster the area with one-and-a-quarter pound scare charges: Osnaz and Spetsnaz troops are strictly instructed during training not to be scared but, undeniably, the explosions are off-putting to say the least. Two of the swimmers are back inside Dornoy before the first bang but the Lieutenant is knocked flat, deafened and bruised by two close charges.

Calmly, he picks himself up off the bottom and completes the job. (His dress is weighted and the weights, unlike those on NATO suits, cannot be slipped — so if he is killed or rendered unconscious his body will not float to the surface. The weights demand a lot of extra energy when swimming, especially when struggling up to the craft's exit/re-entry hatch — but that is just too bad.) He luckily regains the comparative safety of Dornoy before the Swedes become fed up and call in a new 'Göteborg'-class corvette fitted with four ASW 'Elma' grenade launchers and depth-charge racks.

Pavlov thankfully pumps off the bottom and sets course, cautiously at three knots, for the harbor entrance. There is just — but only just — enough water to clear the seabed and allow the ASW ships to pass overhead without colliding.

Soon, heavy ordnance starts to rain down all around. Pavlov feels like a rat being shaken by a terrier in a thunderstorm. He has to increase speed to six knots in order to keep depth — but, true enough, there is no serious damage although one of his gyros topples and doubtless the external equipment is taking a beating. There is only one thing to do — press on blind, trusting to dead-reckoning navigation. If he bottoms again and uses the crawlers (like some of his colleagues in the past when Swedish anti-submarine methods were not so formidable) he will be at much greater risk — and the Swedes are known to be very patient and persistent. He sticks to the main channel, dangerous though it is, to avoid possible nets on either side of it.

Dornoy reaches the open Baltic relatively unscathed — the Swedes were side-tracked by a multitude of 'non-sub' contacts which had to be painstakingly sorted out — and Pavlov has been able to check his position through the periscope from time to time. The remaining gyro has performed superbly and so have the precisely calibrated automatic log and plot.

However, his difficulties are not over yet. The GRU reckoned, reasonably, that it would be unsafe for the ferry-transporter to call at Karlskrona again to re-embark the midget. So a 'Whiskey' is stationed in deep international water North-East of Bornholm to rendezvous with the midget and pass instructions. (Once upon a time a similar boat, the ill-fated No.137, risked the passage right up the harbor with disastrous consequences: that error will not be committed again.)

Contact is duly made with the 'Whiskey' by secure underwater telephone at the RV 35 n miles South of Karlskrona. Pavlov is directed to snorkel-charge as close to the 'Whiskey' as possible which will keep ESM and sonar watch: it also takes over radio guard passing fresh orders on Under Water Telephone.

The second part of the operation, now revealed, is to land the Lieutenant on a shelving beach, away from military installations, in the Kalmar Sound some 50 miles North-East of Karlskrona. The midget is to go in on the crawlers as far as it can without breaking surface. From there the Lieutenant can drag ashore his weighty packages. A KGB man will be waiting for him. At the same time, the 'Whiskey' will create a diversion — a *maskirovka* further down the coast by intermittently transmitting on well-known Snoop Plate radar, thus contributing another incident to the long list of submarine intrusions recorded by the Swedes.

Assuming that all goes well — and there is no reason why it should not — the two boats will again rendezvous out at sea. The 'Whiskey' carries a tow rope in case of need but does not expect to use it. After the RV, and another battery charge, the 'Ugly' partner is to transit South-East towards Polish national waters where the ferry will be ready to swallow the craft and take it back to Vodichka.

(Of course, if the Soviets adopt gst systems, tows are needed: we hope they do not.)

All does go well. A well planned mission, with the strong strategic overtones so often associated with midget operations, has been faultlessly executed.

The Firth of Clyde, Scotland

We are now going to make some assumptions which may be considerably less valid than others. In fact they could be totally invalid. We will deliberately make no attempt to check whether they are right or wrong, partly because the issue is too serious and partly because the only reason for introducing this scenario is to illustrate the operational principles, which might be applied in various places, concerned with a different kind of midget activity.

Having necessarily weasel-worded the introduction, we will imagine how attacks might be directed at American Boomers in the Holy Loch, Scotland and at British Bombers at Faslane not far away. In essence we could equally well imagine — with similar reservations — attacks on other American SSBN bases at Bangor, Washington State or Charleston, South Carolina or at Kings Bay Georgia or, quite possibly, on the French SNLEs at Ile Longue, Brest.

So we will suppose that three GP midgets (one of which is spare) together with a contingent of *Spetsnaz* combat swimmers 20 strong, have been embarked in the Liberian-registered 3000-ton *Latoka*, to all appearances a perfectly normal merchantman plying between the Baltic and various European ports. *Latoka*, like the ferry we examined in the last scenario, has false draught marks. Ferries do not frequent these routes: to send one on a clandestine mission would attract suspicion so *Latoka* has been specially converted at Leningrad's Old Admiralty Yard with workshop facilities and a large opening in the bottom of her main hold attended by gantries, a slipway and transfer beams on which the midgets are secured against rolling.

The Naval Constructor in charge of the conversion made certain changes to her ballasting to ensure adequate buoyancy and stability: the hold, which looks rather like an overgrown swimming pool, can be sealed off and pressurized if necessary. The midgets are high and dry until they are slid into the water, thence down and out into the sea.

The design is based on quite common arrangements in ships carrying diving bells and commercial oceanographic mini-subs: there is nothing complicated or dangerous about it, although the *Latoka* does have to be stopped when midgets leave or enter their cave. Nor is there anything difficult about a midget hovering precisely below the hole, which is surrounded by downward-pointing non-blinding lights. Indeed, the *Latoka* has been used as a practise target on many occasions, involving midgets coming up slowly and quietly underneath her at specific points before moving along under the opening and surfacing at the end of the day. Russian midget-men are taught that the technique was perfected by British X-craft operators way back in 1942.

The weapons selected for an anti-SSBN operation are two-fold. On one side of each midget the side-cargo is standard: on the other it is hollow and filled, so far as accessibility by a diver allows, with limpet mines. A dozen more limpets are stowed under the casing. Every midget has four extra two-meter masts, hinged at casing level and raised hydraulically, each with a springy laminated leaf or flap at the top. These are for resting under a ship's hull like a fly on the ceiling, the flaps allowing for rounded bottoms as well as avoiding undue noise on contact. X-craft used exactly the same method for limpet attacks by divers who, thanks to the 'antenna' masts had plenty of room to climb out of the 'W & D' and go about their business.

Latoka's Captain, accompanied as always by a GRU First Officer, stops his ship at the entrance to the Firth of Clyde off the Mull of Kintyre. His distinctive funnel markings are unnecessarily dirty and seem to be in the process of being repainted because staging covers them entirely. He employs the customary subterfuge of hoisting two black balls to the masthead (the not-under-command warning would be two all-round red lights at night); but he is able to haul the signal down and go on his way in less than half-an-hour. A Nimrod aircraft flies overhead but pays no particular attention: why should it?

Where are the defenses?

This particular operation is a one-way trip for the 2 midgets selected: *Latoka* will not pass by this way again and the two craft will be scuttled. The crews, all in civilian clothes covered by 'dry' diving suits, carry escape kits in waterproof bags and they know where to find friends ashore. Battery capacity is easily enough to cover the 60 or 70 n miles to their destinations: the captains will not be inhibited by lack of amps if they need to make some high-speed dashes; and they can well

afford to pass up the Clyde fully submerged at five knots, slowing down occasionally for periscope fixes, which will take them abeam of Gourock in about 12 hours, soon after sunset.

Here they will find a quiet corner to bottom and rest before coming up to periscope depth at first light to follow their divergent tracks to Holy Loch and Faslane on the Gareloch respectively. There is absolutely no sign of ASW opposition (is it conceivable that this particular assumption for our story is correct?) and intelligence confidently predicted there would be no nets. Magnetic loops — probably; mini-SOSUS chains —

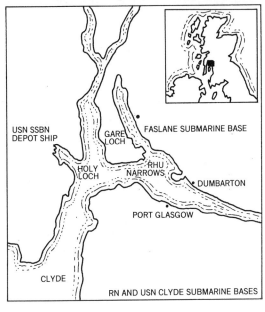

Above: HMS *Neptune*, the RN Submarine Base at Faslane.
Left: The Upper Clyde showing RN and USN Submarine Bases at Faslane and in the Holy Loch.

perhaps. But the GRU has no clear evidence of either. Sharp lookouts — certainly. But even at this time of heightened tension there are plenty of pleasure boats and sailing craft around to say nothing of store vessels, water-boats, picket boats and the like to confuse the picture. What, then, do the ASW defenses consist of? The two Captains are puzzled: perhaps cunning Scotsmen have devised secret methods which nobody has learned about. Or could it be that midget submarines have simply been forgotten?

Not that navigation is all that easy. Tidal streams are fierce and the Rhu Narrows are notoriously hazardous. It is said that British submarine captains dislike the twisted bottle-neck, with its sluicing tides, intensely — the more so because some old seadog in the Yacht Club on the point is bound to be watching through binoculars, hoping gleefully to witness a grounding no doubt. The Faslane-bound midget skipper has taken careful note of that tit-bit from the GRU.

The attacks have been timed to take place at high tide which should leave enough water beneath the SSBN keels for a midget to work its way between them and the bottom. There is no certainty of that: the GRU briefer had remarked contemptuously that years of discarded gin bottles (British) and Coke cans (American) could have raised the seabed artificially. A joke of course (or was it?) but it was one way of saying that the GRU did not really know: there has been a lot of dredging and piling, especially at Faslane, which might make depths marked on Russian charts unre-liable.

In the event, a couple of quick, secure echo-soundings 200 m away from the Bomber jetty at Faslane suggest that trying to worm a way beneath the single monster alongside would be inadvisable.[8] That will mean push-ing out two divers instead of one if the midget bottoms a discreet distance away because the six limpets deemed necessary (there can only be one bite at this cherry) will have to be ferried in six separate trips. No matter. Better safe than sorry.

The Holy Loch midget, on the other hand, reckons there is sufficient water. He goes deep at one-and-a-half knots, 600 m from the American depot ship, USS *Holland*, which has one Boomer alongside. Timing by stopwatch, a vast shape looms blackly overhead just eight seconds before stopwatch time sugges-ted it would appear. That last range by graticule must have been pretty good. 'Stop motor — slow astern — watch the trim —

stop motor — Starboard wheel — slow ahead — stop motor — slow astern — midships — stop motor — WATCH THE COPULATING TRIM *STARPOM* — raise antennae — Port wheel — slow ahead — midships — stop motor — *Kharasho*. We're there. Pump slow-ly. SLOWLY I SAID. STOP PUMPING IDIOT. Gently. Check motion through the water — good, we're stopped'. (A little bit of string sus-pended outside the Starboard viewing port dangles straight down: it is the most primitive of instruments but utterly dependable.) 'Gently, gently — got it.' (The abbreviated fixed periscope shows that the antenna masts are in firm contact and the craft is more or less level.) 'Pump out 50 kilos, *Starpom*: that should anchor us. Out you go comrade diver. Remember, six limpets for the PLARB — you'll find her a few meters on our Port quarter as we're lying. Then I'll release the starboard side cargo for the depot ship. The usual tap signals — don't try talking — if you want your colleague to come and help. Good luck comrade.'

We will not stay to see the results of these two attacks. Perhaps they will be foiled by some means, perhaps they will succeed. Either way the craft will be scuttled quietly by flooding — possibly beneath, or adjacent to, the targets themselves. The crews will have to swim for it — unless they choose to make the final sacrifice by dying in their craft. Were it not for the Squadron Com-mander's unshakeable advice that deliberate suicide missions will fail to achieve their objectives, the second option is what the State would prefer.

END NOTES

1. One reference, Norman Polmar's excellent *Guide to the Soviet Navy* (published by Arms & Armour Press ISBN 0-83568-821-4) suggests that there may be a light forces base in the bay and names it Oranienbaum — but this is not registered on maps or charts and the name is that of another town in central Germany. Whatever the truth may be the little cove described, with the lake behind it, is an ideal spot for midgets.
2. The career described, together with the quotation, is accurately based on a typical young officer's introduction to this kind of work.
3. British X-craft crews operating in Japanese waters during the war were issued with similar capsules. They were never used.
4. Alas, there is evidence of this kind of execution at the place described.
5. This actually happened to HMS *X-6* in 1943.
6. The mine on a captured wartime German midget *Biber* was found to have no less than 13 booby-traps.
7. This account, and much else, is based on the author's personal and painful X-craft memories.
8. HMS *X-3* got stuck for a while under the Japanese cruiser *Takao* at Singapore in 1943.

2.7

SKIRMISHING IN THE PACIFIC

As the days pass by the Soviet Defense Council realises that it may be impossible to limit the war which continues to be fought, predominantly, underwater. Nobody is entirely sure about what is happening because submarines, for tactical reasons, are sending very few messages back to base. Moreover, the codes have not yet been broken by either side. But all the indications are that things are hotting up alarmingly.

NATO and the USSR have fully mobilised their armed forces and France must definitely be counted as an active Western ally. China, although proclaiming neutrality, is tending to side with the West according to KGB reports from Beijing; and, to complicate matters, Japan (whom China is inclined to distrust) is nervously adopting a defensive posture against both the USSR and the People's Republic in case the wind changes and the two giants combine.

The world is, frankly, in a mess. The United Nations Security Council is as impotent as ever while the UN General Assembly is simply an arena for forensic propaganda — a whistle on the boiler but not a sufficient safety valve for blowing off a dangerous head of steam.

Recognising that considerable obstacles are going to be placed in the way of a mass submarine sortie from the Northern Fleet, the Defense Council decides it will be as well to deploy, immediately, as many submarines as possible from the Red Banner Pacific Fleet. Apart from the score or more of SSBNs (including seven 'Delta IIIs') and seven SSBs ('Golf IIs'), the usual proportion of which are on station (with the 'Golfs' now targetting China and Japan), about half the total of 79 attack boats are operationally available. (There are also 65 elderly SSKs in reserve but they are not in fighting trim.)

The ready-to-go boats, which are in the main older than their Northern Fleet comrades, therefore comprise ten SSGNs ('Charlie Is' and 'Echo IIs'); two SSGs ('Julietts'); 15 SSNs (two 'Akulas', three 'Victor IIIs', five 'Victor Is', one 'Echo I' and four 'Novembers'); and 14 SSKs ('Kilos', 'Foxtrots' and 'Romeos'). In addition there is one, 'India' Rescue submarine; one converted 'Golf I' Command, Control and Communications platform; and one 'Bravo' padded target.

The Pacific submarines normally operate out of four bases: Vladivostok (HQ and principal Submarine School), Petropavlovsk (main submarine base) on the Kamchatka Peninsula, Sovyetskaya Gavan (on the mainland inside Sakhalin Island) and Magadan on the Northern shore of the Sea of Okhotsk.

Incidentally, it was revealed during the trial of National Security agent and traitor Ronald Pelton in 1985 that US submarines had intercepted traffic on seabed communication cables between Kamchatka Peninsula and the mainland: the program was known as 'Ivy Bells' and the Russians had evidently been warned about it for some five years by Pelton. Nothing was said during legal proceedings about the method employed by the American boats, nor whether midgets and divers were involved, but 'Ivy Bells' obviously had a relationship to the Karlskrona scenario conjectured in the last chapter.

Russian submariners favor Petropavlovsk as a base because it opens out directly on to the Pacific: submarines from other ports have to pass through narrow straits to reach the sea outside the Soviet-controlled

Kuril Islands which form a chain across the mouth of the Sea of Okhotsk. The snag is that 'Petro' can only be supplied by sea or air: overland transport systems to the Peninsula are non-existent — and there are no railway lines to Magadan either, by the way. In other words, the best submarine base is vulnerable both to submarine attacks on supply vessels and to midget invaders (perhaps robotic) if Japan or the USN are prepared to invest seriously in tiny offensive craft — Japan for the second time.

In the meantime, 'Petro' might well be threatened by the submarine-launched mobile mines which are themselves (rather basic) robotic midgets. Of course, all the Russian bases are open to cruise-missile attack — 'Petro' again being the most vulnerable because the birds will not have to fly over territory where they are more liable to countermeasures than when coming straight in from the sea.

There is thus quite a lot that can be done by American and Japanese submarines (if the latter decide to play) to nullify or at least reduce the Soviet Pacific Fleet's underwater striking power — if action is taken before the majority of available boats deploy. And there, as usual, is the rub.

We will consider two possible cases: one where the Russian C-in-C gets his boats to sea well before hostilities commence; and the other where American and Japanese forces make a pre-emptive underwater strike.

Escaping the net

The first case arises (we will say) from a Defense Council Fleet Directive to deploy all available depot and support ships (there were 81 of them in all the fleets at the last count) to emergency war ports, anchorages and havens. Some, especially the 'Lama' and 'Amga'-class missile support ships which can supply submarines with missiles at sea if conditions are suitable, will simply be sailed to hover somewhere in anticipation of attacks on their home ports; others — 'Ugras', 'Dons' and the rest — will make for destinations throughout the world where the locals have been softened up and are sympathetic or resigned to the Soviet cause.

The USSR currently (1988) has access to ports and anchorages in the Dahlak Islands off Ethiopia, Aden, Cam Ranh Bay in Vietnam, in Angola, West Africa, Mozambique and Cuba; and advances are being made to Tonga and other South Pacific States. It will be routine for the West to keep track of these

movements by satellite observation; but the submarines which follow, fanning out worldwide perhaps, will disappear, most of them only making their presence known if and when it suits them. SOSUS chains are good and getting better but their surveillance is confined to quite small areas and usually choke points. Once past these, submarines may be anywhere. Agreed, such a deployment is the clearest of world-war indicators — but what practical use is that to the West?

We therefore arrive at the second case which, regrettably, is not really on the Western cards — pre-emptive attack. In any event a first strike will achieve nothing against the PLARBs on patrol. It will be easiest to keep our thoughts in the Pacific although they are, in essence, equally applicable to any of the main Soviet fleets.

The pre-emptive strike

It is axiomatic that there are three places to kill wasps; and, by analogy, the logic is relevant to enemy submarines. You can squash them when they gather around the honeypot (a convoy for example); or you can exterminate them in their nest (submarine base); or you can try to swat them on their way from nest to honeypot (submarines in transit) — a strategy that is very likely to result in wasp-comrades stinging the swatter severely while he is attending to one of their number.

There is no doubt about it: go for the nest if you can: smoke it out. Is there any way of doing that without setting light to the surrounding brushwood and finding, too late, that the fire is out of control.

There are, in fact, two ways, neither of which is normally mentioned in polite society — but, then, submariners are not particularly polite in conducting their business affairs.

Option One is to use sabotage. It can be directed at facilities, weapons or at submarines themselves. Sabotage is, by definition, clandestine so directed at Soviet Pacific bases, we are probably in the realm of midget submarine operations again or — if midget submarines, SDVs or whatever are not available — combat swimmers landed from standard boats. The latter should clearly be small if possible. Eighteen Japanese 'Uzushio' and 'Yuushio'-class boats are capable, multi-purpose and not over large: furthermore, the Japanese are supremely good, by tradition, at conducting covert operations. Whether they would be willing to engage in this kind of thing nowadays is another matter — but it does

seem worth considering.

Option Two is, as they used to say of submarining in general, no occupation for a gentleman but a pragmatist might not turn down the idea of employing bacteriological warfare. The danger is tit-for-tat; but along with Option One, it deserves more than a passing thought. Germs do not have to be killers: it is not beyond the wit of man to devise a breed that will incapacitate or induce a moronic mood of apathy. Doctors and scientists, in their (very few) published articles on the subject of germ warfare almost invariably end up by saying that sunlight quickly destroys the agents, or that the wind will carry them away, or that it is impractical to disseminate them on a large scale. As Hamlet remarked of the lady, the medical-scientific fraternity 'doth protest too much, methinks'. If, methinks, our suspicions have some foundation, submarines of some sort will have to carry the disseminators for this literally nauseating form of warfare to the enemy because a submarine base like Petropavlovsk is unapproachable by any other kind of vehicle without certain detection.

In the face of skepticism it might be as well to offer the specific instance, far removed from the Pacific however, of a chronic and debilitating illness which in 1978 started to affect mainly young and healthy adults in the West of Scotland, notably in the seaside town of Helensburgh on the Firth of Clyde. Helensburgh is next door to the SSBN/SSN base at Faslane. For some unexplained reason, only three naval families living in Helensburgh were hit by what turned out to be Coxsackie B group viruses although the majority of sufferers were, like

the naval people, relatively affluent. No more than seven of the 38 patients diagnosed in a particular medical practice lived in local authority housing: the rest were home-owners. There were no obvious connections between cases which occurred in an apparently sporadic fashion. There was no evidence to suggest a seasonal variation or that infection was acquired outside the local area or abroad.

Add these bald documented statements up and it would not be unduly speculative for a layman to suggest that the virus was, so to speak, planted for the results to be observed by an interested party. If this was indeed so (and two doctors[1] have dropped unmistakeable hints to that effect) there was clearly no intention to do widespread damage or debilitate a submarine crew: rather, the object would seem to have been an evaluation of Coxsackie B and/or a means of dissemination. (Tests have shown that an excellent way of spreading germs around the place is to pump them into a bicycle tyre, crack the valve slightly and pedal up and down the streets with a 'slow puncture'; that is scarcely feasible in a Soviet submarine base but there are

Top: Soviet India-class diesel-electric Rescue submarine with its DSRVs. These can be replaced by operational midgets. The 'India' herself is probably not armed.
Above: USS *William H Bates* (SSN 680) with DSRV *Avalon* embarked: any SSN/SSBN, with quite minor modifications, could carry a military midget in the same way.

probably other ways and means!)

All this is apposite to knocking out a submarine crew because the symptoms resulting from Coxsackie B (or some similar unpleasantness) are pretty much what we were looking for when postulating Option Two — headache, vertigo, pain or discomfort in the joints of both hands, facial pain, heart palpitations, shortness of breath, general malaise and — most serious of all for a submariner — marked feelings of apprehension, panic and impending death.

Coxsackie B, as the old English saying goes, it just what the doctor ordered. The problem is how to spread the disease (or something like it) in Soviet submarine bases as remote as those in the Pacific.

Enter the Chinese

It is time to pass on to more enlivening scenarios. We will say that China now takes a leaf out of the Soviet book (as she has so often done in the past) and, fearful with reason of amphibious assault and submarine-launched cruise missiles, she declares the entire Yellow Sea out of bounds to foreign shipping unless specifically authorized. A strong Soviet naval and air force, as well as a rejuvenated Vietnamese Navy, is based no more than 500 miles from China's most southerly extension, Hainan Island. Any force operating eastwards from Cam Ranh Bay will very soon pass only some 300 miles to the South of the Paracel Islands and Macclesfield Bank and very close to the northernmost of the Spratly Islands, all of which are claimed or desired by a far-sighted Chinese government.[2] It is also through this area that China's

swelling trade passes to and from the Malacca Straits.

Thus, in the scenario's high state of tension, China feels obliged to warn that any military vessels which 'appear to have hostile intent' anywhere in these critical areas will be challenged and are liable to attack — primarily by submarines, of course, although that is not specifically included in the warning. However, it is said that submerged foreign submarines will automatically be attacked without warning.

There is no hope of China being able to fulfil these (conjectural) promises over some 400 000 sq sea miles but the Russians would be well advised to take them seriously. It is true that the Chinese PLA(Navy) is outdated in practically every respect and that the published number of combatants is exaggerated — by Western commentators however, not by the thoroughly realistic PLA, but it is catching up fast and is proficient with the material it has.

In the event, we will say, the USSR does not take the Chinese declaration at face value; and one incident in particular demonstrates that, in this, the Russians are rash.

One of the Russian Pacific C-in-C's many tasks is to launch a covert operation against the American West Coast SSBN base at Bangor as well as continuing his efforts to locate and trail the 'Tridents' — a parallel operation to that of C-in-C Northern Fleet. There is no way, in his estimation, that a Soviet merchant ship will be permitted anywhere near the US West Coast: there is nothing like as much Soviet shipping in the Eastern Pacific zone as there is around Europe; and a midget-pregnant merchantman, however well disguised, would be investigated by the efficient US Coast Guard. It was hard enough avoiding USGC attentions while amphibian midgets were gathering intelligence at a time when Russia and America were still smiling at one another across the Nuclear Arms Reduction table.

The only practical and immediate answer is to despatch the Pacific Fleet's diesel-electric 'India' Rescue Submarine with two operational midgets replacing the DSRVs. An 'Echo II' SSN has undergone modification for the same purpose but there is some doubt about its compatibility (it is a brute to trim when embarking or disembarking midgets submerged) and the C-in-C is reluctant to risk the SSN on such a mission at this point.

In light of the complex situation building

Modified 'Golf I' (ex-SSB) Communications submarine for serving as a command and control platform. The 'pillar-box' aft contains raising gear for the associated radio mast.

up, the Russian Admiral decides to sail another important diesel-electric boat — the 'Golf' communications submarine (SSQ) — with his Deputy Chief of Staff and Deputy Chief of the Naval Political Department on board. The SSQ will take up a convenient middling position in the East China Sea from where it can move wherever needed to help control Soviet forces.

Fatal Russian moves

Both these boats, which have minimal weapon systems and are quite noisy with their sundry appendages, duly depart from Vladivostok. They are routed — each in its own moving haven — southwards between Korea and Honshu through the Tsushima Strait, which is deemed safer than other exits from the Sea of Japan, down into the East China Sea where the 'Golf' will establish itself and the 'India' will turn eastwards. The Japanese Maritime Self-Defense Force, well supplied by Intelligence, has correctly appreciated the situation. Understandably not wishing to be involved in a fight if it can be avoided, the Chief of Staff directs the eight submarines on patrol to report but not attack. *Setoshio* (SS 575) and *Nadashio* (SS 577) are straddling the expected Russian track a little to the north of Tsushima. The first indication of the Soviet boats' approach is an ASW 'Bear' flying a search pattern (righteously keeping outside Japanese and South Korean airspace) followed by a pair of 'Krivak I' ASW frigates which announce their presence by blaring out on Spin Trough navigational radar, Head Net air search (to keep tabs on the Bear) and medium frequency sonar.

The Japanese COs are confident that, even if detected, the Russians will not let loose weapons at them; but the highly man-euverable submarines take evasive action nevertheless, utilizing a marked sonar layer to best advantage and bearing in mind that the Russians are towing variable depth sonar (VDS). In theory the Japanese ought to be dis-covered but, knowing that ASW weapons are strictly 'tight', the Russian Captains and sonar operators are not well motivated. Moreover, it is blowing great guns and the crews are seasick, cold and tired after nearly three days of rocking and rolling: they envy the boats snorkelling some 50 miles astern. It is not surprising that they fail to gain contact with the Japanese SSKs which are snug, stable and keeping an alert watch on ZQQ 4 bow sonar while the Captains vary their depth and sidestep professionally.

SOVIET FAR EASTERN BASES

The frigates pass on their way, transmit-ting fruitlessly. It is not long before both the SSKs, 25 n miles apart, pick up distinctive noises to the North and classify them as snorkelling submarines. Prudently, the Cap-tains wait until they are positive — the *Nadashio*'s OOW actually glimpses the 'Golf' broaching in the heavy sea — and then trans-mit Flash enemy reports on UHF to HQ via the communication satellite thoughtfully made available (without undue publicity) by the USA. Naturally, the Chief of Staff returns the compliment by immediately passing the messages to the US Naval Attaché, who in turn transmits them to Washington DC, where they are received and digested within an hour of the original reports. After a brief discus-sion the contents are 'leaked' to the Chinese Naval Attaché who promptly signals Beijing.

The consequence is that not only does the Pentagon have some very useful information, but two Chinese 'Romeos' on patrol about 300 miles East of Shanghai are alerted to what are termed trespassers. Their sonar equip-ment is not the best — centered on 10 kHz it will not detect much in the low frequency bandwidths — but the Russian snorkellers are very wrong to despise the Chinese cap-abilities. Intelligence has told them that PLA(N) ASW weapons are mostly poor qual-ity: although some boats are rumored to be equipped with British Tigerfish by now, only a few of these torpedoes have been purchased due to stringent financial constraints. It is probable, the Russians think, that the dual-purpose Tigerfish boats are retained for home defense in critical areas and the chance

The Far Eastern Soviet submarine bases are exceptionally well protected geographically with only Petropavlovsk directly on the Pacific; but internal communication routes are difficult and the exits from the inland sea of Okhotsk and from inshore of Sakhalin Island could conceivably be blocked.

Overleaf:
Straight-running, elderly, 'unintelligent' torpedoes fired at close range by Chinese 'Romeo' *Great Wall No.32* at a transitting Soviet 'India' midget-carrier, prove entirely effective in this imagined attack — as well they might in real life. Although their SSKs are, for the most part, thirty years out of date by Western standards the simple weapon system available to the very high quality Chinese submariners would be employed to the best possible advantage in a situation like that described here.

of meeting them far out to sea is believed too small to worry about.

It is strange how the mind focusses uniquely on sophisticated weapons. There are circumstances where a bow and arrow will serve just as well as a high velocity rifle. So it is on this occasion.

Outside the Sea of Japan, the weather has moderated to Sea State Three — choppy with a light swell. Han Guisheng, commanding the Chinese-built 'Romeo' *Great Wall No.32*, is an extremely able submariner — as are most of his contemporaries — and totally dedicated to his job. Of late, the rigid drills enforced under Chairman Mao have been relaxed — not least because of candid advice from the Royal Navy gladly given and well taken. Han is flexible, aggressive and determined to do his utmost with the comparatively rudimentary tools at his disposal.

The six bow tubes of *Great Wall No.32* are loaded with straight-running anti-surface 'steam' torpedoes of Russian design manufactured in Xian. The stern tubes carry simple homers which Han distrusts although he would fire them from deep at a menacing ASW ship if necessary. He receives the Japanese contact report (no longer attributed to its source) rather late when the Russian boats have passed out of the straits into 'his' sea; but there is plenty of time to put in a quick battery charge and move into their grain.

Han's vigilance is rewarded at dawn on the following day. Sonar reports a contact bearing 008°, aurally classified as a diesel submarine. It could be a fishing vessel — there are no filters or spectrum analyser associated with the modified Soviet-type Herkules kit — but the operator has done his homework and is fairly sure the contact is what he is listening for. Han agrees and bearings are marked at 20-second intervals on the vertical Time Bearing Plot constructed from an old British drawing. Sonar bearings are much more accurate than they would be with LF equipment: pointing the target, Han's plotter is soon able to draw a smooth curve to measure Bearing Rate.

After 12 minutes on the pointing course, Han alters 90° to Port at ten knots to generate a second bearing rate: this course will also reduce the distance off track and, with any luck, will bring him to a firing position. By comparing the two bearing rates, with a rough propeller revolutions count from Sonar and meticulous plotting on the attack chart by the Navigator, target course is estimated at 170°, speed eight knots.

The range is coming down and the (analog) Torpedo Control Calculator is tracking nicely with inputs from the plot. All bow tubes are brought to the action state and bow caps/bow shutters are opened. The target is making such a din that *Great Wall No.32* can afford to be a little noisy when necessary. Han is soon able to slow to four knots and alter round to a firing course on a 95° torpedo track angle. The Deputy Captain calculates that the range will be a Nelsonian 500 m when the sonar director angle comes on.

Firing by sonar is entirely practicable but Han would dearly like to have a look — so he comes shallow stealthily and risks an observation, after a rapid all-round look, with the periscope 3 m out of the water. And there, right on bearing, is a black protuberance sticking out of the water — an undeniable snorkel-periscope-ESM mast cluster. Lowering the periscope rapidly, Han endeavors to retain the impassive cool for which he is renowned; but his Political Officer excitedly passes the word forward and aft. 'Torpedo depth setting seventeen meters. Ten degrees to go by sonar. Check parallax. Stand by all bow tubes. One degree to go...Stand by One...FIRE. Carry on firing by firing interval.'

The Russian 'India' hears the 45-knot weapons as soon as they are running. The OOW stops snorkelling, launches a decoy, initiates sonar jamming over the 20–40 kHz range, broadcasts 'Emergency Action Stations' and orders hard-a-dive, flood negative, full ahead. His drill is prompt and commendable but it is no use against fast old-fashioned fish with a running time of little more than 20 seconds. The 'India' is only starting to gather speed and head downwards when Number One torpedo in the salvo hits amidships and Number Two explodes against the stern section. *Do Svidanya* to the midget transporter and its valuable deck cargo.

It is tempting to think that Han's colleague Liu in *Great Wall No.43* achieves equal success against the 'Golf' but perhaps that would be pushing Chinese luck too far. There will be those who doubt the feasibility of Han's attack in today's environment but the story, as told, is in fact credible. A determined captain, with a good crew, can work wonders with plain, homely, reliable tools.

END NOTES
1. The doctors do not wish to be named.
2. Chinese troops landed on the Spratlys in March 1988, just after this chapter was written.

2.8

ARCTIC ASSAULT

The underwater battle is still centered in the North, above the Arctic Circle; and new players are continually entering the arena from the USA, UK, France and Canada. We will assume that Canada has, by now, some fully operational SSNs.

Tension has mounted to crisis: in Soviet HQ, Severomorsk, the Operations Board registers *Kraisiz* Day + 12. The C-in-C, Admiral Bigotov, has reinforced the Arctic bastion and further dispersed his strategic forces. One of the 'Typhoons' which was being held in the bunker at Zapadnaya Litsa has moved out deep under the ice (its place being taken by an off-patrol 'Delta IV') where its monstrous sisters are already stationed; the other reserve 'Typhoon' stays in its shelter. The valuable on-duty 'Delta IVs' are also hovering under the ice but they are in *polynya*-populated areas because, with their flat superstructure, they must surface, if they possibly can, in open or thinnish patches.

If the conflict drags on into the winter and *polynyas* start to disappear they will join other PLARBs at the ice-edge, the MIZ, where ambient noise protects them while there are still enough floes, frazil and broken ice to make conventional attack from the air a virtual impossibility. A few more PLARBs are in the White Sea whose entrance, 15 miles across at the narrowest point, is mined and boomed leaving no more than a narrow, well-guarded access channel.

Two brand new Soviet SSGNs, specially configured for breaking through ice and equipped with 20 SS-N-24 land-attack cruise missiles apiece, are *en route* to launching positions in the Beaufort Sea from where they can bombard the North American continent as far South as a line joining Seattle, Washington State and Winnipeg, Manitoba. The GRU is pretty confident that the terrain-hugging SS-N-24 cruise, with the latest stealth technology, will overfly Canada undetected. (Ballistic and cruise missiles are, as normal, targeted on other parts of the USA and Europe but we are concerned specifically with Arctic operations in this chapter.) A converted 'Yankee' is standing by to carpet Norway with SS-N-21 cruise missiles, from a safe position within the Barents bastion, in the event that NATO amphibious forces attempt a major landing there.

None of the older Soviet SSGNs are deployed under the ice because, as a glance at their photographs shows, they are not suitably configured: they confine their activities to anti-ship attacks. Some of the new well-shaped SSNs with a partial load of land-attack cruise missiles are certainly capable of coming up through the ice but their primary duties are ASW and anti-ship operations, so Bigotov is not expected to send them to bombardment stations off Canada.

However, whilst the two latest Russian SSGNs are quietly tracking across the Pole in one direction three American SSNs — a 'Seawolf' and two 'Los Angeles' types (with vertical as well as horizontal tubes and retractable bow planes instead of rotatable sail-mounted planes) are going the opposite way. Their task is twofold: to find and destroy enemy SSBNs and secondly, if ordered, to bring Kola and White Sea naval bases and nearby naval airfields under attack with nuclear Tomahawks.

A pair of Canadian SSNs is prowling in the Beaufort Sea and Canada Deep after the customary hairy passage up through the Bering Strait.

Submarine detection

The chances of any one submarine finding another under the ice are not high in the normal course. Obviously, all the denizens of the deep keep quiet and will only reveal themselves to one another if some kind of unusual activity is forced upon them. So is there any means of detecting them other than by submarine sonar?

It sounds flippant to say that a watch could be kept by a tribe of ASW Eskimos but,

Overleaf:
Massive shelters, more or less proof against nuclear weapons and primarily for PLARBs awaiting deployment, have been drilled out of solid rock at Zapadnaya Litsa not far from the Norwegian border; and bunkers, like those built by the Germans in French harbors during the war for protection against air attack, have probably been constructed in the Kola inlet and White Sea as well.

in principle, that is one solution. (Incidentally, the 18 000 Canadian Eskimos threatened in 1985 to declare a vast expanse of the Arctic independent unless they were allowed to set up their own semi-autonomous province. They wanted — perhaps still do want — to run an area stretching 2000 miles from Baffin Island to the Beaufort Sea and more than 1000 miles North and South. It would be called Nunacut or 'Our Land'.)

The submarine-detection method which 'Eskimos' could use is, theoretically, quite simple: the US Navy is known to have been conducting feasibility studies for several years and doubtless the Russians have already determined its practicability.

Sea-ice readily transmits acoustic energy, particularly at low frequencies; and little reflection occurs at the ice and sea-water interface. A flat transducer laid on the surface of sea-ice can receive acoustic waves through the ice without much attenuation. Similarly, as noted in Chapter 1.9, ice is a very good propagator for radio signals — a hundred times better at 15 kHz than salt water — and this property is used to advantage by submarines streaming a floating wire antenna (FWA) up against the ice overhead.

In about 1986 the Defense Advanced Research Agency (DARPA) launched a small experimental data relay satellite for linking small acoustic sensors on the ice-pack with American shore stations and ships. The satellite, only 16 in across and weighing 150 lb, was cheap at around one million dollars — easily affordable if the experiments, in which it is believed US submarines were involved, have proved successful.

Assuming that this method of ASW detection is indeed practicable, it will be a lot easier for the Russians to employ it than anyone else (because they have much more direct access to the icefield bastion) but it would seem very desirable for Canada to pursue the idea in order to assist her ASW SSNs.

Be that as it may, we will envisage the sort of under-ice engagement which could occur whether stemming initially from fixed acoustic detectors or not.

Contact is made

The *Komsomolskaya Pravda*, a 'Delta IV' PLARB (Captain First Rank I A Kirichenko) is patrolling at minimum speed in deep water to the North of Jan Mayen Island. He is keeping as close as possible to a thin patch with his VLF FWA trailing. Constant watch is maintained on VLF/ELF strategic broadcasts. His towed array sonar is not deployed because it would probably be damaged if he surfaces: he is content, quiet as *Pravda* is, to rely on hull-fitted sonar.

USS *Mendota* (SSN) is scouring the Greenland Sea on a methodical but slow passive search pattern with the new long thin-line towed array streamed. Besides guarding US/NATO submarine broadcasts, the Radio Room is also tuned to the Soviet strategic frequencies: although all signals are coded and traffic is kept at a constant level by meaningless messages, it is just possible that a sudden change in broadcast activity would be apparent and indicative.

So far as *Pravda* is concerned, this is what happens. The Soviet ELF broadcast appears to cease and the VLF broadcast is, for some reason, barely audible. A combination of sabotage — the ELF antennae ashore are kilometers long and potentially vulnerable — and solar interference? Kirichenko is obliged to take urgent action. It is mandatory to regain the broadcast. These are just the sort of circumstances which could arise if the enemy is attempting to frustrate a nuclear strike by the USSR: the cessation of ELF is a bell-ringer in itself.

In accordance with orders, Kirichenko

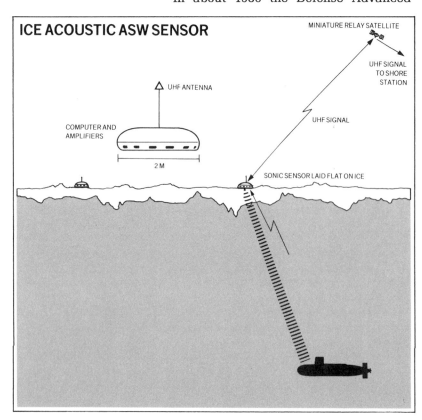

ICE ACOUSTIC ASW SENSOR

MINIATURE RELAY SATELLITE

UHF SIGNAL TO SHORE STATION

UHF SIGNAL

UHF ANTENNA

COMPUTER AND AMPLIFIERS

2 M

SONIC SENSOR LAID FLAT ON ICE

maneuvers as rapidly as possible beneath the nearby *polynya* and prepares to surface in order to make sure of hearing the back-up LF broadcast if VLF is still too weak with antennae fully exposed. There is no time to lose: he can't play around trying this receiver and that, checking for a ground or malfunction. Hence he necessarily abandons stealth: first things come first: the *Rodina* may be calling, in the last resort, on *Komsomolskaya Pravda*'s 16 ballistic missiles, carrying 112 MIRV warheads.

Kirichenko takes the conn himself. Automated trimming (associated with the system used when launching missiles) helps considerably but the moment to pump and start coming up vertically is still a matter of fine judgement. There are some quite large fragments in the frozen pool — the upward-looking echo-sounder and TV display reveals them clearly: it can only be hoped that they are not carried up on the long, broad missile-section amidships. A Muscovite Murphy dictates, however, that they will be. A dozen crewmen armed with crowbars and levers gather in the control room beneath the lower lid, ready to climb out and deal with the problem if necessary.

The *Pravda* is, unavoidably, making a good deal of noise and when the Engineer blows main ballast to achieve full buoyancy, the sound waves travel far and wide. Sure enough, a look aft through the periscope shows two blocks of ice sitting solidly above numbers seven, eight, eleven and twelve tube doors. Out go the men with their tools to dislodge them, immediately clipping their safety harnesses to the casing rails because Chief is about to list the submarine to help dislodge the blocks by flooding three of the Port main ballast tanks — meaning more noise.

Meanwhile, the radio *Michman* reports a long LF message coming in: there are no facilities for automatic decryption except on VLF so it will be some time before the contents are known. VLF is still very difficult to read and too intermittent for the rapid teletype receiver to cope.

Mendota happens (we will say) to be 11 n miles away when the Russian boat starts to sort itself out. The BQQ 5 gains broad band contact suddenly and unmistakeably on the lateral array: there is nothing quite like a submarine blowing main ballast. It has to be assumed that a submarine using great blasts of HP air is an SSBN surfacing — for one deadly purpose. *Mendota* bends on 20 knots: sonar effectiveness is reduced by about 80

per cent but that contact needs very urgent attention.

The SSN's Captain puts together all the fragmentary information at his disposal — intelligence, sound velocity profile, bearing, intensity of the original signal, subsequent analysis of certain narrow band signatures — and estimates that the contact is 10–15 miles distant. After 15 minutes he slows to 12 knots and, as waterflow diminishes, BQQ 5 reports metallic and crew noises bearing 010°. The regular beat of machinery, probably a hydraulic pump, is also showing up on the visual display at 21 Hz. There is naturally no doppler shift: the target cannot be other than stationary.

The final moves

Mendota maneuvers briefly to establish range more accurately: the computer indicates 10 500 yards — just over five miles. No need for undue caution: time is the essence. Numbers One and Two tubes are fired sequentially. The first passive Mk 48 (non-ADCAP) malfunctions but the second apparently runs true. At minute 16 there is a rather muffled explosion on target bearing and sonar contact is temporarily blanked out. *Komsomolskaya Pravda* is fully surfaced in the ever-widening *polynya*, and the missiles have been brought to five minutes notice for launch, when a nearby explosion rocks the huge submarine and causes a couple of the seamen on an already precariously tilted deck to lose their footing: but there is no damage. Kirichenko appreciates, correctly, that an enemy SSN has attacked but that the weapon has detonated against an ice keel. What is he to do now?

The incoming radio message is still being decyphered but, pending the instructions it undoubtedly contains, he must remain ready to fire. Granted the standard order to do so is very brief but maybe, observing that command, control and communications appear to have been disrupted to some degree it could be deliberately wrapped up in a longer signal to deceive hostile interceptors: there is a contingency plan for that. In any event his PLARB is relatively invulnerable on the surface — indeed that has been demonstrated — although the *polynya* is becoming more like a large lake by the minute: the protective keels and ridges are receding to the East.

Mendota's sonar picture clears quite quickly. Broadband noise and some transients are coming in loud and clear — and

USS *Mendota* (SSN) versus **Delta IV-class** *Komsomolskiy Pravda* (SSBN)

DATE: *Kraisiz Day*+12 LOCATION: Arctic Ocean, north of Jan Mayen Island, under ice.

USS *Mendota* (SSN) is tasked to hunt and kill Soviet SSBNs beneath the ice-bastion.

Komsomolskiy Pravda (SSBN) – Captain First Rank I A Kirichenko – is patrolling at minimum speed under ice, keeping as close as possible to a thin patch while constantly maintaining radio watch on the assigned SSBN VLF/ELF broadcasts.

Sequence of Events

USS *Mendota* (SSN) Speed 4 knots, mean course North, depth 200 feet.

0835 Sonar contact bearing 010 – tentatively classified Soviet SSBN.

0837 Alters course towards 010 and prepares to fire 2 Mark 48 (non-ADCAP) torpedoes.

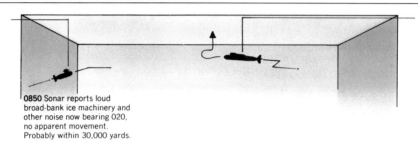

0850 Sonar reports loud broad-bank ice machinery and other noise now bearing 020, no apparent movement. Probably within 30,000 yards.

0852 Sonar reports definite submarine on bearing blowing main ballast. Increases speed to 20 kts for 15 minutes.

Komsomolskiy Pravda (SSBN) Speed 3 knots, course variable, depth 200 feet.

0832 ELF broadcast ceases. VLF broadcast not clearly audible: possible enemy jamming or interference. In accordance with orders Pavlov maneuvers as rapidly as possible beneath the thin patch, finds a *polynya* (open pool) and prepares to surface in order to regain the essential broadcast on VLF or the alternative emergency LF frequency. Pavlov knows he is making detectable noise – but he has no choice.

0915 Fires two Mark 48 torpedoes, wire guided, on bearing. Number One malfunctions. Number Two apparently runs true. Range 10,500 yards.

0931 Explosion on approximate bearing of contact. Sonar contact blanked out.

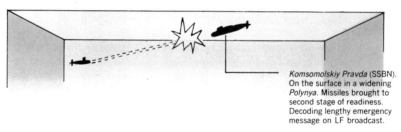

Komsomolskiy Pravda (SSBN). On the surface in a widening *Polynya*. Missiles brought to second stage of readiness. Decoding lengthy emergency message on LF broadcast.

0931 Fairly close explosion to the West. No damage. Pavlov appreciates that an enemy

SSN has attacked but that the weapon has detonated against the ice. Decides to remain on surface where he reckons to be relatively invulnerable – except that the wind has shifted and the small *Polynya* is becoming more like a lake by the minute.

USS Mendota (SSN)

0936 Sonar picture still confused but wide-band noise and transients are still registering now at 300 feet. Closes on bearing with search periscope raised. Underwater visibility excellent. Prepares to fire two more Mark 48s. Bow caps opened slowly and silently by hand control.

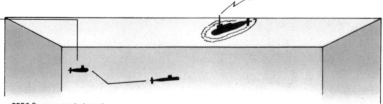

0956 Sonar reports target obviously on the surface and close aboard.

1006 Captain at periscope, now at 150 feet, sees lightening of ice shadow ahead.

USS Mendota (SSN)

1011 Large black shape sighted right ahead and above. *Mendota* slides under. The hull overhead is impressively large. Captain decides to open range to 2000 yards, turn and shoot again.

1023 Commences 'Williamson' turn to bring submarine back on exact reciprocal course.

1027 Fires two sequential Mark 48s, active mode, on precise bearing with initial depth setting shallow but sufficient to pass below any 'stalactites'.

1028 One explosion, very loud. SSN badly shaken. Trim lost: sail hits ice. Primary fire-control U/S. Minor leaks. No damage to reactor.

1036 Forced to withdraw until damage resulting from own torpedo explosion had been rectified and weapon systems are serviceable. Reports indicate at least six hours before the boat is operational again. Meanwhile all masts except the attack periscope

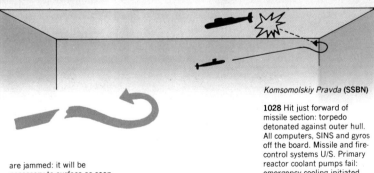

are jammed: it will be necessary to surface as soon as possible to examine the sail. Captain notes that the effect of an under-ice explosion is unpredictable!

Komsomolskiy Pravda (SSBN)

1028 Hit just forward of missile section: torpedo detonated against outer hull. All computers, SINS and gyros off the board. Missile and fire-control systems U/S. Primary reactor coolant pumps fail: emergency cooling initiated. Starboard stern bland leaking badly, Fire behind main electrical switchboard: extinguished promptly but

instrumentation and wiring are damaged.

1036 Pavlov sends Flash report to base on H/F in code. Crew set about repairs. It will be unsafe to dive deeper than 50 meters. One primary coolant pump and a gyro compass should soon be serviceable; and the stern gland will be repacked in a couple of hours sufficiently well to allow speeds of up to 10 knots. It should be possible to prepare three torpedoes for salvo firing in unguided mode; but the missile system can only be repaired in the dockyard where the boat will be out of action for several weeks.

American SSN surfaced in a large *polynya*.

close aboard. The SSN is now at 300 ft (below expected ice keels), speed five knots. Numbers Three and Four tubes are ready: the bow caps were opened silently by hand pump and voices are noticeably kept low. The Captain is at the General Purpose periscope looking upwards from bow to bow: underwater visibility is excellent. The ragged underside of the ice, showing as a dirty greygreen colour with dark specks, starts to lighten — the first hint of a *polynya* — and then a huge dark bulk appears overhead, outlined starkly against the sea-air interface. Even the two seven-bladed propellers are visible: *Mendota*'s Captain presses the integrated camera button — useful intelligence whatever the outcome of the present situation.

OK. *Mendota* will shoot another salvo from about 2000 yards, watching for keels on the way out and executing a Williamson turn to come back on the reciprocal course when the SSN has run for 12 minutes. The Mark 48s are discharged in active mode and steered by wire towards the target at a search depth of 40 ft; that should easily clear minor ice-spikes and put the weapons no deeper than, say, 12

ft beneath the target's keel. They can be controlled accurately in azimuth by wire; and, even if the smart torpedoes are slow to realize they must home upwards and underrun at the first pass, the influence pistols will detonate their warheads.

In the event, the first Mk 48 does steer itself upwards. Its high-pitched pinging is distinctly audible inside the 'Delta IV' but there is nothing that can be done to avoid the hit which comes just forward of the missile section against the outer hull. The second fish is thrown off balance by the explosion and disappears.

On board *Komsomolskaya Pravda* the warning lights on all computers, SINS and gyros glow red; the missile and fire-control systems go wild; electrical supplies to primary coolant pumps on both reactors and most auxiliary systems are cut; the Starboard stern-gland is leaking seriously; and there is a fire behind the main electrical switchboard.

The hull is intact and damage is containable. But it will probably be unsafe to dive deeper than 50 m and the PLARB is unserviceable for any active role. Kirichenko is just about to send a Flash signal to base when the Radio *Michman* hands him the awaited message which has finally been decrypted: 'You are cautioned that an American SSN is operating in your area. Positive detection was made at . . .' He sighs and orders the Flash report to be transmitted 'as is'. No point in complaining: he has a nasty feeling that once again the VLF/ELF reception problem is due to shoddy maintenance. He is right: it is just as well that the LF broadcast constantly functions as a back up. Anyway, there is ample excuse now for anything malfunctioning. The important thing is to dive as soon as his signal is cleared and sneak off before worse befalls.

Worse does not befall because *Mendota* is in difficulties as well. Her own torpedo explosion, almost a mile away, has resulted in remarkably heavy shock damage which seems very unfair in the circumstances. Trim was lost and the sail hit the ice. It will be at least six hours before the SSN is operational again and all masts except the attack periscope are jammed. The boat will have to surface as soon as possible to examine the sail.

Mendota's captain reflects gloomily that the effect of an explosion under the ice is unpredictable — but, then, nothing is certain or predictable in Arctic warfare. We will leave him with that thought.

2.9

RUSSIAN CHESS

The grandest pieces on the Russian chessboard are, for our purposes, on station in the Arctic where they and the under-water NATO Knights are continuing to fight it out in the dark. Regrettably, some of the latter are going to be endangered by smart and novel mines laid, by submarines of course, inside the ice edge.

C-in-C Northern Fleet cannot afford to delay any longer in deploying the mass of his attack submarines out into the Atlantic. The Soviet Defense Council is now assured that the conflict cannot be contained within the Arctic region although there is still some hope, albeit fading, of restricting battles to the sea. Neither does there seem any way, as once intended, of pursuing the most im-mediate military aims in Europe without massive opposition (if full-scale warfare proves unavoidable) or of manipulating politics in such a fashion that the United States declines to participate wholeheartedly in a predominantly Transatlantic affair. Circumstances have changed and long-term strategy will have to be revised.

Yet, the Defense Council believes one chance remains of keeping America from committing more forces, apart from sub-marines, to what is looking more and more like real war. Supposing that some political excuse can be contrived for confronting a major US Task Force with a superior Soviet force. Maybe the excuse could be defense of a Third World nation's interests — an avowed intent to prevent foreign interference in its waters. No matter what, the Politburo will be able to dream up some kind of reason, how-ever implausible. Most probably, the con-frontation would be arranged in South-East Asia although it is not inconceivable that, in Hitlerian style, the Kremlin might announce that it intends to 'protect' Norway or Iceland or wherever. The place is not important; but the confrontation, with conventional and nu-clear odds overwhelmingly stacked against the American Fleet (for no action would be taken unless they were) could be crucial to Soviet strategy as the Defense Council sees it.

What will the American Task Force Commander do in such a situation? What will Washington order him to do? We in the West are confident that he will fight; but it could be that the Soviet Defense Council, believing its navy to be superior, expects him to back down with all the consequences that retreat implies.

Hence it is not impossible that vast Russian air, surface and sub-surface armadas will appear in the Pacific and/or Atlantic at some stage of our imagined conflict with one object in mind — to force a showdown. The Endgame (a term familiar to chess-players) would follow, directed at the American economy and trade routes, if and when NATO is fragmented and Europe is largely neutralized. At least, wishful thinking or not, that is what the USSR might logically be expected to hope from its massive fleets if the Politburo is in militant mood.

We will therefore conjecture that the Russian Admiral is tasked not only to send his attack submarines into the Atlantic but also to assemble the largest Battle Group he can muster, together with shore-based naval aviation support. Besides the ships and air-craft engaged on defending the bastion and those undergoing overhaul or maintenance, it is reasonable to reckon that he could assemble (in our time scale) two carriers (CVN and CV), two battle-cruisers (CGN), four cruisers (CG), six guided-missile destroyers (DDG), three guided-missile frigates and 15 ASW/AA escorts.

All the ships have anti-submarine and anti-aircraft/anti-missile armament; but the Battle Group will not be sailed South until the attack submarine force has cleared the Norwegian Sea and until selected SSGNs/SSNs are, hopefully, nearing a posi-tion from which to weaken the NATO (mainly US) Striking Fleet maneuvering in dispersed formation in the Eastern Atlantic.

The awesome Fleet gathers in the Barents Sea with replenishment ships and a ring-fence of light ASW vessels and aircraft — an irresistible target for NATO submarines if only the politicians will let them loose. That time must come but attacks on surface ships are not our direct concern. Suffice to say that an importunate COMSUBEASTLANT (Flag Officer Submarines) is beating on the door of his C-in-C at Northwood, begging him to seek ministerial approval for the two 'Trafalgar' SSNs close inshore off North Cape to be let loose. With American submarines coming down from the North and French SSNs approaching, besides more British boats (armed with Sub-Harpoon as well as ASW weapons) which can be diverted from ASW patrols if priorities change, the Russian Battle Group is liable to take a hammering before it leaves the Barents Sea. Furthermore, history suggests that the thicker a force is the easier it is for a submarine, once in amongst it, to deal blow after blow and escape retaliation: the physical proximity of so many ships, the noise they make and the confusion caused by weapon explosions all work in favor of an aggressive shark.

Breaking into the Atlantic

To return to C-in-C Northern Fleet's submarine surge he must plan, somehow, to overcome or circumvent two major obstacles — the NATO ASW submarine barrier across the Norwegian Sea (which is probably deep and extensive) and the CAPTOR minefield which the USA claims to have laid in the Denmark Strait between Greenland and Iceland: the American Ambassador to the UN has politely warned of this and, although Intelligence believes it could be bluff at present, it will soon become an established fact.

Bigotov does not, in fact, have as great a problem as the Comrade Vice-Admiral C-in-C in the Baltic where West German and Danish ships and submarines (hoping that the Kiel-based boats have not fallen foul of midget-planted mines) are realistically expected to block the narrow exits completely.

The Northern Staff has thought the problem through for many years: it is decided to adopt Plan M for *Maskirovka* (which translates as deception or trickery).

The attack submarines are divided into six groups. Two groups are committed to wide-ranging bastion defense; one to opposing NATO landings in Norway; one (as we saw earlier) to a Norwegian Sea ASW barrier; and two large groups — *Bitva* and *Glava* — are destined for the Atlantic.

Bitva, comprising ten SSGNs and seven SSNs, is to attack the Striking Fleet. *Glava*, consisting of three SSGNs, two SSGs and 15 SSKs, with a second wave — mainly SSKs — to follow will straddle Atlantic supply routes, lay mines around Europe and conduct inshore operations. War outfits are 25 per cent nuclear warheads, 75 per cent conventional.

Spetsnaz units, including those in midgets, are supporting the mass deployment by disrupting NATO communications; and Bigotov is asking the Defense Council's permission for an old SSBN to launch a megaton warhead set to detonate one hundred miles above the earth's atmosphere in a carefully calculated position — say South of Iceland at the latitude of Glasgow — such that the Eastern Atlantic, UK and Western Europe, North Sea and Norwegian Sea approaches are subjected to electromagnetic pulse (EMP) effect. Would this by itself trigger a nuclear exchange?

The probability is that it probably would not. But it would immediately have a devastating effect on unshielded shipboard, airborne and shore devices which use integrated or printed circuits, semi-conductors and micro-electric chips, including digital computers and electronic sensors. High-power, high-current systems like radar are not affected by EMP although there will be a lengthy radar, as well as communications, blackout. Soviet equipment is, in the main, shielded or else has relatively old-fashioned EMP-proof vacuum tubes rather than solid state electronics.

An enormous Western effort is going into 'hardening' ships, aircraft and systems against EMP; and fiber optics, which do not conduct electricity, can be employed instead

Fairly typical ice hummocks and tilted floes bordering a *polynya*. They imply that ridges and keels project down into the water beneath but it is impossible to estimate, from the jumble on the surface, how deep these might extend.

of wiring — but the cost is very high and the Russians are probably betting on a sizeable proportion of NATO equipment ashore and afloat being unprotected. Submarines are not susceptible to EMP and have no need of expensive hardening.

This lengthy digression is entirely relevant to any Soviet deployment scheme: and EMP at the right time will contribute importantly to the *Maskirovka* by making a temporary shambles of enemy communications. In turn that should mean that if the enemy is not, after all, deceived no warnings will be received at Northwood during the critical period.

Necessary casualties

The plan is simple but involves certain sacrifices. Eleven antique 'Whiskey' and 'Romeo' SSKs, not normally listed in the Order of Battle, have been called out of retirement. Their captains are selected from prospective commanding officers who have only just embarked on the tactical command course: they have been flown to Murmansk from Leningrad and can hardly believe their luck when the C-in-C personally greets them and announces their appointments. The *Rodina* has great need of these fine young comrades: they are to take their boats into action forthwith, out into the Atlantic to destroy the enemy wherever he may be.

Ingenuous and starry-eyed, the new Commanding Officers have no inkling of their real task which is wholly concealed from them: their boats are to be expendable decoys — no more than that. They know, of course, that they will be standing into danger when they snorkel down the Norwegian Sea but the Motherland's submariners must be fearless. Air cover will be provided and that quells any doubts they may have.

They are sent off with rousing cheers. C-in-C sighs deeply. He hates, as a submariner himself, to see them go to almost certain death — but the *Maskirovka* demands that they are sunk. He is in fact, treating these boys like wrong-doers in the penal battalions which invariably precede the main armies through minefields or sop up the enemy's initial fire.

The doomed 'Whiskeys' and 'Romeos' dive before they round North Cape and all but two then snorkel southwards at eight knots. A comforting number of ASW 'Bears' cross and recross the sea ahead and over the moving havens. All boats and aircraft are equipped with IFF to differentiate friend from foe: the whole point of the *Maskirovka* would be lost if the SSKs were sunk by their own forces.

What the young COs do not know is that the bulk of Groups *Bitva* and *Glava* are silently following in their wake, their individual units linked by secure underwater telephone.

The inevitable happens. First one and then another of the decoys goes down to NATO barrier SSNs. Then another — and another. On each occasion, clearly signalled and located by the torpedo explosions, Divisional Commanders in *Bitva* and *Glava* assign one, sometimes two, SSNs to take out the attacker — with varying success — while the other submarines continue their stealthy transit.

The 'Bears' are 'weapons tight' unless specifically directed on a Subair vector. They will get out of the way if the EMP ploy is approved; but until then their primary job is to try, by dropping active sonobuoys, to force enemy submarines to take evasive action and thereby, perhaps, reveal themselves if not already located by Soviet SSNs investigating what in the surface world would be called flaming datums.

Plan M is brutally callous but war is war, and the C-in-C believes it will succeed. He could be right.

However, to hedge his bet he sends the two remaining decoy boats down the Denmark Strait, a real penal battalion tactic, to take the brunt of mines with six (modern) SSKs, temporarily detached from Group *Glava*, following in line astern: all these submarines follow the same track, very precisely, by bottom-contour navigation.

At the last moment, we will say, C-in-C is ordered to transfer, as quickly as possible, one SSGN to the Pacific Fleet via the North Pole and Bering Strait to strengthen another possible Soviet-American confrontation in the Far East. It is a 3000-nautical mile transit: no problem until the submarine reaches the Chukchi Sea where it should arrive in seven or eight days given a relatively quiet but still potentially detectable speed of advance (SOA) of 15 knots.

The role of the Canadians

The move is made purely for our convenience to raise again the question of what purpose the Canadian SSNs are tasked to serve. We have implied earlier that at least some of them seem to be intended to attack Soviet submarines under the ice in the Canadian Arctic; and that sounds fine. But what will their prob-

DANGEROUS STRAITS AND SHALLOWS

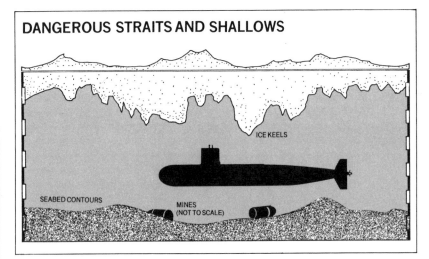

ICE KEELS

SEABED CONTOURS

MINES
(NOT TO SCALE)

There are places leading to the Arctic Ocean where there is barely room for an SSN to squeeze between the seabed and ice keels overhead — as USS *Nautilus* discovered (on the first attempt in June 1958 to cross the North Pole) in the square area shown on the chart at left. Such places could be mined and so could relatively narrow and sometimes tortuous Straits leading from the Pacific and Atlantic Oceans, adding greatly to the hazards because ground, as opposed to moored, mines seem unlikely to be detected by a submarine's normal ice or mine-detection sonar. Moreover, midgets can bury ground mines. Although on-board mine countermeasures (eg, degaussing) may be quite effective, some considerable risks are implied in wartime: it could be that robotic or remotely controlled submersible mine-hunters are called for.

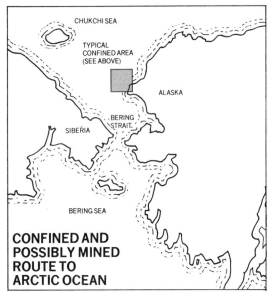

CHUKCHI SEA

TYPICAL
CONFINED AREA
(SEE ABOVE)

ALASKA

BERING
STRAIT

SIBERIA

BERING SEA

CONFINED AND POSSIBLY MINED ROUTE TO ARCTIC OCEAN

ability of success be against boats on station, unless assisted by fixed sensors, in such a vast expanse of water? The only choke points are in the Bering Strait and its approaches — the Soviets have no need of the Northwest passage — where the water is so shallow and the ice is frequently so thick that there is very little room to maneuver. Surely no SSN captain would be happy to patrol there? There is also a real danger of the Straits being mined by Soviet submarines when (or if) they no longer need the passages themselves. In other words, Canadian SSN useage beneath the icefield for purely national defense begs even more important questions than those regarding American and British operations in the Arctic.

Needless to say, if the Canadian government is indeed altruistic, and offers to join the fray in order to support other NATO forces,

the SSNs will doubtless be extremely welcome. But public enthusiasm for their mounting guard in the Canadian Arctic could be thought a little over the top. Few Russian chessmen are likely to be moved in that direction: and those that are sent (eg, SSGNs) will be very hard to find. That is, unless a Soviet transitter (ie, a boat making a certain amount of noise) wants to pass fairly speedily between the Arctic and the Pacific — and we have only been able to contrive a rather feeble excuse for that.

Anyway, we will suppose, for argument's sake, that the Canadian government (in consort, of course, with NATO) opts for defense at a distance and that some of the available Canadian SSNs are deployed, early, to the most forward possible positions in the Barents Sea off the Russian Kola bases. The patrol zone here seems highly hazardous on the face of it but in practise the huge amount of Soviet naval activity expected in the area, as well as other factors, may well confuse Soviet ASW control.

At the time of writing the type of SSNs selected by Canada — British 'Trafalgars' or the French 'Rubis'-class — has not been announced. However, a great deal is known about Canadian submariners: they are first-class, aggressive and innovative. Without much doubt they would welcome a forward deployment and, as always, it will be men and morale who decide the issue. (The same can be said about Australian submariners but they are not, unfortunately, being given the best material which they arguably need and deserve — that is, a nuclear submarine force.)

So we can imagine the Canadian SSN *Moosonee*, to give her a name, sitting in the plum position North of Ribachiy through which a large proportion of Soviet submarine traffic will doubtless pass. Her Captain, Commander Chuck Gatineau, is a forceful pragmatical character with a French Canadian father and a flexibly Jewish mother who adopted the Catholic faith when the family moved to Quebec. Chuck has trained the crew with ruthless professionalism and without undue regard for dogma. They do things his way — or else. He is a firm believer in getting close to the enemy and he is certainly close enough now. He carries a full load of American Mark 48 torpedoes and he intends to make every one of them count if he possibly can.

There are ships everywhere, it seems, and flocks of aircraft fly overhead. But

Chuck's task is strictly ASW for the moment and with any luck some Russky submarines will soon show.

The 'Whiskey' and 'Romeo' decoys have rounded North Cape by the time that *Moosonee* arrives on station ten days after sailing from Halifax, Nova Scotia. But the important units are now clearing the Kola, heavily escorted by ASW frigates who have previously swept through the Canadian patrol zone and declared it free of enemy submarines — correctly because the Canadian SSNs had not yet reached their patrol positions as it happened. Admiral Bigotov's plot therefore displays a safe transit lane for Groups *Bitva* and *Glava* as far as the Longitude of Vardo, some 60 miles West of Ribachiy. In order to retain full control and avoid mutual interference, the submarines will remain on the surface until they reach this point.

Soviet miscalculation

Bigotov has fallen into the old, old trap of plot-fixation. If the transit lane is shown as safe, then safe it must be. The escorts and the submarines themselves are equally mesmerised — so when one of the frigate captains excitedly reports a sonar contact he is told by the ASW Commander to shut up. No enemy submarines are included in the Plan for the Day — and that is that. Chuck, in *Moosonee*, is thankful but not particularly surprised when dangerous sonar transmissions pass him by: the Soviets would not expect him to be so far forward. He has been counting on that and on the rigidity implied if the Russians decide on a mass deployment.

When the first submarine looms up, sheathed in ice, it looks enormous through the periscope. The Arctic air has a tendency to magnify images. Visibility is good: the morning steam-like vapors have blown away and a nice choppy sea, with no swell, makes it extremely unlikely that a cautiously raised periscope will be detected. Chuck is an ardent periscope man: his sonar is excellent but nothing beats a good look in busy conditions like this. He has, incidentally, decided — despite orders — to torpedo any ASW vessel that menaces his boat; but, so far, the situation has not arisen and he doubts if it will.

His first target is the 'Victor' *Sixty Years of Young Communist League Patronage*[1]. The Captain and Navigator, dressed in heavy parkas and fur hats, are sitting on a raised and padded seat, rather like a park bench, athwart the top of the sail. A lookout stands in the well immediately forward of the two officers and a glass shield protects them all from spray. A signalman is ensconced with his lamp above the upper conning tower hatch a little further aft in the sail. Everybody is sublimely confident in the massive surface and air escort: there can be no need to worry with so many ASW units all round.

Of course, that is where *Sixty Years of YCL Patronage* is wrong. The fact is that she and her followers really have too much protection and too much organisation for their own good. *Moosonee*'s salvo, straight down the throat, results in two successive hits. Chuck, entirely unfettered by classical SSN tactics, remains at periscope depth and keeps very close to his dying victim. He is confident that alarm and despondency will ensue over the whole area: he will stand into much more danger is he runs away into clear water than if he centers himself in what will soon be a scene of chaos and confusion. He will change his tactics when it suits him to do so — when the next target presents himself. Already a couple more firm surface-submarine sonar contacts are being plotted although it is quite difficult to hear them through the noise created by Russian escorts racing hither and thither.

Assuming that Canadian nuclear personnel retain their admirable flexibility and are not 'Rickoverized' by their powerplants, they can be expected to do great execution in forward areas: hopefully, that is where they will be sent.

Admittedly, there could be some Canadian or Soviet strategy that has not been made public and which we have not been able to conjecture. Perhaps, for some reason, it is deemed desirable to patrol the Chukchi Sea and Bering Strait. Or maybe Canadian Intelligence suggests it is necessary to provide a dense system of defense in the Beaufort Sea against missile-launchers. If so, particularly in shallow water, could not a sizeable number of the small nuclear hybrid boats discussed in Chapter 1.3, suitably armed, do the job better than a strictly limited number of big, prestigious but expensive SSNs?

Meanwhile, there could be pawns of this kind, hidden so far, on the Soviet chessboard. If so, the game will be played according to new rules in some places; and, as is well known, a Pawn can take a King.

END NOTES

1. This is an actual 'Victor' name! The description of the arrangements on the sail which follows is accurate.

Overleaf:
The 'Victor' *Sixty Years of Young Communist League Patronage* is hit by two successive Mk 48 torpedoes fired down the throat by the Canadian SSN *Moosonee*. Soviet submarines are quite likely to transit on the surface for a considerable distance from the base if several are deployed at one time: the area off and around the Kola Peninsula and Ribachiy could be a rich hunting ground for a skilful and daring NATO submarine captain, despite a plethora of ASW units.

2.10

THE SURVIVORS

We come at last to imagine the unimaginable. A Head of Government makes a mistake and orders SSBNs to launch a nuclear first strike. It could not be other than a mistake, an appalling totally catastrophic error of judgement, because as all concerned must realize (or do they?) a ballistic-missile firing is bound to be suicidal. Even worse, as pointed out in Chapter 1.8, submarine-launched ballistic missiles are unidentifiable: so their appearance on radar screens at, say, Krasnoyarsk will almost inevitably result in global retaliation, whatever blandishments are proffered on the hot lines.

If we proclaim the invisibility and relative invulnerability of SSBNs (compared with shore-based silos) we ought, at the same time, to recognize two of their dangers — anonimity and an unimpaired second- or even third-strike capability.

Submarines armed with cruise missiles are also well cloaked but, until more nations acquire them, their nationality will not be much in doubt if their birds take wing. For that reason and because they do not alert long-range warning devices, automatically triggered to respond, cruise missiles are a great deal less likely to provoke a world-wide holocaust. Nevertheless, although less powerful than their ballistic cousins, they can strike deadly blows to supplement — or perhaps demonstrate by way of a final threat — the results of a massed ballistic attack.

There is no call to dwell on the unspeakable scenes of carnage and corpses, fire and utter devastation after a full-scale nuclear attack. Whether or not a nuclear winter will follow, how many human beings will continue to exist after a given number of megatons, in what way genetic chains will be twisted and what mutations will occur — all these questions are academic. Life in any tolerable form on land will simply cease: the lucky ones will die abruptly; the less lucky will linger; and the least fortunate of all will be left trying to put the few remaining pieces together as best they can with no acceptable future ahead of them.

Nor, predictably, will nuclear weapons alone be employed for, or after, the first strike. If war is all-out it will be just that.

Chemical and biological/bacteriological carriers will be brought into play on a massive scale, probably disseminated by the Russian West wind over China and, of course, amongst those surface ships which are still afloat after tactical nuclear engagements.

This appears to be the logical conclusion — conclusion in a hideously literal sense — of unrestricted warfare. And it stems largely from the fact that missile-submarines cannot be written off by a pre-emptive strike. We can envisage some being sunk, disabled or sabotaged (the French and British boats are, on the face of it, somewhat susceptible to a concentrated anti-SSBN campaign by reason of their small numbers) but enough will stay in business to wreck the planet: any hope that, on either side, a sufficiency of American Boomers or Russian PLARBs will be destroyed to avoid catastrophe is a chimera.

In short, nuclear submarines — SSBNs, SSGNs, SSNs — will be the active survivors of Armageddon. It is said that secret tests have shown that diesel boats (SSKs), needing to draw in air occasionally from the atmosphere, stand little more chance than surface fleets. So what will happen if or when nuclear submarines find themselves virtually alone in being able to continue a conflict?

That question begs another. Who, if anyone, will be capable of directing operations? The Defense Council embedded in the Zhiguli monolith can be expected to outlast the rest but whether its members will have the stomach for further fighting seems doubtful. Why bother? Western pockets of resistance may continue in being for a while

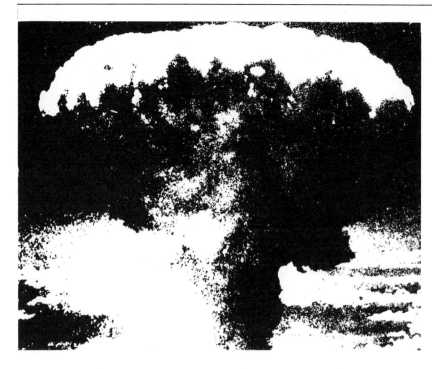

Finis — a strategic nuclear warhead explosion. If this were the first, it could be followed by anything up to 24 000 more because that is the approximate number of strategic warheads in the world pending Arms Limitation agreements. Of that total there are currently (1988) about 10 000 warheads carried by some 1500 submarine-launched ballistic missiles available for American and Soviet SSBNs without counting British and French deterrent submarines. By no means all these could be deployed simultaneously; but then there are submarine-launched cruise missiles as yet uncounted......

The task of anti-submarine submariners on all sides is, to say the least, challenging.

— but, again, what purpose will there be in carrying on the struggle? Maybe, a few countries in the southern hemisphere will escape the immediate consequences of an exchange but eventually they, too, will succumb to the effects of poisonous radiation. It will simply be a case of each man for himself: warlike ambitions will be irrelevant.

We might imagine some Soviet support ships making their way unscathed to, say, the Antarctic and gathering around them a brood of nuclear submarines. So, in the ultimate scenario, the inclusion of a few female officers in some Soviet surface vessels might prove more popular than seems usual, if only to help perpetuate the species. But, feminine company apart, the long-term prospects look bleak all round.

In other words, there is no point, in our context, in stretching imagination beyond the final nuclear exchange. However, it is just possible — albeit only just — to conceive a situation where, by some miracle, the use of cruise rather than ballistic missiles would succeed in limiting war to a fairly small theater — especially if the warheads were in the main non-nuclear and nuclear weapons were more or less confined to the sea.

In that case, gas and bacteria might well bring civilian populations and armed forces to their knees. Again, the only units left with a meaningful fighting capability would be submarines; and on this strictly limited stage, where death-dealing or disabling poisons are not necessarily widespread, SSKs might remain as operational as nuclear boats. Naturally, the same would be true for both victor and vanquished if they both have a submarine force. The stronger power would presumably employ his boats to quash any resistance remaining, or, if the outcome is equally devastating on both sides, to tip the balance in his favor by more land-attack missiles or by strangulation of maritime supply routes. The weaker or weakened power would then have to rely on submarine-versus-submarine warfare — like as not regretting bitterly that more effort had not been devoted to submarine ASW in the piping times of peace.

It will, rightly, be said that much of what we have discussed or suggested is sheer speculation. Speculation it is, but not sheer. The fact is that every act of forward planning depends upon speculation, founded on the best intelligence available and a thorough understanding of the relevant historical background.

Unfortunately, there is no significant case history concerning submarine-versus-submarine engagements — which by itself makes speculation unavoidable.

Meanwhile two things are as sure as ever such murky matters can be. Submarines will be foremost amongst the survivors in practically any type of future confrontation involving naval forces; and their deadliest enemies are to be found amongst their own kind.

INDEX

A

AMPS (ECS) 30, 31, *31*
Anti-air missiles (SAM) 23, 24, 106, *106*; SIAM 106; SLAM 105, 106
Asdic 8

B

Batteries 24, *25*
Bayerlein, Lt Gen 11
Burke, Adm Arleigh 19

C

Chernavin, Adm 6, *13*, 16, 20, 22, 106
Closed-cycle engines 24, *25*
Cryogenics 26

D

Decima Flottiglia Mas (It. *maiale*) 87
Diesel-electric propulsion 23, *25*

E

Eccles, Adm 18

F

Falklands confrontation 30, 52
Ferranti FISCS *59*
Flywheel energy storage *25*, 26
Fuel Cells 24

G

Gee, Ethel, Portland spy 13
Glomar Explorer 75, *113*

H

Hicks Transmissions (flywheel) 31 (note)
Holland, USS 164
Holy Loch, USN SSBN base 162 et seq (imagined scenario)
Houghton, Ron, Portland spy 13
HTP propulsion *25*
Hybrid propulsion *25*; ECS AMPS 30, 31, *31*

I

Ivy Bells program 165

K

Kockums (Sw) designs *25*, *26*; Type 471 (Aus) 137
Kuznetsov, Adm *13*, 16

L

Launders, Lt, HMS *Venturer* 8

M

Maksimov, C-in-C RSVN 20
Maritalia (Italy) gst designs *25*, *98–99*; note 101
MHD propulsion 28,29
Midgets, see Maritalia and Submarines (various nations)
Mine Types:
  AMD – 1000 (Sov) 61
  CAPTOR (US) 62–64; under ice 85
  Rising (Sov) 61, *62*, 63
  UEP (Sov) 63
Missile launch, early *17*
Missiles, strategic, numbers (Sov) 66
Missiles, strategic warhead numbers 189
Missile types (see also anti-air):
  Chinese SLCMs 133
  M–4 (Fr) 73
  MSBSM (Fr) 73
  Polaris (US, Br) 70, 72, 73, 74
  Poseidon (US) 70
  Regulus (US) 77, *77*
  Sea Lance (US) 57
  SIAM (US) 106
  SLAM (Br) 105, 106
  SM–39 (Fr) 78, 139
  SSM–N–9 (US) 77
  SS–N–3a (Sov) 77, *78*
  SS–N–6 (Sov) 66
  SS–N–7 (Sov) 77
  SS–N–8 (Sov) 66
  SS–N–9 (Sov) 77
  SS–N–12 (Sov) 77
  SS–N–15 (Sov) 57, 59
  SS–N–16 (Sov) 57–60
  SS–N–17 (Sov) 66
  SS–N–20 (Sov) 67, 69, 75
  SS–N–21 (Sov) 59, 60, 68
  SS–N–24 (Sov) 77, 150, 173
Subroc (US) 57
Sub Harpoon (US, Br, Aus, Jap) 59
Tomahawk (US) 59, 71, *76*, 77, 136, 173
Trident I (US) *69*, 70, 71
Trident II D5 (US, Br) 71, 73, 74
V–1 (Ger) 75
Mountbatten, Lord 19

N

Neptune, HMS, Faslane submarine base 162 et seq (imagined scenario); *163*, 167
Nuclear power and variants 27–31,28–29; *Vanguard* PWR 2 72
Nyon agreement, submarine piracy 138

O

Olterra, MV, clandestine *maiale* base 87

P

Pigeons, communications 48
PUFFS sonar passive ranging 19, 148

Q

Queen Elizabeth, HMS, damaged by *maiale* 87

R

Ramillies, HMS, damaged by Japanese midget 91
Rickover, Adm 19, 28, 107, 185

S

SKINC, small nuclear torpedo warhead 60
SMCS integrated fire control system (Br) 64
SPUR proposed robotic midget (Br) *98*
Sonar, Soviet conjectural *36*, *37*
SOSUS and conjectural Soviet equivalent *38*, 40, 66, *118*, 163
Stalin 13, 16
Stirling engine *25*, 26
Storozhevoy, absconding Soviet destroyer 110
SUBACS integrated fire-control system (US) 64
SUBAIR tactics 15, 19, 57, 106
Submarines:
  American:
    Archerfish 79
    Avalon (DSRV) *167*
    Billfish 79, 81
    Ethan Allen 12
    George Washington 12
    Grayback 77
    Growler 77
    Halibut 77
    Hawkbill 79
    'Los Angeles' class 22, 32, 52, 127, *149*, 173
    'Mendota' 176 et seq
    Michigan 70
    Moccasin, periscope 42
    Nautilus (old), Arctic 84; (SSN) Arctic 84; 184
    0–12 (*Nautilus*), Arctic 84
    Ohio 70, *111*
    'Ohio' class, radio room 50; *70*, 71, 150
    Phoenix 70, *147*
    Ray 79
    Sargo 84
    Scorpion, disaster 29
    Sea Devil 79, 81
    Seadragon 84
    Seawolf 28; new class 32, 55, 129, 173
    Skate, hits bottom 45; Arctic 79, 84
    Skipjack, 'Albacore' hull 16, 19, *19*
    SSBN (FBM) numbers 69, 71
    SSBN (FBM) types, first three groups 69, 70
    'Sturgeon' class 42, 127 et seq
    Tautog, prayers to Mecca 110
    Thresher disaster 22, 29
    William H Bates carrying DSRV *167*
    Woodrow Wilson 12

X–1 midget 93, *93*
Argentinian:
  San Luis, Falklands
    torpedo failures 52
Australian:
  General 30, 108, 184;
    Kockums 'Type
    471' 109, 137;
    'Oxley' class 137
British:
  A-class, crushing
    depth tested 22
  Aeneas SSG 105
  Churchill, pump jet 55
  Dreadnought, design
    debt to USN 19
  E 41 minelayer 61
  Excalibur (HTP) 26
  Explorer (HTP) *26*
  Grampus, Arctic 84
  Holland 1, first RN
    submarine,
    periscope *42*
  K–4 (steam) aground
    47
  Meteorite (HTP) 26
  Minnow (X-craft) 92
  'Oberon' class 32, 57
  Onyx, Falklands
    conflict 30
  'Piranha' miniature
    type proposed
    (VSEL) 88, 93
  Renown, accident
    prone 72
  Resolution 72, 111
  'Resolution' class
    (Polaris) 65, 72
  Springer rams
    dunking sonar 105
  Stickleback (X–craft)
    92
  Superb, loses towed
    array 54; Arctic 79,
    81
  'Swiftsure' class 55,
    104
  'Tantivy' 129 et seq
    (imagined scenario)
  Tenth Submarine
    Flotilla (Malta) 11
  Trafalgar 111
  'Trafalgar' class 32,
    129 et seq, 185
  Tribune 42, 111
  'Trident' SSBNs 65,
    72, 73, 74
  Type 2400 32, 34
  U-Class 11
  'Upholder' class (Type
    2400) 32, 34
  Vanguard, PWR 72;
    149
  Venturer, sinks *U–864*
    8
  X-craft 91 et seq; 153
  X–23 92
Canadian:
  Canadian ECS group,
    suitability of
    AMPS 30, 31, *31*

Difficulties in
  patrolling Arctic
  183, 184
Efficiency of
  submarines 108,
  184
Intelligence gathering
  145
'Moosonee' 184, 185
  (imagined scenario)
SSN Arctic patrols
  173
Chinese:
  'Romeo' SSK types
    ('Great Walls') 109,
    145, *146*, 149; 168
    et seq (imagined
    scenario)
  'Xia' class SSBNs 74
Dutch:
  Notable efficiency
    108
French:
  Casabianca 139 et seq
    (imagined scenario)
  Logic 108
  Rubis (SSN) 78
  'Rubis' class 28, 121,
    124
  SNLEs (SSBNs) 71, 72
German:
  Neger midgets 89
  Seehund midgets 90,
    90
  Seeteufel amphibious
    midget 90, *90*
  Skilful U-boats 153
  Type 206 25, 153
  Type 211 153
  Type 1500 (in Indian
    navy) 52
  U–71 attacked by
    aircraft 44
  U–864 sunk by
    Venturer 8
  U–972 (HTP) 24
Indian:
  German Type 1500 52
  Soviet 'Charlie I',
    leased 146
Iranian:
  Midgets, possibly
    based on X-craft 93
Israeli:
  SSKs 136
Italian:
  CB midgets 90
  Guiliano Prini 140,
    144 (imagined
    scenario)
  Maiale 87, *89*
  Maritalia midgets,
    revolutionary gst
    design 25, *98–99*;
    note 101
  Salvatore Pelosi 140,
    140
Japanese:
  Aircraft carrying
    submarines *20*
  Kaiten midgets 88, 89

Koryu midgets 89
  SSKs *137*, 166 et seq
  Type A midgets 91,
    100
Libyan:
  Al Hunein 138 et seq
    (imagined scenario)
  Al Khyber 138 et seq
    (imagined scenario)
  'Foxtrot' class 139,
    142–143
Soviet:
  Academy of Sciences'
    117 et seq
    (imagined scenario)
  'Akula' (Shark) class
    22, 29, 35, 56, 165
  'Alfa' class 22, 28, 30,
    34, 56, *56*, 109
  'Argus' midget 91
  'Bravo' class 165
  'Charlie' class 77, *78*,
    165; leased to India
    146
  'Dekabrist' 125 et seq
    (imagined scenario)
  'Delta' class 66, 68;
    176 et seq
    (imagined scenario)
  'Dornoy' amphibious
    midget 157 et seq
    (imagined scenario)
  'Echo' class 77, 165
  'Foxtrot' class 23, 57,
    105, 149, 165;
    Libyan 138 et seq,
    142–143
  'Golf' class lost and
    partly salvaged 75,
    113, *113*, 165;
    communications
    platform *168*, 169
    et seq (imagined
    scenario)
  'Hotel' class 18
  'India' class 93, 132;
    165 et seq
    (imagined scenario)
  'Ivan Rogov' 146 et
    seq (imagined
    scenario)
  'Juliett' class 77, *78*,
    165
  K–21 14, *14*, *111*
  K–22 14
  'Kilo' class 23, 56,
    106; 117 et seq
    (imagined
    scenario); *119*, 165
  'Komsomolskaya
    Pravda' 176 et seq
    (imagined scenario)
  Leninskiy
    Komsomolets 16;
    Arctic 85
  M–172 14, *14*
  'Mike' class 22, 35,
    56, 57, 146
  'November' class 16,
    17, *18*; weapon

system 52; Arctic
  79; 165
Numbers, various
  types 10, 16, 17, 20,
  66, 165
'Oscar' class 35, 77,
  103
'Piskar' midget 152 et
  seq (imagined
  scenario)
'Quebec' class 17
'Rebyonok' midget
  152 et seq
  (imagined scenario)
'Romeo' class 17, *18*,
  20, 88, 165, 183;
  see also Chinese
S–13 wartime
  successes 15
'Shch' class 14
Shch–421 14
'Sierra' class 22, 29,
  29, 55–57; 125 et
  seq (imagined
  scenario); 146
'Tango' class *18*, 23,
  24, 56, 106, 149;
  120 et seq
  (imagined scenario)
'Typhoon' class 21,
  35, *67*, 68–70, 173
'U' class (ex-RN) 112
'Victor' class (Types I,
  II, III) 28, 35;
  collision 54; 55–57,
  59, 60, 77; 146 et
  seq (imagined
  scenario); 148; 165
'Whiskey' class 17;
  twin cylinder 18,
  18; 88; on the rocks
  109; 153, 183
'Yankee' class 12, 66;
  loss 29, 66, 75; 69;
  'wasp-waisted' *150*,
  173
'Yaroslavsky
  Komsomolets' 120
  et seq (imagined
  scenario)
YCL Patronage
  ('Victor') 185 et seq
  (imagined scenario)
'Zulu' class 17
Syrian:
  'Kilo' class newly
    acquired 145 (note)
  'Romeo' class, elderly
    138
Submarine Development
  Group Two (USN) 19
Swimmer Delivery
  Vehicles (SDVs) 23
Swimmers, SBS, SEALS
  etc *27*, 30

T

Tirpitz (German
  battleship) 14
Toroidal hull

construction: see
  Maritalia
Torpedo failures:
  Argentinian 52;
  wartime U-boat 52
Torpedo types:
  E 15 (Fr) 139, 141
  L 5 (Fr) 139 et seq
    (imagined scenario)
  Mk VIII (Br) 8
  Mk 24 (Br Tigerfish) 51,
    57, *58*, 59; 129 et seq
    (imagined scenario)
  Mk 37 (US) 19
  Mk NT 37C (US/Nor)
    137
  Mk NT 37E (US/Israel)
    136
  Mk 48 and ADCAP (US)
    59, 60; under ice 82;
    105, 137; 178 et seq,
    184, 185 (imagined
    scenario)
  Mk 50 (US) 57
  Seeschlanger (Ger) 153
  Spearfish (Br) 59; under
    ice 72; 105
  SUT (Ger) 153
  Tigerfish (Br): see Mk
    24

V

Valiant, HMS damaged by
  maiali 87
Viribus Unitis (Austrian)
  sunk 1918 by Italian
  human torpedo 88

W

Walter plant (HTP) 24, 25
Wien (Austrian) sunk
  1918 by Italian
  human torpedo 88

X

X-craft (Br midgets) 91,
  92, 93; Iranian copies
  93; *94*, 153; W and D
  lock *155*; 164 (notes)